Derivatives and Alternative Investments

CFA® PROGRAM CURRICULUM • VOLUME 6

LEVEL I
2008

Printed in the United States of America

10 9 8 7 6 5 4 3 2 1

ISBN 0-536-34228-8

2006160828

AG/JS

Please visit our web site at *www.pearsoncustom.com*

PEARSON CUSTOM PUBLISHING
501 Boylston Street, Suite 900, Boston, MA 02116
A Pearson Education Company

CONTENTS

HOW TO USE THE CFA PROGRAM CURRICULUM

Congratulations on your decision to enter the Chartered Financial Analyst (CFA®) Program. This exciting and rewarding program of study reflects your desire to become a serious investment professional. You are embarking on a program noted for its high ethical standards and the breadth of knowledge, skills, and abilities it develops. Your commitment to the CFA Program should be educationally and professionally rewarding.

The credential you seek is respected around the world as a mark of accomplishment and dedication. Each level of the program represents a distinct achievement in professional development. Successful completion of the program is rewarded with membership in a prestigious global community of investment professionals. CFA charterholders are dedicated to life-long learning and maintaining currency with the ever-changing dynamics of a challenging profession.

The CFA examination measures your degree of mastery of the assigned CFA Program curriculum. Effective study and preparation based on that curriculum are keys to your success on the examination.

Curriculum Development

The CFA Program curriculum is grounded in the practice of the investment profession. CFA Institute regularly conducts a practice analysis survey of investment professionals around the world to determine the knowledge, skills, and abilities that are relevant to the profession. The survey results define the Candidate Body of Knowledge (CBOK™), an inventory of knowledge and responsibilities expected of the investment management professional at the level of a new CFA charterholder. The survey also determines how much emphasis each of the major topic areas receives on the CFA examinations.

A committee made up of practicing charterholders, in conjunction with CFA Institute staff, designs the CFA Program curriculum to deliver the CBOK to candidates. The examinations, also written by practicing charterholders, are designed to allow you to demonstrate your mastery of the CBOK as set forth in the CFA Program curriculum. As you structure your personal study program, you should emphasize mastery of the CBOK and the practical application of that knowledge. For more information on the practice analysis, CBOK, and development of the CFA Program curriculum, please visit www.cfainstitute.org/toolkit.

Organization

The Level I CFA Program curriculum is organized into 10 topic areas. Each topic area begins with a brief statement of the material and the depth of knowledge expected.

Each topic area is then divided into one or more study sessions. These study sessions—18 sessions in the Level I curriculum—should form the basic structure of your reading and preparation.

Each study session includes a statement of its structure and objective, and is further divided into specific reading assignments. The outline on the inside front cover of each volume illustrates the organization of these 18 study sessions.

The reading assignments are the basis for all examination questions, and are selected or developed specifically to teach the CBOK. These readings are drawn from textbook chapters, professional journal articles, research analyst reports, CFA Program-commissioned content, and cases. Many readings include problems and solutions as well as appendices to help you learn.

Reading-specific Learning Outcome Statements (LOS) are listed in the pages introducing each study session as well as at the beginning of each reading. These LOS indicate what you should be able to accomplish after studying the reading. We encourage you to review how to properly use LOS, and the descriptions of commonly used LOS "command words," at www.cfainstitute.org/toolkit. The command words signal the depth of learning you are expected to achieve from the reading. You should use the LOS to guide and focus your study, as each examination question is based on an assigned reading and one or more LOS. However, the readings provide context for the LOS and enable you to apply a principle or concept in a variety of scenarios. It is important to study the whole of a required reading.

Features of the Curriculum

- **Required vs. Optional Segments** - You should read all of the pages for an assigned reading. In some cases, however, we have reprinted an entire chapter or article and marked those parts of the reading that are not required as "optional." The CFA examination is based only on the required segments, and the optional segments are included only when they might help you to better understand the required segments (by seeing the required material in its full context). When an optional segment begins, you will see an icon and a solid vertical bar in the outside margin that will continue until the optional segment ends, accompanied by another icon. *Unless the material is specifically marked as optional, you should assume it is required.* Keep in mind that the optional material is provided strictly for your convenience and will not be tested. You should rely on the required segments and the reading-specific LOS in preparing for the examination.

- **Problems/Solutions** - *All questions and problems in the readings as well as their solutions (which are provided in an appendix at the end of each volume) are required material.* When appropriate, we have included problems after the readings to demonstrate practical application and reinforce your understanding of the concepts presented. The questions and problems are designed to help you learn these concepts. Many of the questions are in the same style and format as the actual CFA examination and will give you test-taking experience in that format. Examination questions that come from a past CFA examination are marked with the CFA logo in the margin.

- **Margins** - The wide margins in each volume provide space for your note-taking.

- **Two-color Format** - To enrich the visual appeal and clarity of the exhibits, tables, and text, the curriculum is printed in a two-color format.

- **Six-volume Structure** - For portability of the curriculum, the material is spread over six volumes.

- **Glossary and Index** - For your convenience, we have printed a comprehensive glossary and index in each volume. Throughout the curriculum, a **bolded blue** word in a reading denotes a term defined in the glossary.

Designing Your Personal Study Program

Create a Schedule - An orderly, systematic approach to examination preparation is critical. You should dedicate a consistent block of time every week to reading and studying. Complete all reading assignments and the associated problems and solutions in each study session. Review the LOS both before and after you study each reading to ensure that you have mastered the applicable content and can demonstrate the knowledge, skill, or ability described by the LOS and the assigned reading.

CFA Institute estimates that you will need to devote a minimum of 10–15 hours per week for 18 weeks to study the assigned readings. Allow a minimum of one week for each study session, and plan to complete them all at least 30–45 days prior to the examination. This schedule will allow you to spend the final four to six weeks before the examination reviewing the assigned material and taking multiple online sample examinations.

At CFA Institute, we believe that candidates need to commit to a *minimum* of 250 hours reading and reviewing the curriculum, and taking online sample examinations, to master the material. This recommendation, however, may substantially underestimate the hours needed for appropriate examination preparation depending on your individual circumstances, relevant experience, and academic background.

You will undoubtedly adjust your study time to conform to your own strengths and weaknesses, and your educational and professional background. You will probably spend more time on some study sessions than on others. You should allow ample time for both in-depth study of all topic areas and additional concentration on those topic areas for which you feel least prepared.

Preliminary Readings - The reading assignments in Economics assume candidates already have a basic mastery of the concepts typically presented in introductory university-level economics courses. Information on suggested readings to improve your knowledge of these topics precedes the relevant study sessions.

Candidate Preparation Toolkit - We have created the online toolkit to provide a single comprehensive location for resources and guidance for candidate preparation. In addition to in-depth information on study program planning, the CFA Program curriculum, and the online sample examinations, the toolkit also contains curriculum errata, printable study session outlines, sample examination questions, and more. Errata identified in the curriculum are corrected and listed periodically in the errata listing in the toolkit. We encourage you to use the toolkit as your central preparation resource during your tenure as a candidate. Visit the toolkit at www.cfainstitute.org/toolkit.

Online Sample Examinations - After completing your study of the assigned curriculum, use the CFA Institute online sample examinations to measure your knowledge of the topics and to improve your examination-taking skills. After each question, you will receive immediate feedback noting the correct response and indicating the assigned reading for further study. The sample examinations are designed by the same people who create the actual CFA examinations, and reflect the question formats, topics, and level of difficulty of the actual CFA examinations, in a timed environment. Aggregate data indicate that the CFA examination pass rate was higher among candidates who took one or more online sample examinations than among candidates who did not take the online sample examinations. For more information on the online sample examinations, please visit www.cfainstitute.org/toolkit.

Preparatory Providers - After you enroll in the CFA Program, you may receive numerous solicitations for preparatory courses and review materials. Although preparatory courses and notes may be helpful to some candidates, you should view these resources as *supplements* to the assigned CFA Program curriculum. The CFA examinations reference only the CFA Institute assigned curriculum—no preparatory course or review course materials are consulted or referenced.

Before you decide on a supplementary prep course, do some research. Determine the experience and expertise of the instructors, the accuracy and currency of their content, the delivery method for their materials, and the provider's claims of success. Most importantly, make sure the provider is in compliance with the CFA Institute Prep Provider Guidelines Program. Three years of prep course products can be a significant investment, so make sure you're getting a sufficient return. Just remember, there are no shortcuts to success on the CFA examinations. Prep products can enhance your learning experience, but the CFA curriculum is the key to success. For more information on the Prep Provider Guidelines Program, visit www.cfainstitute.org/cfaprog/resources/prepcourse.html.

SUMMARY

Every question on the CFA examination is based on specific pages in the required readings and on one or more LOS. Frequently, an examination question is also tied to a specific example highlighted within a reading or to a specific end-of-reading question/problem and its solution. To make effective use of the curriculum, please remember these key points:

1. All pages printed in the Custom Curriculum are required reading for the examination except for occasional sections marked as optional. You may read optional pages as background, but you will not be tested on them.

2. All questions/problems printed at the end of readings and their solutions in the appendix to each volume are required study material for the examination.

3. Make appropriate use of the CFA Candidate Toolkit, the online sample examinations, and preparatory courses and review materials.

4. Commit sufficient study time to cover the 18 study sessions, review the materials, and take sample examinations.

Feedback

At CFA Institute, we are committed to delivering a comprehensive and rigorous curriculum for the development of competent, ethically grounded investment professionals. We rely on candidate and member feedback as we work to incorporate content, design, and packaging improvements. You can be assured that we will continue to listen to your suggestions. Please send any comments or feedback to curriculum@cfainstitute.org. Ongoing improvements in the curriculum will help you prepare for success on the upcoming examinations, and for a lifetime of learning as a serious investment professional.

ANALYSIS OF DERIVATIVE INVESTMENTS

STUDY SESSION

Study Session 17 Derivative Investments

TOPIC LEVEL LEARNING OUTCOME

The candidate should be able to demonstrate a working knowledge of the analysis of derivative investments, including forwards, futures, options, and swaps.

$4\frac{5}{8}$ $4^{7/..}$ $-^{5/8}$

$5\frac{1}{2}$ $5\frac{1}{2}$ $-\frac{1}{8}$

$5\frac{1}{2}$ $21\frac{3}{16}$ $-\frac{1}{16}$

$20\frac{5}{8}$ $21\frac{3}{16}$ $-\frac{1}{16}$

$17\frac{3}{8}$ $18\frac{1}{8}$ $+\frac{7}{8}$

$18\frac{1}{2}$ $17\frac{3}{8}$ $18\frac{1}{8}$ $+$

$6\frac{1}{2}$ $6\frac{1}{2}$ $-\frac{1}{2}$

$7\frac{1}{4}$ $6\frac{1}{2}$

$3\frac{1}{32}$ $-\frac{1}{8}$

$15/16$

$9/16$ $9/16$

$9/16$ $9/16$

$1\frac{5}{32}$ $7\frac{13}{16}$ $7\frac{15}{16}$

$7\frac{15}{16}$ $7\frac{13}{16}$ $7\frac{15}{16}$

$25/8$ $2\frac{11}{32}$ $2\frac{1}{2}$ $+$

27 $2\frac{3}{4}$ $2\frac{1}{4}$ $2\frac{1}{4}$

$61/8$ $12\frac{1}{16}$ $11\frac{3}{8}$ $11\frac{3}{4}$ $+$

87 $33\frac{3}{4}$ 33 $33\frac{1}{8}$ $-$

502 $25\frac{5}{8}$ $24\frac{9}{16}$ $25\frac{3}{8}$ $+$

833 12 $11\frac{5}{8}$ $11\frac{7}{8}$ $+$

16 $10\frac{1}{2}$ $10\frac{1}{2}$ $10\frac{1}{2}$ $-$

78 $15\frac{7}{8}$ $15\frac{13}{16}$ $15\frac{7}{16}$ $-$

4608 $9\frac{1}{16}$ $8\frac{1}{4}$ $8\frac{7}{8}$ $+$

430 $11\frac{1}{4}$ $10\frac{1}{8}$

$4\frac{1}{8}$ $4\frac{5}{8}$

STUDY SESSION 17
DERIVATIVE INVESTMENTS

Derivatives—financial instruments that offer a return based on the return of some underlying asset—have become increasingly important and fundamental in effectively managing financial risk and creating synthetic exposures to asset classes. As in other security markets, arbitrage and market efficiency play a critical role in establishing prices and maintaining parity.

This study session builds the conceptual framework for understanding derivative investments (forwards, futures, options, and swaps), derivative markets, and the use of options in risk management.

READING ASSIGNMENTS

Reading 70 Derivative Markets and Instruments
Reading 71 Forward Markets and Contracts
Reading 72 Futures Markets and Contracts
Reading 73 Option Markets and Contracts
Reading 74 Swap Markets and Contracts
Reading 75 Risk Management Applications of Option Strategies

LEARNING OUTCOMES

Reading 70: Derivative Markets and Instruments
The candidate should be able to:

a. define a derivative and differentiate between exchange-traded and over-the-counter derivatives;

b. define a forward commitment and a contingent claim, and describe the basic characteristics of forward contracts, futures contracts, options (calls and puts), and swaps;

c. discuss the purposes and criticisms of derivative markets;

d. explain arbitrage and the role it plays in determining prices and promoting market efficiency.

Reading 71: Forward Markets and Contracts
The candidate should be able to:

a. differentiate between the positions held by the long and short parties to a forward contract in terms of delivery/settlement and default risk;

b. describe the procedures for settling a forward contract at expiration, and discuss how termination alternatives prior to expiration can affect credit risk;

c. differentiate between a dealer and an end user of a forward contract;

d. describe the characteristics of equity forward contracts and forward contracts on zero-coupon and coupon bonds;

e. describe the characteristics of the Eurodollar time deposit market, define LIBOR and Euribor;

f. describe the characteristics of forward rate agreements (FRAs);

g. calculate and interpret the payoff of an FRA and explain each of the component terms;

h. describe the characteristics of currency forward contracts.

Reading 72: Futures Markets and Contracts
The candidate should be able to:

a. describe the characteristics of futures contracts, and distinguish between futures contracts and forward contracts;

b. differentiate between margin in the securities markets and margin in the futures markets; and define initial margin, maintenance margin, variation margin, and settlement price;

c. describe price limits and the process of marking to market, and compute and interpret the margin balance, given the previous day's balance and the change in the futures price;

d. describe how a futures contract can be terminated by a close-out (i.e., offset) at expiration (or prior to expiration), delivery, an equivalent cash settlement, or an exchange-for-physicals;

e. describe the characteristics of the following types of futures contracts: Eurodollar, Treasury bond, stock index, and currency.

Reading 73: Option Markets and Contracts
The candidate should be able to:

a. define European option, American option, and moneyness, and differentiate between exchange-traded options and over-the-counter options;

b. identify the types of options in terms of the underlying instruments;

c. compare and contrast interest rate options to forward rate agreements (FRAs);

d. define interest rate caps, floors, and collars;

e. compute and interpret option payoffs, and explain how interest rate option payoffs differ from the payoffs of other types of options;

f. define intrinsic value and time value, and explain their relationship;

g. determine the minimum and maximum values of European options and American options;

h. calculate and interpret the lowest prices of European and American calls and puts based on the rules for minimum values and lower bounds;

i. explain how option prices are affected by the exercise price and the time to expiration;

j. explain put-call parity for European options, and relate put-call parity to arbitrage and the construction of synthetic options;

k. contrast American options with European options in terms of the lower bounds on option prices and the possibility of early exercise;

l. explain how cash flows on the underlying asset affect put-call parity and the lower bounds of option prices;

m. indicate the directional effect of an interest rate change or volatility change on an option's price.

Reading 74: Swap Markets and Contracts
The candidate should be able to:

a. describe the characteristics of swap contracts and explain how swaps are terminated;

b. define and give examples of currency swaps, plain vanilla interest rate swaps, and equity swaps, and calculate and interpret the payments on each.

Reading 75: Risk Management Applications of Option Strategies
The candidate should be able to:

a. determine the value at expiration, profit, maximum profit, maximum loss, breakeven underlying price at expiration, and general shape of the graph of the strategies of buying and selling calls and puts, and indicate the market outlook of investors using these strategies;

b. determine the value at expiration, profit, maximum profit, maximum loss, breakeven underlying price at expiration, and general shape of the graph of a covered call strategy and a protective put strategy, and explain the risk management application of each strategy.

4⅝
5½ 5½ −
5½
20⅝ 21³⁄₁₆ − ¹⁄₁₆
17³⁄₈ 18⅛ + ⅞
18½
7¼ 6½ 6½ − ½
15⁄₁₆ 31⁄₃₂ − ⅛
9⁄₁₆ 9⁄₁₆
1⁹⁄₃₂
7¹⁵⁄₁₆ 7¹³⁄₁₆ 7¹⁵⁄₁₆
2⅝ 2¹¹⁄₃₂ 2½ +
2¾ 2¼ 2¼
6⅛ 12¹⁄₁₆ 11⅜ 11¾ +
87 33¾ 33 33¹⁄₁₆ −
602 25⅝ 24⁹⁄₁₆ 25⅜ +
833 12 11⅝ 11⅞ +
16 10½ 10½ 10⅛ −
78 15⅞ 15¹³⁄₁₆ 15⅞ −
608 9¹⁄₁₆ 8¼ 8⅛ +
430 11¼ 10⅛
163 5 4⅝

DERIVATIVE MARKETS AND INSTRUMENTS

by Don M. Chance

LEARNING OUTCOMES

The candidate should be able to:

a. define a derivative and differentiate between exchange-traded and over-the-counter derivatives;

b. define a forward commitment and a contingent claim, and describe the basic characteristics of forward contracts, futures contracts, options (calls and puts), and swaps;

c. discuss the purposes and criticisms of derivative markets;

d. explain arbitrage and the role it plays in determining prices and promoting market efficiency.

INTRODUCTION 　　1

The concept of risk is at the heart of investment management. Financial analysts and portfolio managers continually identify, measure, and manage risk. In a simple world where only stocks and bonds exist, the only risks are the fluctuations associated with market values and the potential for a creditor to default. Measuring risk often takes the form of standard deviations, betas, and probabilities of default. In the above simple setting, managing risk is limited to engaging in stock and bond transactions that reduce or increase risk. For example, a portfolio manager may hold a combination of a risky stock portfolio and a risk-free bond, with the relative allocations determined by the investor's tolerance for risk. If for some reason the manager desires a lower level of risk, the only transactions available to adjust the risk downward are to reduce the allocation to the risky stock portfolio and increase the allocation to the risk-free bond.

Analysis of Derivatives for the CFA® Program, by Don M. Chance. Copyright © 2003 by AIMR. Reprinted with permission.

But we do not live in a simple world of only stocks and bonds, and in fact investors can adjust the level of risk in a variety of ways. For example, one way to reduce risk is to use insurance, which can be described as the act of paying someone to assume a risk for you. The financial markets have created their own way of offering insurance against financial loss in the form of contracts called **derivatives.** *A derivative is a financial instrument that offers a return based on the return of some other underlying asset.* In this sense, its return is *derived* from another instrument—hence, the name.

As the definition states, a derivative's performance is based on the performance of an underlying asset. This underlying asset is often referred to simply as the **underlying.**[1] It trades in a market in which buyers and sellers meet and decide on a price; the seller then delivers the asset to the buyer and receives payment. The price for immediate purchase of the underlying asset is called the **cash price** or **spot price** (in this book, we will use the latter term). A derivative also has a defined and limited life: A derivative contract initiates on a certain date and terminates on a later date. Often the derivative's payoff is determined and/or made on the expiration date, although that is not always the case. In accordance with the usual rules of law, a derivative contract is an agreement between two parties in which each does something for the other. In some cases, as in the simple insurance analogy, a derivative contract involves one party paying the other some money and receiving coverage against potential losses. In other cases, the parties simply agree that each will do something for the other at a later date. In other words, no money need change hands up front.

We have alluded to several general characteristics of derivative contracts. Let us now turn to the specific types of derivatives that we will cover in this book.

2   TYPES OF DERIVATIVES

In this section, we take a brief look at the different types of derivative contracts. This brief treatment serves only as a short introduction to familiarize you with the general ideas behind the contracts. We shall examine these derivatives in considerable detail in later readings.

Let us start by noting that derivative contracts are created on and traded in two distinct but related types of markets: exchange traded and over the counter. Exchange-traded contracts have standard terms and features and are traded on an organized derivatives trading facility, usually referred to as a **futures exchange** or an options exchange. Over-the-counter contracts are any transactions created by two parties anywhere else. We shall examine the other distinctive features of these two types of contracts as we proceed.

Derivative contracts can be classified into two general categories: forward commitments and **contingent claims.** In the following section, we examine for-

---

[1] On behalf of the financial world, we apologize to all English teachers. "Underlying" is not a noun, but in the world of derivatives it is commonly used as such. To be consistent with that terminology, we use it in that manner here.

ward commitments, which are contracts in which the two parties enter into an agreement to engage in a transaction at a later date at a price established at the start. Within the category of forward commitments, two major classifications exist: exchanged-traded contracts, specifically futures, and over-the-counter contracts, which consist of forward contracts and swaps.

2.1 Forward Commitments

The forward contract is an agreement between two parties in which one party, the buyer, agrees to buy from the other party, the seller, an underlying asset at a future date at a price established at the start. The parties to the transaction specify the forward contract's terms and conditions, such as when and where delivery will take place and the precise identity of the underlying. In this sense, the contract is said to be *customized*. Each party is subject to the possibility that the other party will default.

Many simple, everyday transactions are forms of forward commitments. For example, when you order a pizza for delivery to your home, you are entering into an agreement for a transaction to take place later ("30 minutes or less," as some advertise) at a price agreed on at the outset. Although default is not likely, it could occur—for instance, if the party ordering the pizza decided to go out to eat, leaving the delivery person wondering where the customer went. Or perhaps the delivery person had a wreck on the way to delivery and the pizza was destroyed. But such events are extremely rare.

Forward contracts in the financial world take place in a large and private market consisting of banks, investment banking firms, governments, and corporations. These contracts call for the purchase and sale of an underlying asset at a later date. The underlying asset could be a security (i.e., a stock or bond), a foreign currency, a commodity, or combinations thereof, or sometimes an interest rate. In the case of an interest rate, the contract is not on a bond from which the interest rate is derived but rather on the interest rate itself. Such a contract calls for the exchange of a single interest payment for another at a later date, where at least one of the payments is determined at the later date.[2]

As an example of someone who might use a forward contract in the financial world, consider a pension fund manager. The manager, anticipating a future inflow of cash, could engage in a forward contract to purchase a portfolio equivalent to the S&P 500 at a future date—timed to coincide with the future cash inflow date—at a price agreed on at the start. When that date arrives, the cash is received and used to settle the obligation on the forward contract.[3] In this manner, the pension fund manager commits to the position in the S&P 500 without having to worry about the risk that the market will rise during that period. Other common forward contracts include commitments to buy and sell a foreign currency or a commodity at a future date, locking in the exchange rate or commodity price at the start.

The forward market is a private and largely unregulated market. Any transaction involving a commitment between two parties for the future purchase/sale of an asset is a forward contract. Although pizza deliveries are generally not considered forward contracts, similar transactions occur commonly in the financial world. Yet we cannot simply pick up *The Wall Street Journal* or *The Financial Times* and read

---

[2] These instruments are called forward rate agreements and will be studied in detail in Reading 71.

[3] The settling of the forward contract can occur through delivery, in which case the buyer pays the agreed-upon price and receives the asset from the seller, or through an equivalent cash settlement. In the latter case, the seller pays the buyer the difference between the market price and the agreed-upon price if the market price is higher. The buyer pays the seller the difference between the agreed-upon price and the market price if the agreed-upon price is higher.

about them or determine how many contracts were created the previous day.[4] They are private transactions for a reason: The parties want to keep them private and want little government interference. This need for privacy and the absence of regulation does not imply anything illegal or corrupt but simply reflects a desire to maintain a prudent level of business secrecy.

Recall that we described a forward contract as an agreement between two parties in which one party, the buyer, agrees to buy from the other party, the seller, an underlying asset at a future date at a price agreed upon at the start. A **futures contract** is a variation of a forward contract that has essentially the same basic definition but some additional features that clearly distinguish it from a forward contract. For one, a futures contract is not a private and customized transaction. Instead, it is a public, standardized transaction that takes place on a futures exchange. A futures exchange, like a stock exchange, is an organization that provides a facility for engaging in futures transactions and establishes a mechanism through which parties can buy and sell these contracts. The contracts are standardized, which means that the exchange determines the expiration dates, the underlying, how many units of the underlying are included in one contract, and various other terms and conditions.

Probably the most important distinction between a futures contract and a forward contract, however, lies in the default risk associated with the contracts. As noted above, in a forward contract, the risk of default is a concern. Specifically, the party with a loss on the contract could default. Although the legal consequences of default are severe, parties nonetheless sometimes fall into financial trouble and are forced to default. For that reason, only solid, creditworthy parties can generally engage in forward contracts. In a futures contract, however, the futures exchange guarantees to each party that if the other fails to pay, the exchange will pay. In fact, the exchange actually writes itself into the middle of the contract so that each party effectively has a contract with the exchange and not with the other party. The exchange collects payment from one party and disburses payment to the other.

The futures exchange implements this **performance guarantee** through an organization called the **clearinghouse**. For some futures exchanges, the clearinghouse is a separate corporate entity. For others, it is a division or subsidiary of the exchange. In either case, however, the clearinghouse protects itself by requiring that the parties settle their gains and losses to the exchange on a daily basis. This process, referred to as the **daily settlement** or marking to market, is a critical distinction between futures and forward contracts. With futures contracts, profits and losses are charged and credited to participants' accounts each day. This practice prevents losses from accumulating without being collected. For forward contracts, losses accumulate until the end of the contract.[5]

One should not get the impression that forward contracts are rife with credit losses and futures contracts never involve default. Credit losses on forward contracts are extremely rare, owing to the excellent risk management practices of participants. In the case of futures contracts, parties do default on occasion. In fact, it is likely that there are more defaults on futures contracts than on forward

---

[4] In Section 4 of this reading, we will look at some ways to measure the amount of this type of trading.

[5] Although this process of losses accumulating on forward contracts until the expiration day is the standard format for a contract, modern risk management procedures include the possibility of forcing a party in debt to periodically pay losses accrued prior to expiration. In addition, a variety of risk-reducing techniques, such as the use of collateral, are used to mitigate the risk of loss. We discuss these points in more detail in Reading 71.

contracts.[6] Nonetheless, the exchange guarantee has never failed for the party on the other side of the transaction. Although the possibility of the clearinghouse defaulting does exist, the probability of such a default happening is extremely small. Thus, we can generally assume that futures contracts are default-free. In contrast, the possibility of default, although relatively small, exists for forward contracts.

Another important distinction between forward contracts and futures contracts lies in the ability to engage in offsetting transactions. Forward contracts are generally designed to be held until expiration. It is possible, however, for a party to engage in the opposite transaction prior to expiration. For example, a party might commit to purchase one million euros at a future date at an exchange rate of \$0.85/€. Suppose that later the euro has a forward price of \$0.90/€. The party might then choose to engage in a new forward contract to sell the euro at the new price of \$0.90/€. The party then has a commitment to buy the euro at \$0.85 and sell it at \$0.90. The risk associated with changes in exchange rates is eliminated, but both transactions remain in place and are subject to default.[7]

In futures markets, the contracts have standardized terms and trade in a market that provides sufficient liquidity to permit the parties to enter the market and offset transactions previously created. The use of contracts with standardized terms results in relatively widespread acceptance of these terms as homogeneous agreed-upon standards for trading these contracts. For example, a U.S. Treasury bond futures contract covering \$100,000 face value of Treasury bonds, with an expiration date in March, June, September, or December, is a standard contract. In contrast, if a party wanted a contract covering \$120,000 of Treasury bonds, he would not find any such instrument in the futures markets and would have to create a nonstandard instrument in the forward market. The acceptance of standardized terms makes parties more willing to trade futures contracts. Consequently, futures markets offer the parties liquidity, which gives them a means of buying and selling the contracts. Because of this liquidity, a party can enter into a contract and later, before the contract expires, enter into the opposite transaction and offset the position, much the same way one might buy or sell a stock or bond and then reverse the transaction later. This reversal of a futures position completely eliminates any further financial consequences of the original transaction.[8]

A **swap** is a variation of a forward contract that is essentially equivalent to a series of forward contracts. Specifically, a swap is an agreement between two parties to exchange a series of future cash flows. Typically at least one of the two series of cash flows is determined by a later outcome. In other words, one party agrees to pay the other a series of cash flows whose value will be determined by the unknown future course of some underlying factor, such as an interest rate, exchange rate, stock price, or commodity price. The other party promises to make a series of payments that could also be determined by a second unknown factor or, alternatively, could be preset. We commonly refer to swap payments as being "fixed" or "floating" (sometimes "variable").

---

[6] Defaults are more likely for futures contracts than for forward contracts because participants in the forward markets must meet higher creditworthiness standards than those in the futures markets. Indeed, many individuals participate in the futures markets; forward market participants are usually large, creditworthy companies. But the forward markets have no guarantor of performance, whereas the futures markets do. Therefore, participants in the forward markets have incurred credit losses in the past, while participants in the futures markets have not.

[7] It is possible for the party engaging in the first transaction to engage in the second transaction with the same party. The two parties agree to cancel their transactions, settling the difference in value in cash and thereby eliminating the risk associated with exchange rates as well as the possibility of default.

[8] A common misconception is that, as a result of their standardized terms, futures contracts are liquid but nonstandardized forward contracts are illiquid. This is not always the case; many futures contracts have low liquidity, and many forward contracts have high liquidity.

We noted that a forward contract is an agreement to buy or sell an underlying asset at a future date at a price agreed on today. A swap in which one party makes a single fixed payment and the other makes a single floating payment amounts to a forward contract. One party agrees to make known payments to the other and receive something unknown in return. This type of contract is like an agreement to buy at a future date, paying a fixed amount and receiving something of unknown future value. That the swap is a *series* of such payments distinguishes it from a forward contract, which is only a single payment.[9]

Swaps, like forward contracts, are private transactions and thus not subject to direct regulation.[10] Swaps are arguably the most successful of all derivative transactions. Probably the most common use of a swap is a situation in which a corporation, currently borrowing at a floating rate, enters into a swap that commits it to making a series of interest payments to the swap counterparty at a fixed rate, while receiving payments from the swap counterparty at a rate related to the floating rate at which it is making its loan payments. The floating components cancel, resulting in the effective conversion of the original **floating-rate loan** to a fixed-rate loan.

Forward commitments (whether forwards, futures, or swaps) are firm and binding agreements to engage in a transaction at a future date. They obligate each party to complete the transaction, or alternatively, to offset the transaction by engaging in another transaction that settles each party's financial obligation to the other. Contingent claims, on the other hand, allow one party the flexibility to not engage in the future transaction, depending on market conditions.

2.2 Contingent Claims

Contingent claims are derivatives in which the payoffs occur if a specific event happens. We generally refer to these types of derivatives as options. Specifically, an **option** is a financial instrument that gives one party the right, but not the obligation, to buy or sell an underlying asset from or to another party at a fixed price over a specific period of time. An option that gives the right to buy is referred to as a call; an option that gives the right to sell is referred to as a put. The fixed price at which the underlying can be bought or sold is called the **exercise price**, **strike price**, **striking price**, or **strike**, and is determined at the outset of the transaction. In this book, we refer to it as the exercise price, and the action of buying or selling the underlying at the exercise price is called exercising the option. The holder of the option has the right to exercise it and will do so if conditions are advantageous; otherwise, the option will expire unexercised. Thus, the payoff of the option is contingent on an event taking place, so options are sometimes referred to as contingent claims.

In contrast to participating in a forward or futures contract, which represents a *commitment* to buy or sell, owning an option represents the *right* to buy or sell. To acquire this right, the buyer of the option must pay a price at the start to the option seller. This price is called the **option premium** or sometimes just the option price. In this book, we usually refer to it as the option price.

Because the option buyer has the right to buy or sell an asset, the seller of the option has the potential commitment to sell or buy this asset. If the option

---

[9] A few other distinctions exist between swaps and forward contracts, such as the fact that swaps can involve both parties paying a variable amount.

[10] Like all over-the-counter derivatives transactions, swaps are subject to indirect regulatory oversight in that the companies using them could be regulated by securities or banking authorities. In addition, swaps, like all contracts, are subject to normal contract and civil law.

buyer has the right to buy, the option seller may be obligated to sell. If the option buyer has the right to sell, the option seller may be obligated to buy. As noted above, the option seller receives the amount of the option price from the option buyer for his willingness to bear this risk.

An important distinction we made between forward and futures contracts was that the former are customized private transactions between two parties without a guarantee against losses from default. The latter are standardized contracts that take place on futures exchanges and are guaranteed by the exchange against losses from default. For options, both types of contracts—over-the-counter customized and exchange-listed standardized—exist. In other words, the buyer and seller of an option can arrange their own terms and create an **option contract**. Alternatively, the buyer and seller can meet directly, or through their brokers, on an options exchange and trade standardized options. In the case of customized options, the buyer is subject to the possibility of the seller defaulting when and if the buyer decides to exercise the option. Because the option buyer is not obligated to do anything beyond paying the original price, the seller of any type of option is not subject to the buyer defaulting. In the case of a standardized option, the buyer does not face the risk of the seller defaulting. The exchange, through its clearinghouse, guarantees the seller's performance to the buyer.

A variety of other instruments contain options and thus are forms of contingent claims. For instance, many corporations issue convertible bonds offering the holder an optionlike feature that enables the holder to participate in gains on the market price of the corporation's stock without having to participate in losses on the stock. Callable bonds are another example of a common financial instrument that contains an option, in this case the option of the issuer to pay off the bond before its maturity. Options themselves are often characterized in terms of standard or fairly basic options and more advanced options, often referred to as exotic options. There are also options that are not even based on assets but rather on futures contracts or other derivatives. A very widely used group of options is based on interest rates.

Another common type of option is contained in asset-backed securities. An asset-backed security is a claim on a pool of securities. The pool, which might be mortgages, loans, or bonds, is a portfolio assembled by a financial institution that then sells claims on the portfolio. Often, the borrowers who issued the mortgages, loans, or bonds have the right to pay off their debts early, and many choose to do so when interest rates fall significantly. They then refinance their loans by taking out a new loan at a lower interest rate. This right, called a prepayment feature, is a valuable option owned by the borrower. Holders of asset-backed securities bear the risk associated with prepayment options and hence are sellers of those options. The holders, or option sellers, receive a higher promised yield on their bond investment than they would have received on an otherwise equivalent bond without the option.

With an understanding of derivatives, there are no limits to the types of financial instruments that can be constructed, analyzed, and applied to achieve investment objectives. What you learn from this book and the CFA Program will help you recognize and understand the variety of derivatives that appear in many forms in the financial world.

Exhibit 1 presents a classification of the types of derivative contracts as we have described them. Note that we have partitioned derivatives into those that are exchange-traded and those that trade in the over-the-counter market. The exhibit also notes some other categories not specifically mentioned above. These instruments are included for completeness, but they are relatively advanced and not covered in this first reading.

EXHIBIT 1	A Classification of Derivatives

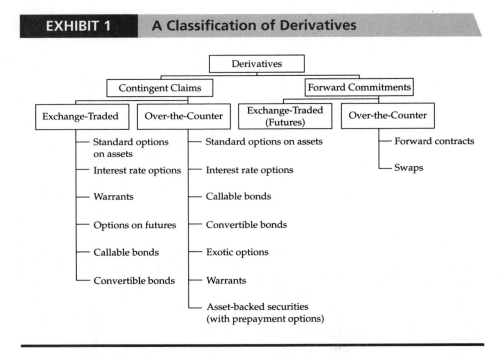

We have now looked at the basic characteristics of derivative contracts. In order to better understand and appreciate derivatives, we should take a quick look at where they came from and where they are now. Accordingly, we take a brief look at the history and current state of derivative markets.

3   DERIVATIVE MARKETS: PAST AND PRESENT

Derivative markets have an exciting and colorful history. Examining that history gives insights that help us understand the structure of these markets as they exist today.

The basic characteristics of derivative contracts can be found throughout the history of humankind. Agreements to engage in a commercial transaction as well as agreements that provide the right to engage in a commercial transaction date back hundreds of years. In medieval times, contracts for the future delivery of an asset with the price fixed at the time of the contract initiation were frequent. Early indications of futures markets were seen in Japan many hundreds of years ago. The futures markets generally trace their roots, however, to the 1848 creation of the Chicago Board of Trade, the first organized futures market. Its origins resulted from the burgeoning grain markets in Chicago, which created a need for a farmer to secure a price at one point in time, store the grain, and deliver it at a later point in time. At around the same time, customized option transactions were being offered, including some by the well-known financier Russell Sage, who found a clever way to offer combinations of customized options that replicated a loan at a rate that exceeded the maximum allowable rate under the then-existing usury laws.[11]

---

[11] Sage was perhaps the first options arbitrageur. Of course, usury laws are rare these days and most investors understand **put–call parity**, so do not expect to make any money copying Sage's scheme.

In the century that followed, the futures industry grew rapidly. Institutions such as the Chicago Board of Trade, the Chicago Mercantile Exchange, and later, the New York Mercantile Exchange and the Chicago Board Options Exchange became the primary forces in the global derivatives industry. These exchanges created and successfully marketed many innovative derivative contracts.[12] Although the first 100 years of futures exchanges were dominated by trading in futures on agricultural commodities, the 1970s saw the introduction of futures on financial instruments such as currencies, bonds, and stock indices. These "financial futures," as well as newly introduced options on individual stocks, currencies, bonds, and stock indices, ushered in a new era in which financial derivatives dominated agricultural derivatives—a situation that continues today. Although the commodity derivatives market includes very active contracts in oil and precious metals, financial derivatives have remained the primary force in the worldwide derivatives market.

Exchange-listed standardized derivatives, however, have hardly been the only instruments in the derivatives world. As noted, customized options have been around since at least the 19th century. The customized-options market flourished until the early 1970s, largely as a retail product. With the introduction of standardized options in 1973, however, the customized options market effectively died. But something else was going on at the time that would later revive this market. In the early 1970s, foreign exchange rates were deregulated and allowed to float freely. This deregulation led not only to the development of a futures, and later options, market for currencies but also to a market for customized forward contracts in foreign currencies. This market became known as the interbank market because it was largely operated within the global banking community, and it grew rapidly. Most importantly, it set the stage for the banking industry to engage in other customized derivative transactions.

Spurred by deregulation of their permitted activities during the 1980s, banks discovered that they could create derivatives of all forms and sell them to corporations and institutions that had risks that could best be managed with products specifically tailored for a given situation. These banks make markets in derivative products by assuming the risks that the corporations want to eliminate. But banks are not in the business of assuming unwanted risks. They use their vast resources and global networks to transfer or lay off the risk elsewhere, often in the futures markets. If they successfully lay off these risks, they can profit by buying and selling the derivatives at a suitable bid–ask spread. In addition to banks, investment banking firms also engage in derivatives transactions of this sort. The commercial and investment banks that make markets in derivatives are called **derivatives dealers**. Buying and selling derivatives is a natural extension of the activity these banks normally undertake in financial markets. This market for customized derivatives is what we refer to as the over-the-counter derivatives market.

By the end of the 20th century, the derivatives market reached a mature stage, growing at only a slow pace but providing a steady offering of existing products and a continuing slate of new products. Derivatives exchanges underwent numerous changes, often spurred by growing competition from the over-the-counter market. Some merged; others that were formerly nonprofit corporations have since become profit making. Some derivatives exchanges have even experimented with offering somewhat customized transactions. Nearly all have lobbied heavily for a reduction in the level or structure of the regulations imposed on them. Some derivatives exchanges have altered the manner in which trading takes place, from the old system of face-to-face on a trading floor (in sections called pits) to off-floor electronic trading in which participants communicate

---

[12] It is probably also important to note that the futures and options exchanges have introduced many unsuccessful contracts as well.

through computer screens. This type of transacting, called electronic trading, has even been extended to the Internet and, not surprisingly, is called e-trading. Pit trading is still the primary format for derivatives exchanges in the United States, but electronic trading is clearly the wave of the future. As the dominant form of trading outside the United States, it will likely replace pit trading in the United States in coming years.

Exhibit 2 lists all global derivatives exchanges as of January 2002. Note that almost every country with a reasonably advanced financial market system has a derivatives exchange.

EXHIBIT 2	Global Derivatives Exchanges

North America
American Stock Exchange
Bourse de Montreal
BrokerTec Futures Exchange
Chicago Board Options Exchange
Chicago Board of Trade
Chicago Mercantile Exchange
International Securities Exchange (New York)
Kansas City Board of Trade
Minneapolis Grain Exchange
New York Board of Trade
New York Mercantile Exchange
Pacific Exchange (San Francisco)
Philadelphia Stock Exchange
Winnipeg Commodity Exchange

Asia
Central Japan Commodity Exchange
Dalian Commodity Exchange
Hong Kong Exchanges & Clearing
Kansai Commodities Exchange (Osaka)
Korea Futures Exchange
Korea Stock Exchange
Malaysia Derivatives Exchange
New Zealand Futures & Options Exchange
Osaka Mercantile Exchange
Shanghai Futures Exchange
Singapore Commodity Exchange
Singapore Exchange
Tokyo Commodity Exchange
Tokyo Grain Exchange
Tokyo International Financial Futures Exchange
Tokyo Stock Exchange
Zhengzhou Commodity Exchange

Europe
Bolsa de Valores de Lisboa e Porto
Borsa Italiana
Budapest Commodity Exchange
Eurex Frankfurt
Eurex Zurich
Euronext Amsterdam
Euronext Brussels
Euronext Paris
FUTOP Market (Copenhagen)
Helsinki Exchanges Group
International Petroleum Exchange of London
London International Financial Futures and Options Exchange
London Metal Exchange
MEFF Renta Fija (Barcelona)
MEFF Renta Variable (Madrid)
OM London Exchange
OM Stockholm Exchange
Romanian Commodity Exchange
Sibiu Monetary–Financial and Commodities Exchange (Romania)
Tel Aviv Stock Exchange
Wiener Borse AG (Vienna)

South America
Bolsa de Mercadorias & Futuros (Sao Paulo)
Mercado a Termino de Buenos Aires
Santiago Stock Exchange

Africa
South African Futures Exchange

Australia
Australian Stock Exchange
Sydney Futures Exchange

Source: Futures [magazine] *2002 Sourcebook.*

We cannot technically identify where over-the-counter derivatives markets exist. These types of transactions can conceivably occur anywhere two parties can agree to engage in a transaction. It is generally conceded, however, that London and New York are the primary markets for over-the-counter derivatives; considerable activity also takes place in Tokyo, Paris, Frankfurt, Chicago, Amsterdam, and many other major world cities.

Now we know where the derivative markets are, but are they big enough for us to care about? We examine this question in Section 4.

HOW BIG IS THE DERIVATIVES MARKET?

4

Good question. And the answer is: We really do not know. Because trading in exchange-listed contracts, such as futures and some options, is recorded, volume figures for those types of contracts are available. Exhibit 3 presents summary statistics for contract volume of global futures and options for 2000 and 2001. Note that in 2001, the largest category is equity indices. In 2000, the largest category was individual equities, followed by interest rates. In prior years, the largest category had been interest rates.

Currently, the United States accounts for approximately 35 percent of global futures and options volume. The largest exchange in the world, however, is the Korea Stock Exchange, which trades an exceptionally large volume of options on a Korean stock index. The second-largest exchange (and the largest exchange in terms of futures volume only) is the combined German–Swiss exchange called Eurex. The other largest exchanges (in order of 2001 volume) are the Chicago Mercantile Exchange, the Chicago Board of Trade, the London International Financial Futures and Options Exchange, the Paris Bourse, the New York Mercantile Exchange, the Bolsa de Mercadorias & Futuros of Brazil, and the Chicago Board Options Exchange. All of these exchanges traded at least 70 million contracts in 2001.[13]

EXHIBIT 3	Global Exchange-Traded Futures and Options Contract Volume (in millions of contracts)	
Contract Type	**2000**	**2001**
Equity indices	674.8	1,470.3
Interest rates	844.3	1,216.1
Individual equities	969.7	1,112.7
Energy	154.8	166.9
Agricultural	185.7	156.5
Nonprecious metals	75.7	70.2
Currencies	47.0	49.2
Precious metals	36.2	39.1
Other	1.3	0.8
Overall Total	2,989.5	4,281.8

Source: Futures Industry (January/February 2002).

---

[13] *Futures Industry* (January/February 2002).

One important factor that must be considered, however, in looking at trading volume as a measure of activity is that the futures and options exchanges influence their own volume by designating a contract's size. For example, a standard option in the United States covers 100 shares of the underlying stock. If an investor takes a position in options on 1,000 shares of stock, the investor would trade 10 options. If the options exchange had designated that the contract size be 200 options, then the investor would trade only five contracts. Although there are often good reasons for setting a contract size at a certain level, volume comparisons must be taken with a degree of skepticism.[14]

The over-the-counter derivatives market is much more difficult to measure. Because the transactions are private, unregulated, and can take place virtually anywhere two parties can enter into an agreement, no official tabulation exists that allows us to identify the size of the market. Information is available, however, from semiannual surveys conducted by the Bank for International Settlements (BIS) of Basel, Switzerland, an international organization of central banks. The BIS publishes this data in its semiannual report "Regular OTC Derivatives Market Statistics," available on its website at www.bis.org/publ/regpubl.htm.

Exhibit 4 presents two charts constructed from the 30 June 2001 BIS survey and shows figures for foreign exchange, interest rate, equity, and commodity derivatives transactions. The "other" category, however, does include transactions of these types and reflects the BIS's estimates of positions taken by parties that do not report in this survey. It is used primarily to obtain an estimate for the overall size of the market and is not broken down by category.

For over-the-counter derivatives, notional principal is the most widely used measure of market size. Notional principal measures the amount of the underlying asset covered by a derivative contract. For example, a swap involving interest payments on ¥500 million has a notional principal of ¥500 million. The actual payments made in the swap, however, are merely interest payments on ¥500 million and do not come close to ¥500 million.[15] Thus, although notional principal is a commonly used measure of the size of the market, it can give a misleading impression by suggesting that it reflects the amount of money involved.[16]

Nonetheless, we would be remiss if we failed to note the market size as measured by notional principal. Based on Exhibit 4A, the total notional principal summing over these five categories is almost $100 trillion. Also note that interest rate derivatives are the most widely used category by far.

Exhibit 4B gives another picture of the size of the market by indicating the market value of over-the-counter derivatives. Market value indicates the

---

[14] For example, in 1999 the volume of Treasury bond futures on the Chicago Board of Trade was about 90 million contracts while the volume of Eurodollar futures on the Chicago Mercantile Exchange was about 93 million contracts. Consequently, at that time these two contracts appeared to have about the same amount of activity. But the Treasury bond contract covers Treasury bonds with a face value of $100,000, while the Eurodollar contract covers Eurodollars with a face value of $1,000,000. Thus, the Eurodollar futures market was arguably 10 times the size of the Treasury bond futures market. In 2002, about three Eurodollar futures contracts were traded for every Treasury bond futures contract traded.

[15] In fact, the payments on a swap are even smaller than the interest payments on the notional principal. Swap interest payments usually equal only the difference between the interest payments owed by the two parties.

[16] The over-the-counter derivatives industry originally began the practice of measuring its size by notional principal. This was a deliberate tactic designed to make the industry look larger so it would be more noticed and viewed as a significant and legitimate force. As it turns out, this tactic backfired, resulting in fears that more money was involved and at risk of loss than really was. Calls for increased scrutiny of the industry by government authorities resulted in the industry backpedaling on its use of notional principal and focusing more on market value as a measure of its size. Nonetheless, notional principal continues to be used as one, if not the primary, measure of the industry's size.

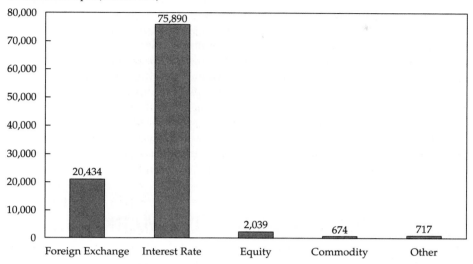

EXHIBIT 4A — Outstanding Notional Principal of Global Over-the-Counter Derivatives, 30 June 2001 (billions)

Notional Principal (billions of $)

	Notional Principal
Foreign Exchange	20,434
Interest Rate	75,890
Equity	2,039
Commodity	674
Other	717

Source: Bank for International Settlements, www.bis.org/publ/regpubl.htm.

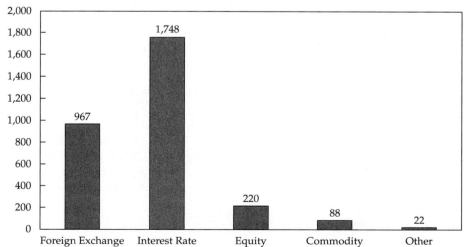

EXHIBIT 4B — Outstanding Market Value of Global Over-the-Counter Derivatives, 30 June 2001 (billions)

Market Value (billions of $)

	Market Value
Foreign Exchange	967
Interest Rate	1,748
Equity	220
Commodity	88
Other	22

Source: Bank for International Settlements, www.bis.org/publ/regpubl.htm.

economic worth of a derivative contract and represents the amount of money that would change hands if these transactions were terminated at the time of the report. The total market value for all categories is about $3 trillion. Market value is a better indication of the size of the market because it more accurately represents the actual money involved. Nonetheless, market value is subject to greater errors in estimation and thus is a less reliable measure than notional principal.

Although it is impossible to determine where these contracts originate, dollar-denominated derivatives represented about 34 percent of the global interest rate derivatives market in 2001, with euro-denominated derivatives accounting for about 27 percent and yen-denominated derivatives representing 17 percent.

Whether notional principal or market value is used, it is clear that the derivatives industry is large by any standard. Derivatives are widely available in global asset markets, and consequently, understanding derivatives is essential to operating in these markets, whether one chooses to use them or not.

Because derivative markets have been created around the world, there must be a reason for their continued existence. Let us now look at why derivative markets exist.

5 THE PURPOSES OF DERIVATIVE MARKETS

Derivative markets serve a variety of purposes in global social and economic systems. One of the primary functions of futures markets is **price discovery**. Futures markets provide valuable information about the prices of the underlying assets on which futures contracts are based. They provide this information in two ways. First, many of these assets are traded in geographically dispersed markets. Recall that the current price of the underlying asset is called the spot price. With geographically dispersed markets, many different spot prices could exist. In the futures markets, the price of the contract with the shortest **time to expiration** often serves as a proxy for the price of the underlying asset. Second, the prices of all futures contracts serve as prices that can be accepted by those who trade contracts in lieu of facing the risk of uncertain future prices. For example, a company that mines gold can hedge by selling a futures contract on gold expiring in two months, which locks in the price of gold two months later. In this manner, the two-month futures price substitutes for the uncertainty of the price of gold over the next two months.[17]

Futures contracts are not, however, the only derivatives that serve this purpose. In fact, forward contracts and swaps allow users to substitute a single locked-in price for the uncertainty of future spot prices and thereby permit the same form of price discovery as do futures.

Options work in a slightly different manner. They are used in a different form of hedging, one that permits the holder to protect against loss while allowing participation in gains if prices move favorably. Options do not so much reveal *prices* as they reveal *volatility*. As we shall see in Reading 73, the volatility of the underlying asset is a critical factor in the pricing of options. It is possible, therefore, to infer what investors feel about volatility from the prices of options.

---

[17] Some people view futures prices as revealing expectations of future spot prices of the underlying asset, and in that sense, leading to price discovery. This view, however, is incorrect. Futures prices are not necessarily expectations of future spot prices. As we discussed above, they allow a substitution of the futures price for the uncertainty of future spot prices of the asset. In that sense they permit the acceptance of a sure price and the avoidance of risk.

Perhaps the most important purpose of derivative markets is **risk management**. We define risk management as the process of identifying the desired level of risk, identifying the actual level of risk, and altering the latter to equal the former. Often this process is described as hedging, which generally refers to the reduction, and in some cases the elimination, of risk. On the other side is the process called speculation. Traditional discussions of derivatives refer to hedging and speculation as complementary activities. In general, hedgers seek to eliminate risk and need speculators to assume risk, but such is not always the case. Hedgers often trade with other hedgers, and speculators often trade with other speculators. All one needs to hedge or speculate is a party with opposite beliefs or opposite risk exposure. For example, a corporation that mines gold could hedge the future sale of gold by entering into a derivative transaction with a company that manufactures jewelry. Both of these companies are hedgers, seeking to avoid the uncertainty of future gold prices by locking in a price for a future transaction. The mining corporation has concerns about a price decrease, and the jewelry manufacturer is worried about a price increase.

An unfortunate consequence of the use of the terms "hedging" and "speculating" is that hedgers are somehow seen as on the high moral ground and speculators are sometimes seen as evil—a distortion of the role of speculators. In fact, there need be very little difference between hedgers and speculators. To restate an example we used when discussing swaps, consider a corporation that currently borrows at a floating rate. A common response to a fear of rising interest rates is for the corporation to use an interest rate swap in which it will make payments at a fixed rate and receive payments at a floating rate. The floating-rate payments it receives from the swap offset the floating-rate payments on the loan, thereby effectively converting the loan to a fixed-rate loan. The company is now borrowing at a fixed rate and, in the eyes of many, hedging.

But is the company really hedging? Or is it simply making a bet that interest rates will increase? If interest rates decrease, the company will be losing money in the sense of the lost opportunity to borrow at a lower rate. From a budgeting and cash flow standpoint, however, its fixed interest payments are set in stone. Moreover, the market value of a fixed-rate loan is considerably more volatile than that of a floating-rate loan. Thus, our "hedging" corporation can be viewed as taking more risk than it originally had.

The more modern view of the reason for using derivatives does not refer to hedging or speculation. Although we shall sometimes use those terms, we shall use them carefully and make our intentions clear. In the grander scheme of things, derivatives are tools that enable companies to more easily practice risk management. In the context of our corporation borrowing at the floating rate, it made a conscious decision to borrow at a fixed rate. Engaging in the swap is simply an activity designed to align its risk with the risk it wants, given its outlook for interest rates. Whether one calls this activity hedging or speculation is not even very important. The company is simply managing risk.

Derivative markets serve several other useful purposes. As we show later when exploring the pricing of derivative contracts, they improve market efficiency for the underlying assets. Efficient markets are fair and competitive and do not allow one party to easily take money from another. As a simple example, buying a stock index fund can be replicated by buying a futures on the fund and investing in risk-free bonds with the money that otherwise would have been spent on the fund. In other words, the fund and the combination of the futures and risk-free bond will have the same performance. But if the fund costs more than the combination of the futures and risk-free bond, investors have the opportunity to avoid the overpriced fund and take the combination.[18] This decreased demand for the fund will lower its price. The benefits to investors who do not even use derivatives should be clear: They can now invest in the fund at a more attractive price, because the derivatives market forced the price back to its appropriate level.

Derivative markets are also characterized by relatively low transaction costs. For example, the cost of investing in a stock index portfolio is as much as 20 times the cost of buying a futures contract on the index and a risk-free bond as described above. One might reasonably ask why derivatives are so much less expensive in terms of transaction costs. The answer is that derivatives are designed to provide a means of managing risk. As we have previously described, they serve as a form of insurance. Insurance cannot be a viable product if its cost is too high relative to the value of the insured asset. In other words, derivatives must have low transaction costs; otherwise, they would not exist.

It would be remiss to overlook the fact that derivative markets have been subject to many criticisms. We next present some of these complaints and the reasons behind them.

6   CRITICISMS OF DERIVATIVE MARKETS

Derivatives have been highly controversial for a number of reasons. For one, they are very complex. Much of the criticism has stemmed from a failure to understand derivatives. When derivatives fail to do their job, it is often the derivatives themselves, rather than the users of derivatives, that take the blame. Yet, in many cases, the critics of derivatives simply do not understand them well enough. As described in Section 2, when homeowners take out mortgages, they usually receive a valuable option: the right to prepay their mortgages. When interest rates fall, homeowners often pay off their mortgages, refinancing them at lower rates. The holders of these mortgages usually sell them to other parties, which can include small organizations and individuals. Thus, we often find unsophisticated investors holding securities based on the payments from mortgages. When homeowners refinance, they capture huge interest savings. Where does this money come from? It comes from the pockets of the holders of mortgage securities. When these unsophisticated investors lose a lot of money, derivatives usually get the blame. Yet these losses went into the pockets of homeowners in the form of interest savings. Who is to blame? Probably the brokers, who sold the securities to investors who did not know what they were buying—which leads us to the next common criticism of derivatives.

The complexity of derivatives means that sometimes the parties that use them do not understand them well. As a result, they are often used improperly, leading to potentially large losses. Such an argument can, however, be used to describe fire, electricity, and chemicals. Used improperly, perhaps in the hands of a child or someone who does not know how to use them, all of these can be extremely dangerous. Yet, we know that sufficient knowledge of fire, electricity, and chemicals to use them properly is not very difficult to obtain. The same is true for derivatives; treat them with respect and healthy doses of knowledge.

Derivatives are also mistakenly characterized as a form of legalized gambling. Although gambling is certainly legal in many parts of the world, derivatives

---

[18] Some investors, called arbitrageurs, will even find ways to sell the fund short to eliminate the risk of holding the futures and the bond, earning a profit from any discrepancy in their prices. We shall cover this type of transaction later in this reading.

are often viewed as a government's sanction of gambling via the financial markets. But there is an important distinction between gambling and derivatives: The benefits of derivatives extend much further across society. By providing a means of managing risk along with the other benefits discussed above, derivatives make financial markets work better. The organized gambling industry affects the participants, the owners of casinos, and perhaps some citizens who benefit from state lotteries. Organized gambling does not, however, make society function better, and it arguably incurs social costs.

We have taken a look at what derivatives are, where they come from, where they are now, why we have them, and what people think of them. Understanding derivatives, however, requires a basic understanding of the market forces that govern derivative prices. Although we shall cover derivative pricing in more detail in later readings, here we take a brief look at the process of pricing derivatives by examining some important fundamental principles.

ELEMENTARY PRINCIPLES OF DERIVATIVE PRICING

7

In this section, we take a preliminary glance at how derivative contracts are priced. First, we introduce the concept of **arbitrage**. Arbitrage occurs when equivalent assets or combinations of assets sell for two different prices. This situation creates an opportunity to profit at no risk with no commitment of money. Let us start with the simplest (and least likely) opportunity for arbitrage: the case of a stock selling for more than one price at a given time. Assume that a stock is trading in two markets simultaneously. Suppose the stock is trading at $100 in one market and $98 in the other market. We simply buy a share for $98 in one market and immediately sell it for $100 in the other. We have no net position in the stock, so it does not matter what price the stock moves to. We make an easy $2 at no risk and we did not have to put up any funds of our own. The sale of the stock at $100 was more than adequate to finance the purchase of the stock at $98. Naturally, many market participants would do this, which would create downward pressure on the price of the stock in the market where it trades for $100 and upward pressure on the price of the stock in the market where it trades for $98. Eventually the two prices must come together so that there is but a single price for the stock. Accordingly, the principle that no arbitrage opportunities should be available is often referred to as the **law of one price**.

Recall that we mentioned in Section 5 that an asset can potentially trade in different geographic markets and, therefore, have several spot prices. This potential would appear to violate the law of one price, but in reality, the law is still upheld. A given asset selling in two different locations is not necessarily the same asset. If a buyer in one location discovered that it is possible to buy the asset more cheaply in another location, the buyer would still have to incur the cost of moving the asset to the buyer's location. Transportation costs could offset any such price differences.[19]

Now suppose we face the situation illustrated in Exhibit 5. In Exhibit 5A, observe that we have one stock, AXE Electronics, which today is worth $50 and which, one period later, will be worth either $75 or $40. We shall denote these

---

[19] One might reasonably wonder if finding a consumer article selling in Wal-Mart at a lower price than in Target is not a violation of the law of one price. It certainly is, but we make no claim that the market for consumer products is efficient. Our focus is on the financial markets where, for example, Goldman Sachs can hardly offer shares of IBM at one price while Merrill Lynch offers them at another.

EXHIBIT 5A	Arbitrage Opportunity with Stock AXE, Stock BYF, and a Risk-Free Bond

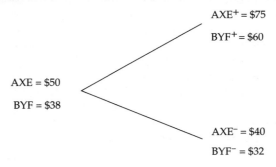

$AXE^+ = \$75$

$BYF^+ = \$60$

$AXE = \$50$

$BYF = \$38$

$AXE^- = \$40$

$BYF^- = \$32$

Note: The risk-free rate is 4 percent.

EXHIBIT 5B	Execution of Arbitrage Transaction with Stock AXE, Stock BYF, and a Risk-Free Bond

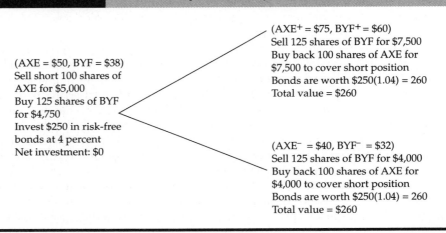

($AXE = \$50$, $BYF = \$38$)
Sell short 100 shares of
AXE for $5,000
Buy 125 shares of BYF
for $4,750
Invest $250 in risk-free
bonds at 4 percent
Net investment: $0

($AXE^+ = \$75$, $BYF^+ = \$60$)
Sell 125 shares of BYF for $7,500
Buy back 100 shares of AXE for
$7,500 to cover short position
Bonds are worth $250(1.04) = 260
Total value = $260

($AXE^- = \$40$, $BYF^- = \$32$)
Sell 125 shares of BYF for $4,000
Buy back 100 shares of AXE for
$4,000 to cover short position
Bonds are worth $250(1.04) = 260
Total value = $260

prices as $AXE = 50$, $AXE^+ = 75$, and $AXE^- = 40$. Another stock, BYF Technology, is today worth $38 and one period later will be worth $60 or $32. Thus, $BYF = 38$, $BYF^+ = 60$, and $BYF^- = 32$. Let us assume the risk-free borrowing and lending rate is 4 percent. We assume no dividends on either stock during the period covered by this example.

The opportunity exists to make a profit at no risk without committing any of our funds, as demonstrated in Exhibit 5B. Suppose we borrow 100 shares of stock AXE, which is selling for $50, and sell short, thereby receiving $5,000. We take $4,750 and purchase 125 shares of stock BYF. We invest the remaining $250 in risk-free bonds at 4 percent. This transaction will not require us to put up any funds of our own: The short sale will be sufficient to fund the investment in BYF and leave money to invest in risk-free bonds.

If the top outcome in Exhibit 5 occurs, we sell the 125 shares of BYF for 125 × $60 = $7,500. This amount is sufficient to buy back the 100 shares of AXE, which is selling for $75. But we will also have the bonds, which are worth

$250 × 1.04 = $260. If the bottom outcome occurs, we sell the 125 shares of BYF for 125 × $32 = $4,000—enough money to buy back the 100 shares of AXE, which is selling for $40. Again, we will have the risk-free bonds, worth $260. Regardless of the outcome, we end up with $260.

Recall that we put up no money of our own and ended up with a sure $260. It should be apparent that this is an extremely attractive transaction, so everyone would do it. The combined actions of multiple investors would drive down the price of AXE and/or drive up the price of BYF until an equilibrium was reached at which this transaction would not be profitable. Assuming stock BYF's price remained constant, stock AXE would fall to $47.50. Or assuming stock AXE's price remained constant, stock BYF would rise to $40.

Of course, this example is extremely simplified. Clearly a stock price can change to more than two other prices. Also, if a given stock is at one price, another stock may be at any other price. We have created a simple case here to illustrate a point. When derivatives are involved, the simplification here is relatively safe. In fact, it is quite appropriate.

Now we look at another type of **arbitrage opportunity**, which involves a forward contract and will establish an appropriate price for the forward contract. Let stock AXE sell for $50. We borrow $50 at 4 percent interest by issuing a risk-free bond, use the money to buy one share of stock AXE, and simultaneously enter into a forward contract to sell this share at a price of $54 one period later. The stock will then move to either $75 or $40 in the next period; the forward contract will require that we deliver the stock and accept $54 for it; and we shall owe $50 × 1.04 = $52 on the loan.

Let us look at the two outcomes. Suppose stock AXE goes to $75. We deliver the stock to settle the obligation on the forward contract and receive $54 for it. We use $52 of the $54 to pay back the loan, leaving a gain of $2. Now suppose AXE goes to $40. We deliver the stock, fulfilling the obligation of the forward contract, and receive $54. Again, we use $52 of the $54 to pay back the loan, leaving a gain of $2.

In either case we made $2, free and clear. In fact, we can even accommodate the possibility of more than two future prices for AXE. The key point is that we faced no risk and did not have to put up any of our own money, but we ended up with $2—clearly a good deal. In fact, this is what we would call an arbitrage profit. But from where did it originate?

It turns out that the forward price we received, $54, was an inappropriate price given current market conditions. In fact, it was just an arbitrary price, made up to illustrate the point. To eliminate the opportunity to earn the $2 profit, the forward price should be $52—equal, not coincidentally, to the amount owed on the loan. It is also no coincidence that $52 is the price of the asset increased by the rate of interest.

In this example, many market participants would do this transaction as long it generates an arbitrage profit. These forces of arbitrage would either force the forward price down or force the price of the stock up until an equilibrium is reached that eliminates the opportunity to profit at no risk with no commitment of one's own funds.

We have just had a taste of not only the powerful forces of arbitrage but also a pricing model for one derivative, the forward contract. In this simple example, according to the pricing model, the forward price should be the spot price increased by the interest rate. Although there is a lot more to derivative pricing than shown here, the basic principle remains the same regardless of the type of instrument or the complexity of the setting: *Prices are set to eliminate the opportunity to profit at no risk with no commitment of one's own funds.* There are no opportunities for arbitrage profits.

Lest we be too naive, however, we must acknowledge that there is a large industry of arbitrageurs. So how can such an industry exist if there are no opportunities for riskless profit? One explanation is that most of the arbitrage transactions are more complex than this simple example and involve estimating information, which can result in differing opinions. Arbitrage involving options, for example, usually requires estimates of a stock's volatility. Different participants have different opinions about this volatility. It is quite possible that two counterparties trading with each other can believe that each is arbitraging against the other.

But more importantly, the absence of arbitrage opportunities is upheld, ironically, only if participants believe that arbitrage opportunities *do* exist. If market traders believe that no opportunities exist to earn arbitrage profits, then they will not follow market prices and compare these prices with what they ought to be, as in the forward contract example given above. Without participants watching closely, prices would surely get out of line and offer arbitrage opportunities. Thus, eliminating arbitrage opportunities requires that participants be vigilant to arbitrage opportunities. In other words, strange as it may sound, disbelief and skepticism concerning the absence of arbitrage opportunities are required in order that it hold as a legitimate principle.

Markets in which arbitrage opportunities are either nonexistent or are quickly eliminated are relatively efficient markets. Recall from your study of portfolio theory and investment analysis that efficient markets are those in which it is not possible, except by chance, to earn returns in excess of those that would be fair compensation for the risk assumed. Although abnormal returns can be earned in a variety of ways, arbitrage profits are definitely examples of abnormal returns, relatively obvious to identify and easy to capture. Thus, they are the most egregious violations of the principle of market efficiency. A market in which arbitrage profits do not exist is one in which the most obvious violations of market efficiency have been eliminated.

Throughout this study session, we shall study derivatives by using the principle of arbitrage as a guide. We will assume that arbitrage opportunities cannot exist for any significant length of time. Thus, prices must conform to models that assume no arbitrage. On the other hand, we do not want to take the absence of arbitrage opportunities so seriously that we give up and believe that arbitrage opportunities never exist. Otherwise, they will arise, and someone else will take them from us.

We have now completed this introductory reading, which has touched only lightly on the world of derivatives. The remainder of the study session is organized as follows: Reading 71 on forwards, Reading 72 on futures, Reading 73 on options, and Reading 74 on swaps provide details describing the types of instruments and how they are priced. Reading 75 is on options. We now proceed to Reading 71, which looks at forward markets and contracts.

SUMMARY

- A derivative contract is a financial instrument with a return that is obtained from or "derived" from the return of another underlying financial instrument.

- Exchange-traded derivatives are created, authorized, and traded on a derivatives exchange, an organized facility for trading derivatives. Exchange-traded derivatives are standardized instruments with respect to certain terms and conditions of the contract. They trade in accordance with rules and specifications prescribed by the derivatives exchange and are usually subject to governmental regulation. Exchange-traded derivatives are guaranteed by the exchange against loss resulting from the default of one of the parties. Over-the-counter derivatives are transactions created by any two parties off of a derivatives exchange. The parties set all of their own terms and conditions, and each assumes the credit risk of the other party.

- A forward commitment is an agreement between two parties in which one party agrees to buy and the other agrees to sell an asset at a future date at a price agreed on today. The three types of forward commitments are forward contracts, futures contracts, and swaps.

- A forward contract is a forward commitment created in the over-the-counter market. A futures contract is a forward commitment created and traded on a futures exchange. A swap is an over-the-counter transaction consisting of a series of forward commitments.

- A contingent claim is a derivative contract with a payoff dependent on the occurrence of a future event. The primary types of contingent claims are options, but other types involve variations of options, often combined with other financial instruments or derivatives.

- An option is a derivative contract giving one party the right to buy or sell an underlying asset at a fixed price over a period of time or at a specific point in time. The party obtaining the right pays a premium (the option price) at the start and receives the right to buy or sell, as prescribed by the contract. The two types of options are a call (the right to buy) and a put (the right to sell).

- The size of the global derivatives market can be measured by notional principal, which is the amount of the underlying on which a derivative is based, and by market value, which is the economic worth of the derivative.

- Derivative markets serve many useful purposes such as providing price discovery, facilitating risk management, making markets more efficient, and lowering transaction costs. Derivatives are often criticized as being excessively dangerous for unknowledgeable investors and have been inappropriately likened to gambling.

- Arbitrage is a process through which an investor can buy an asset or combination of assets at one price and concurrently sell at a higher price, thereby earning a profit without investing any money or being exposed to any risk. The combined actions of many investors engaging in arbitrage results in rapid price adjustments that eliminate these opportunities, thereby bringing prices back in line and making markets more efficient.

PRACTICE PROBLEMS FOR READING 70

1. For all parties involved, which of the following financial instruments is *not* an example of a forward commitment?

   A. Swap.

   B. Call option.

   C. Futures contract.

   D. Forward contract.

2. The main risk faced by an individual who enters into a forward contract to buy the S&P 500 Index is that

   A. the market may rise.

   B. the market may fall.

   C. market volatility may rise.

   D. market volatility may fall.

3. Which of the following statements is *most* accurate?

   A. Futures contracts are private transactions.

   B. Forward contracts are marked to market daily.

   C. Futures contracts have more default risk than forward contracts.

   D. Forward contracts require that both parties to the transaction have a high degree of creditworthiness.

4. Which of the following statements is *least* accurate?

   A. Futures contracts are easier to offset than forward contracts.

   B. Forward contracts are generally more liquid than futures contracts.

   C. Forward contracts are easier to tailor to specific needs than futures contracts.

   D. Futures contracts are characterized by having a clearinghouse as an intermediary.

5. A swap is *best* characterized as a

   A. series of forward contracts.

   B. derivative contract that has not gained widespread popularity.

   C. single fixed payment in exchange for a single floating payment.

   D. contract that is binding on only one of the parties to the transaction.

6. Which of the following is *most* representative of forward contracts and contingent claims?

	Forward Contracts	Contingent Claims
A.	Premium paid at inception	Premium paid at inception
B.	Premium paid at inception	No premium paid at inception
C.	No premium paid at inception	Premium paid at inception
D.	No premium paid at inception	No premium paid at inception

7. For the **long position**, the *most likely* advantage of contingent claims over forward commitments is that contingent claims

   A. are easier to offset than forward commitments.

   B. have lower default risk than forward commitments.

   C. permit gains while protecting against losses.

   D. are typically cheaper to initiate than forward commitments.

8. For derivative contracts, the notional principal is *best* described as

   A. the amount of the underlying asset covered by the contract.

   B. a measure of the actual payments made and received in the contract.

   C. tending to underestimate the actual payments made and received in the contract.

   D. being, conceptually and in aggregate, the best available measure of the size of the market.

9. By volume, the most widely used group of derivatives is the one with contracts written on which of the following types of underlying assets?

   A. Financial.

   B. Commodities.

   C. Energy-related.

   D. Precious metals.

10. Which of the following is *least* likely to be a purpose served by derivative markets?

   A. Arbitrage.

   B. Price discovery.

   C. Risk management.

   D. Hedging and speculation.

11. The *most likely* reason derivative markets have flourished is that

   A. derivatives are easy to understand and use.

   B. derivatives have relatively low transaction costs.

   C. the pricing of derivatives is relatively straightforward.

   D. strong regulation ensures that transacting parties are protected from fraud.

12. A private transaction in which one party agrees to make a single fixed payment in the future and another party agrees to make a single floating payment in the future is *best* characterized as a(n):

   A. futures contract.

   B. forward contract.

   C. exchange-traded contingent claim.

   D. over-the-counter contingent claim.

13. A public, standardized transaction that constitutes a commitment between two parties to transfer the underlying asset at a future date at a price agreed upon now is *best* characterized as a(n):

   A. swap.

   B. futures contract.

   C. exchange-traded contingent claim.

   D. over-the-counter contingent claim.

2005 exam

14. Assume the probability of bankruptcy for the underlying asset is high. Compared to the price of an American put option on the same underlying asset, the price of an equivalent European put option will *most likely* be:

   A. lower.

   B. higher.

   C. the same because the probability of bankruptcy does not affect pricing.

   D. the same because the possibility of early exercise only affects the pricing of call options.

FORWARD MARKETS
AND CONTRACTS
by Don M. Chance

LEARNING OUTCOMES

The candidate should be able to:

a. differentiate between the positions held by the long and short parties to a forward contract in terms of delivery/settlement and default risk;

b. describe the procedures for settling a forward contract at expiration, and discuss how termination alternatives prior to expiration can affect credit risk;

c. differentiate between a dealer and an end user of a forward contract;

d. describe the characteristics of equity forward contracts and forward contracts on zero-coupon and coupon bonds;

e. describe the characteristics of the Eurodollar time deposit market, define LIBOR and Euribor;

f. describe the characteristics of forward rate agreements (FRAs);

g. calculate and interpret the payoff of an FRA and explain each of the component terms;

h. describe the characteristics of currency forward contracts.

INTRODUCTION   1

In Reading 70, we gave a general overview of global derivative markets. We identified those markets as forward markets, futures markets, options markets, and swap markets. The following series of readings focuses individually on those markets. We begin with forward markets.

First recall our definition of a forward contract: *A forward contract is an agreement between two parties in which one party, the buyer, agrees to buy from the other party, the seller, an underlying asset or other derivative, at a future date at a price established at the start of the contract.* Therefore, it is a

Analysis of Derivatives for the CFA® Program, by Don M. Chance. Copyright © 2003 by AIMR. Reprinted with permission.

31

commitment by two parties to engage in a transaction at a later date with the price set in advance. The buyer is often called the **long** and the seller is often called the **short**.[1] Although any two parties can agree on such a contract, in this book we are interested only in forward contracts that involve large corporations, financial institutions, nonprofit organizations, or governments.

Recalling an example from Reading 70, a pension fund manager, anticipating the receipt of cash at a future date, might enter into a commitment to purchase a stock portfolio at a later date at a price agreed on today. By doing so, the manager's position is unaffected by any changes in the value of the stock portfolio between today and the date of the actual investment in the stock portfolio. In this sense, the manager is hedged against an increase in stock prices until the cash is received and invested. The disadvantage of such a transaction is that the manager is also hedged against any decreases in stock prices. If stock prices fall between the time the commitment is established and the time the cash is received, the manager will regret having entered into the forward contract because the stock could have been acquired at a lower price. But that is the nature of a forward contract hedge: It locks in a price.

An important feature of a forward contract is that neither party pays any money at the start. The parties might require some collateral to minimize the risk of default, but for most of this book, we shall ignore this point. So keep in mind this very important aspect of forward contracts: *No money changes hands at the start.*

1.1 Delivery and Settlement of a Forward Contract

When a forward contract expires, there are two possible arrangements that can be used to settle the obligations of the parties. A deliverable forward contract stipulates that the long will pay the agreed-upon price to the short, who in turn will deliver the underlying asset to the long, a process called **delivery**. An alternative procedure, called **cash settlement**, permits the long and short to pay the net cash value of the position on the delivery date. For example, suppose two parties agree to a forward contract to deliver a zero-coupon bond at a price of $98 per $100 par. At the contract's expiration, suppose the underlying zero-coupon bond is selling at a price of $98.25. The long is due to receive from the short an asset worth $98.25, for which a payment to the short of $98.00 is required. In a cash-settled forward contract, the short simply pays the long $0.25. If the zero-coupon bond were selling for $97.50, the long would pay the short $0.50. Delivery of a zero-coupon bond is not a difficult thing to do, however, and cash-settled contracts are more commonly used in situations where delivery is impractical.[2] For example, if the underlying is the Russell 3000 Index, the short would have to deliver to the long a portfolio containing each of the Russell 3000

---

[1] As pointed out in Reading 70 with respect to the word *underlying*, the derivatives industry often uses nouns, verbs, adjectives, and adverbs as parts of speech other than what they are. Hence, words like *long* and *short* are used not as adjectives but as nouns.

[2] Be aware, however, that the choice of delivery or cash settlement is not an option available at expiration. It is negotiated between the parties at the start.

stocks proportionate to its weighting in the index. Consequently, cash settlement is much more practical. Cash-settled forward contracts are sometimes called **NDFs**, for **nondeliverable forwards**, although this term is used predominately with respect to foreign exchange forwards.

1.2 Default Risk and Forward Contracts

An important characteristic of forward contracts is that they are subject to default. Regardless of whether the contract is for delivery or cash settlement, the potential exists for a party to default. In the zero-coupon bond example above, the long might be unable to pay the $98 or the short might be unable to buy the zero-coupon bond and make delivery of the bond to the long. Generally speaking, however, forward contracts are structured so that only the party owing the greater amount can default. In other words, if the short is obligated to deliver a zero-coupon bond selling for more than $98, then the long would not be obligated to make payment unless the short makes delivery. Likewise, in a cash settled contract, only one party—the one owing the greater amount—can default. We discuss the nature of this credit risk in the following section and in Section 5 after we have determined how to value forward contracts.

1.3 Termination of a Forward Contract

Let us note that a forward contract is nearly always constructed with the idea that the participants will hold on to their positions until the contract expires and either engage in delivery of the asset or settle the cash equivalent, as required in the specific contract. The possibility exists, however, that at least one of the participants might wish to terminate the position prior to expiration. For example, suppose a party goes long, meaning that she agrees to buy the asset at the expiration date at the price agreed on at the start, but she subsequently decides to terminate the contract before expiration. We shall assume that the contract calls for delivery rather than cash settlement at expiration.

To see the details of the contract termination, suppose it is part of the way through the life of the contract, and the long decides that she no longer wishes to buy the asset at expiration. She can then re-enter the market and create a new forward contract expiring at the same time as the original forward contract, taking the position of the seller instead. Because of price changes in the market during the period since the original contract was created, this new contract would likely have a different price at which she would have to commit to sell. She would then be long a contract to buy the asset at expiration at one price and short a contract to sell the asset at expiration at a different price. It should be apparent that she has no further exposure to the price of the asset.

For example, suppose she is long to buy at $40 and short to deliver at $42. Depending on the characteristics of the contract, one of several possibilities could occur at expiration. Everything could go as planned—the party holding the short position of the contract on which she is long at $40 delivers the asset to her, and she pays him $40. She then delivers the asset to the party who is long the contract on which she is short at $42. That party pays her $42. She nets $2. The transaction is over.

There is always a possibility that her counterparty on the long contract could default. She is still obligated to deliver the asset on the short contract, for which she will receive $42. But if her counterparty on the long contract defaults, she has to buy the asset in the market and could suffer a significant loss. There is also a possibility that the counterparty on her short contract could fail to pay her the $42. Of course, she would then not deliver the asset but would be exposed to the risk of changes in the asset's price. This type of problem illustrates the credit risk in a forward contract.

To avoid the credit risk, when she re-enters the market to go short the forward contract, she could contact the same counterparty with whom she engaged in the long forward contract. They could agree to cancel both contracts. Because she would be owed $2 at expiration, cancellation of the contract would result in the counterparty paying her the present value of $2. This termination or offset of the original forward position is clearly desirable for both counterparties because it eliminates the credit risk.[3] It is always possible, however, that she might receive a better price from another counterparty. If that price is sufficiently attractive and she does not perceive the credit risk to be too high, she may choose to deal with the other counterparty and leave the credit risk in the picture.

2 THE STRUCTURE OF GLOBAL FORWARD MARKETS

The global market for forward contracts is part of a vast network of financial institutions that make markets in these instruments as well as in other related derivatives, such as swaps and options. Some dealers specialize in certain markets and contracts, such as forward contracts on the euro or forward contracts on Japanese equity products. These dealers are mainly large global banking institutions, but many large non-banking institutions, such as Goldman Sachs and Merrill Lynch, are also big players in this market.

Dealers engage in transactions with two types of parties: end users and other dealers. An end user is typically a corporation, nonprofit organization, or government.[4] An end user is generally a party with a risk management problem that is searching for a dealer to provide it with a financial transaction to solve that problem. Although the problem could simply be that the party wants to take a position in anticipation of a market move, more commonly the end user has a risk it wants to reduce or eliminate.

As an example, Hoffman-LaRoche, the large Swiss pharmaceutical company, sells its products globally. Anticipating the receipt of a large amount of cash in U.S. dollars and worried about a decrease in the value of the dollar relative to the Swiss franc, it could buy a forward contract to sell the dollar and buy Swiss francs. It might seek out a dealer such as UBS Warburg, the investment firm affiliated with the large Swiss bank UBS, or it might approach any of the other large multinational banks with which it does business. Or it might end up dealing with a nonbank entity, like Merrill Lynch. Assume that Hoffman-LaRoche enters into this contract with UBS Warburg. Hoffman-LaRoche is the end user; UBS Warburg is the dealer.

---

[3] This statement is made under the assumption that the parties do not want the credit risk. Credit risk, like other risks, however, can be a risk that some parties want because of the potential for earning attractive returns by using their expertise in measuring the actual credit risk relative to the credit risk as perceived by the market. In addition, credit risk offers diversification benefits.

[4] The U.S. government does not transact in forward contracts or other derivatives, but some foreign governments and central banks do. Within the United States, however, some state and local governments do engage in forward contracts and other derivatives.

Transactions in forward contracts typically are conducted over the phone. Each dealer has a quote desk, whose phone number is well known to the major participants in the market. If a party wishes to conduct a transaction, it simply phones the dealer for a quote. The dealer stands ready to take either side of the transaction, quoting a bid and an ask price or rate. The bid is the price at which the dealer is willing to pay for the future purchase of the asset, and the ask is the price at which the dealer is willing to sell. When a dealer engages in a forward transaction, it has then taken on risk from the other party. For example, in the aforementioned transaction of Hoffman-LaRoche and UBS Warburg, by entering into the contract, UBS Warburg takes on a risk that Hoffman-LaRoche has eliminated. Specifically, UBS Warburg has now committed to buying dollars and selling Swiss francs at a future date. Thus, UBS Warburg is effectively long the dollar and stands to gain from a strengthening dollar/weakening Swiss franc. Typically dealers do not want to hold this exposure. Rather, they find another party to offset the exposure with another derivative or spot transaction. Thus, UBS Warburg is a wholesaler of risk—buying it, selling it, and trying to earn a profit off the spread between its buying price and selling price.

One might reasonably wonder why Hoffman-LaRoche could not avoid the cost of dealing with UBS Warburg. In some cases, it might be able to. It might be aware of another party with the exact opposite needs, but such a situation is rare. The market for financial products such as forward contracts is made up of wholesalers of risk management products who use their technical expertise, their vast network of contacts, and their access to critical financial market information to provide a more efficient means for end users to engage in such risk management transactions.

Dealers such as UBS Warburg lay off the risk they do not wish to assume by transacting with other dealers and potentially other end users. If they do this carefully, quickly, and at accurate prices, they can earn a profit from this market-making activity. One should not get the impression, however, that market making is a highly profitable activity. The competition is fierce, which keeps bid–ask spreads very low and makes it difficult to earn much money on a given transaction. Indeed, many market makers do not make much money on individual transactions—they typically make a small amount of money on each transaction and do a large number of transactions. They may even lose money on some standard transactions, hoping to make up losses on more-complicated, nonstandard transactions, which occur less frequently but have higher bid–ask spreads.

Risk magazine conducts annual surveys to identify the top dealers in various derivative products. Exhibit 1 presents the results of those surveys for two of the forward products we cover here, currency and interest rate forwards. Interest rate forwards are called forward rate agreements (FRAs). In the next section, we shall study the different types of forward contracts and note that there are some others not covered in the *Risk* surveys.

One of these surveys was sent to banks and investment banks that are active dealers in over-the-counter derivatives. The other survey was sent to end users. The tabulations are based on respondents' simple rankings of who they think are the best dealers. Although the identities of the specific dealer firms are not critical, it is interesting and helpful to be aware of the major players in these types of contracts. Most of the world's leading global financial institutions are listed, but many other big names are not. It is also interesting to observe that the perceptions of the users of these dealer firms' services differ somewhat from the dealers' self-perceptions. Be aware, however, that the rankings change, sometimes drastically, each year.

| EXHIBIT 1 | *Risk* Magazine Surveys of Banks, Investment Banks, and Corporate End Users to Determine the Top Three Dealers in Currency and Interest Rate Forwards |

	Respondents	
Currencies	**Banks and Investment Banks**	**Corporate End Users**
Currency Forwards		
$/€	UBS Warburg	Citigroup
	Deutsche Bank	Royal Bank of Scotland
	JP Morgan Chase	JP Morgan Chase/Bank of America
$/¥	UBS Warburg	Citigroup
	Citigroup	Bank of America
	JP Morgan Chase	JP Morgan Chase/UBS Warburg
$/£	UBS Warburg	Royal Bank of Scotland
	Royal Bank of Scotland	Citigroup
	Hong Kong Shanghai Banking Corporation	UBS Warburg
$/SF	UBS Warburg	UBS Warburg
	Credit Suisse First Boston	Citigroup
	BNP Paribas	Credit Suisse First Boston
Interest Rate Forwards (FRAs)		
$	JP Morgan Chase	JP Morgan Chase
	Bank of America	Royal Bank of Scotland
	Deutsche Bank	Bank of America
€	Deutsche Bank	Royal Bank of Scotland
	Intesa BCI	JP Morgan Chase
	Royal Bank of Scotland	Deutsche Bank
¥	Mizuho Securities	Citigroup
	JP Morgan Chase	Merrill Lynch
	BNP Paribas	Hong Kong Shanghai Banking Corporation
£	Royal Bank of Scotland	Royal Bank of Scotland
	Commerzbank	Bank of America/ING Barings
	Deutsche Bank	
SF	Credit Suisse First Boston	UBS Warburg
	UBS Warburg	Credit Suisse First Boston
	Deutsche Bank	Citigroup/ING Barings

Note: $ = U.S. dollar, € = euro, ¥ = Japanese yen, £ = U.K. pound sterling, SF = Swiss franc.

Source: Risk, September 2002, pp. 30–67 for banks and investment banking dealer respondents, and June 2002, pp. 24–34 for end user respondents. The end user survey provides responses from corporations and asset managers. The above results are for corporate respondents only.

TYPES OF FORWARD CONTRACTS 3

In this section, we examine the types of forward contracts that fall within the scope of this book. By the word "types," we mean the underlying asset groups on which these forward contracts are created. Because the CFA Program focuses on the asset management industry, our primary interest is in equity, interest rate and fixed-income, and currency forwards.

3.1 Equity Forwards

An **equity forward** is a contract calling for the purchase of an individual stock, a stock portfolio, or a stock index at a later date. For the most part, the differences in types of equity forward contracts are only slight, depending on whether the contract is on an individual stock, a portfolio of stocks, or a stock index.

3.1.1 Forward Contracts on Individual Stocks

Consider an asset manager responsible for the portfolio of a high-net-worth individual. As is sometimes the case, such portfolios may be concentrated in a small number of stocks, sometimes stocks that have been in the family for years. In many cases, the individual may be part of the founding family of a particular company. Let us say that the stock is called Gregorian Industries, Inc., or GII, and the client is so heavily invested in this stock that her portfolio is not diversified. The client notifies the portfolio manager of her need for $2 million in cash in six months. This cash can be raised by selling 16,000 shares at the current price of $125 per share. Thus, the risk exposure concerns the market value of $2 million of stock. For whatever reason, it is considered best not to sell the stock any earlier than necessary. The portfolio manager realizes that a forward contract to sell GII in six months will accomplish the client's desired objective. The manager contacts a forward contract dealer and obtains a quote of $128.13 as the price at which a forward contract to sell the stock in six months could be constructed. In other words, the portfolio manager could enter into a contract to sell the stock to the dealer in six months at $128.13. We assume that this contract is deliverable, meaning that when the sale is actually made, the shares will be delivered to the dealer. Assuming that the client has some flexibility in the amount of money needed, let us say that the contract is signed for the sale of 15,600 shares at $128.13, which will raise $1,998,828. Of course when the contract expires, the stock could be selling for any price. The client can gain or lose on the transaction. If the stock rises to a price above $128.13 during the six-month period, the client will still have to deliver the stock for $128.13. But if the price falls, the client will still get $128.13 per share for the stock.

3.1.2 Forward Contracts on Stock Portfolios

Because modern portfolio theory and good common sense dictate that investors should hold diversified portfolios, it is reasonable to assume that forward contracts on specific stock portfolios would be useful. Suppose a pension fund manager knows that in three months he will need to sell about $20 million of stock to make payments to retirees. The manager has analyzed the portfolio and determined the precise identities of the stocks he wants to sell and the number of shares of each that he would like to sell. Thus the manager has designated a specific subportfolio to be sold. The problem is that the prices of these stocks in three months are uncertain. The manager can, however, lock in the sale prices by entering into a forward contract to sell the portfolio. This can be done one of two ways.

The manager can enter into a forward contract on each stock that he wants to sell. Alternatively, he can enter into a forward contract on the overall portfolio. The first way would be more costly, as each contract would incur administrative costs, whereas the second way would incur only one set of costs.[5] Assume that the manager chooses the second method. He provides a list of the stocks and number of shares of each he wishes to sell to the dealer and obtains a quote. The dealer gives him a quote of $20,200,000. So, in three months, the manager will sell the stock to the dealer and receive $20,200,000. The transaction can be structured to call for either actual delivery or cash settlement, but in either case, the client will effectively receive $20,200,000 for the stock.[6]

3.1.3 Forward Contracts on Stock Indices

Many equity forward contracts are based on a stock index. For example, consider a U.K. asset manager who wants to protect the value of her portfolio that is a Financial Times Stock Exchange 100 index fund, or who wants to eliminate a risk for which the FTSE 100 Index is a sufficiently accurate representation of the risk she wishes to eliminate. For example, the manager may be anticipating the sale of a number of U.K. blue chip shares at a future date. The manager could, as in our stock portfolio example, take a specific portfolio of stocks to a forward contract dealer and obtain a forward contract on that portfolio. She realizes, however, that a forward contract on a widely accepted benchmark would result in a better price quote, because the dealer can more easily hedge the risk with other transactions. Moreover, the manager is not even sure which stocks she will still be holding at the later date. She simply knows that she will sell a certain amount of stock at a later date and believes that the FTSE 100 is representative of the stock that she will sell. The manager is concerned with the systematic risk associated with the U.K. stock market, and accordingly, she decides that selling a forward contract on the FTSE 100 would be a good way to manage the risk.

Assume that the portfolio manager decides to protect £15,000,000 of stock. The dealer quotes a price of £6,000 on a forward contract covering £15,000,000. We assume that the contract will be cash settled because such index contracts are nearly always done that way. When the contract expiration date arrives, let us say that the index is at £5,925—a decrease of 1.25 percent from the forward price. Because the manager is short the contract and its price went down, the transaction makes money. But how much did it make on a notional principal of £15,000,000?

---

[5] Ignoring those costs, there would be no difference in doing forward contracts on individual stocks or a single forward contract on a portfolio. Because of the non-linearity of their payoffs, this is not true for options. A portfolio of options is not the same as an option on a portfolio, but a portfolio of forward contracts is the same as a forward contract on a portfolio, ignoring the aforementioned costs.

[6] If, for example, the stock is worth $20,500,000 and the transaction calls for delivery, the manager will transfer the stocks to the dealer and receive $20,200,000. The client effectively takes an opportunity loss of $300,000. If the transaction is structured as a cash settlement, the client will pay the dealer $300,000. The client would then sell the stock in the market, receiving $20,500,000 and netting $20,200,000 after settling the forward contract with the dealer. Similarly, if the stock is selling for less than the amount guaranteed by the forward contract, the client will deliver the stock and receive $20,200,000 or, if the transaction is cash settled, the client will sell the stock in the market and receive a cash payment from the dealer, making the effective sale price still $20,200,000.

The index declined by 1.25 percent. Thus, the transaction should make $0.0125 \times £15{,}000{,}000 = £187{,}500$. In other words, the dealer would have to pay £187,500 in cash. If the portfolio were a FTSE 100 index fund, then it would be viewed as a portfolio initially worth £15,000,000 that declined by 1.25 percent, a loss of £187,500. The forward contract offsets this loss. Of course, in reality, the portfolio is not an index fund and such a hedge is not perfect, but as noted above, there are sometimes reasons for preferring that the forward contract be based on an index.

3.1.4 The Effect of Dividends

It is important to note the effect of dividends in equity forward contracts. Any equity portfolio nearly always has at least a few stocks that pay dividends, and it is inconceivable that any well-known equity index would not have some component stocks that pay dividends. Equity forward contracts typically have payoffs based only on the price of the equity, value of the portfolio, or level of the index. They do not ordinarily pay off any dividends paid by the component stocks. An exception, however, is that some equity forwards on stock indices are based on total return indices. For example, there are two versions of the well-known S&P 500 Index. One represents only the market value of the stocks. The other, called the S&P 500 Total Return Index, is structured so that daily dividends paid by the stocks are reinvested in additional units of the index, as though it were a portfolio. In this manner, the rate of return on the index, and the payoff of any forward contract based on it, reflects the payment and reinvestment of dividends into the underlying index. Although this feature might appear attractive, it is not necessarily of much importance in risk management problems. The variability of prices is so much greater than the variability of dividends that managing price risk is considered much more important than worrying about the uncertainty of dividends.

In summary, equity forwards can be based on individual stocks, specific stock portfolios, or stock indices. Moreover, these underlying equities often pay dividends, which can affect forward contracts on equities. Let us now look at bond and **interest rate forward** contracts.

3.2 Bond and Interest Rate Forward Contracts

Forward contracts on bonds are similar to forward contracts on interest rates, but the two are different instruments. Forward contracts on bonds, in fact, are no more difficult to understand than those on equities. Drawing on our experience of Section 3.1, we simply extend the notion of a forward contract on an individual stock, a specific stock portfolio, or a stock index to that of a forward contract on an individual bond, a specific bond portfolio, or a bond index.[7]

3.2.1 Forward Contracts on Individual Bonds and Bond Portfolios

Although a forward contract on a bond and one on a stock are similar, some basic differences nonetheless exist between the two. For example, the bond may pay a coupon, which corresponds somewhat to the dividend that a stock might pay. But unlike a stock, a bond matures, and a forward contract on a bond must

---

[7] It may be useful to review Chapters 1 and 3 of *Fixed Income Analysis for the Chartered Financial Analyst Program* by Frank J. Fabozzi, New Hope, PA: Frank J. Fabozzi Associates (2000).

90 days, the rate on 180-day LIBOR is 6 percent. That 6 percent interest will be paid 180 days later. Therefore, the present value of a Eurodollar time deposit at that point in time would be

$$\frac{\$10,000,000}{1 + 0.06\left(\dfrac{180}{360}\right)}$$

At expiration, then, the end user, the party going long the FRA in our example, receives the following payment from the dealer, which is the party going short:

$$\$10,000,000\left[\frac{(0.06 - 0.055)\left(\dfrac{180}{360}\right)}{1 + 0.06\left(\dfrac{180}{360}\right)}\right] = \$24,272$$

If the underlying rate is less than 5.5 percent, the payment is calculated based on the difference between the 5.5 percent rate and the underlying rate and is paid by the long to the short. It is important to note that even though the contract expires in 90 days, the rate is on a 180-day LIBOR instrument; therefore, the rate calculation adjusts by the factor 180/360. The fact that 90 days have elapsed at expiration is not relevant to the calculation of the payoff.

Before presenting the general formula, let us review the calculations in the numerator and denominator. In the numerator, we see that the contract is obviously paying the difference between the actual rate that exists in the market on the contract expiration date and the agreed-upon rate, adjusted for the fact that the rate applies to a 180-day instrument, multiplied by the notional principal. The divisor appears because when Eurodollar rates are quoted in the market, they are based on the assumption that the rate applies to an instrument that accrues interest at that rate with the interest paid a certain number of days (here 180) later. When participants determine this rate in the London Eurodollar market, it is understood to apply to a Eurodollar time deposit that begins now and matures 180 days later. So the interest on an actual Eurodollar deposit would not be paid until 180 days later. Thus, it is necessary to adjust the FRA payoff to reflect the fact that the rate implies a payment that would occur 180 days later on a standard Eurodollar deposit. This adjustment is easily done by simply discounting the payment at the current LIBOR, which here is 6 percent, prorated over 180 days. These conventions are also followed in the market for FRAs with other underlying rates.

In general, the FRA payoff formula (from the perspective of the party going long) is

$$\text{Notional principal}\left[\frac{(\text{Underlying rate at expiration} - \text{Forward contract rate})\left(\dfrac{\text{Days in underlying rate}}{360}\right)}{1 + \text{Underlying rate at expiration}\left(\dfrac{\text{Days in underlying rate}}{360}\right)}\right]$$

where *forward contract rate* represents the rate the two parties agree will be paid and *days in underlying rate* refers to the number of days to maturity of the instrument on which the underlying rate is based.

One somewhat confusing feature of FRAs is the fact that they mature in a certain number of days and are based on a rate that applies to an instrument maturing in a certain number of days measured from the maturity of the FRA.

EXHIBIT 2	FRA Descriptive Notation and Interpretation	
Notation	**Contract Expires in**	**Underlying Rate**
1 × 3	1 month	60-day LIBOR
1 × 4	1 month	90-day LIBOR
1 × 7	1 month	180-day LIBOR
3 × 6	3 months	90-day LIBOR
3 × 9	3 months	180-day LIBOR
6 × 12	6 months	180-day LIBOR
12 × 18	12 months	180-day LIBOR

Note: This list is not exhaustive and represents only the most commonly traded FRAs.

Thus, there are two day figures associated with each contract. Our example was a 90-day contract on 180-day LIBOR. To avoid confusion, the FRA markets use a special type of terminology that converts the number of days to months. Specifically, our example FRA is referred to as a 3 × 9, reflecting the fact that the contract expires in three months and that six months later, or nine months from the contract initiation date, the interest is paid on the underlying Eurodollar time deposit on whose rate the contract is based.[9]

FRAs are available in the market for a variety of maturities that are considered somewhat standard. Exhibit 2 presents the most common maturities. Most dealers follow the convention that contracts should expire in a given number of exact months and should be on the most commonly traded Eurodollar rates such as 30-day LIBOR, 60-day LIBOR, 90-day LIBOR, 180-day LIBOR, and so on. If a party wants a contract expiring in 37 days on 122-day LIBOR, it would be considered an exception to the standard, but most dealers would be willing to make a market in such an instrument. Such nonstandard instruments are called *off the run*. Of course, FRAs are available in all of the leading currencies.

The FRA market is large, but not as large as the swaps market. It is important, however, to understand FRAs before trying to understand swaps. As we will show in Reading 74, a swap is a special combination of FRAs. But let us now turn to another large forward market, the market for currency forwards.

3.3 Currency Forward Contracts

Spurred by the relaxation of government controls over the exchange rates of most major currencies in the early 1970s, a currency forward market developed and grew extremely large. Currency forwards are widely used by banks and corporations to manage foreign exchange risk. For example, suppose Microsoft has a European subsidiary that expects to send it €12 million in three months. When Microsoft receives the euros, it will then convert them to dollars. Thus, Microsoft is essentially long euros because it will have to sell euros, or equivalently, it is short dollars because it will have to buy dollars. A currency forward contract is especially useful in this situation, because it enables Microsoft to lock in the rate at which it will sell euros and buy dollars in three months. It can do this by going

---

[9] The notation "3 × 9" is pronounced "three by nine."

short the forward contract, meaning that it goes short the euro and long the dollar. This arrangement serves to offset its otherwise long-euro, short-dollar position. In other words, it needs a forward contract to sell euros and buy dollars.

For example, say Microsoft goes to JP Morgan Chase and asks for a quote on a currency forward for €12 million in three months. JP Morgan Chase quotes a rate of $0.925, which would enable Microsoft to sell euros and buy dollars at a rate of $0.925 in three months. Under this contract, Microsoft would know it could convert its €12 million to 12,000,000 × $0.925 = $11,100,000. The contract would also stipulate whether it will settle in cash or will call for Microsoft to actually deliver the euros to the dealer and be paid $11,100,000. This simplified example is a currency forward hedge.

Now let us say that three months later, the spot rate for euros is $0.920. Microsoft is quite pleased that it locked in a rate of $0.925. It simply delivers the euros and receives $11,100,000 at an exchange rate of $0.925.[10] Had rates risen, however, Microsoft would still have had to deliver the euros and accept a rate of $0.925.

A few variations of currency forward contracts exist, but most of them are somewhat specialized and beyond the objectives of this book. Let us now take a very brief look at a few other types of forward contracts.

3.4 Other Types of Forward Contracts

Although this book focuses primarily on the financial derivatives used by asset managers, we should mention here some of the other types. **Commodity forwards**—in which the underlying asset is oil, a precious metal, or some other commodity—are widely used. In addition, the derivatives industry has created forward contracts and other derivatives on various sources of energy (electricity, gas, etc.) and even weather, in which the underlying is a measure of the temperature or the amount of disaster damage from hurricanes, earthquakes, or tornados.

Many of these instruments are particularly difficult to understand, price, and trade. Nonetheless, through the use of derivatives and indirect investments, such as hedge funds, they can be useful for managing risk and investing in general. They are not, however, the focus of this book.

In the examples and illustrations used, we have made reference to certain prices. Determining appropriate prices and fair values of financial instruments is a central objective of much of the process of asset management. Accordingly, pricing and valuation occupies a major portion of the CFA Program.

---

[10] Had the contract been structured to settle in cash, the dealer would have paid Microsoft 12,000,000 × ($0.925 − $0.920) = $60,000. Microsoft would have converted the euros to dollars at the current spot exchange rate of $0.920, receiving 12,000,000 × $0.920 = $11,040,000. Adding the $60,000 payment from the dealer, Microsoft would have received $11,100,000, an effective rate of $0.925.

SUMMARY

▶ The holder of a long forward contract (the "long") is obligated to take delivery of the underlying asset and pay the forward price at expiration. The holder of a short forward contract (the "short") is obligated to deliver the underlying asset and accept payment of the forward price at expiration.

▶ At expiration, a forward contract can be terminated by having the short make delivery of the underlying asset to the long or having the long and short exchange the equivalent cash value. If the asset is worth more (less) than the forward price, the short (long) pays the long (short) the cash difference between the market price or rate and the price or rate agreed on in the contract.

▶ A party can terminate a forward contract prior to expiration by entering into an opposite transaction with the same or a different counterparty. It is possible to leave both the original and new transactions in place, thereby leaving both transactions subject to credit risk, or to have the two transactions cancel each other. In the latter case, the party owing the greater amount pays the market value to the other party, resulting in the elimination of the remaining credit risk. This elimination can be achieved, however, only if the counterparty to the second transaction is the same counterparty as in the first.

▶ A dealer is a financial institution that makes a market in forward contracts and other derivatives. A dealer stands ready to take either side of a transaction. An end user is a party that comes to a dealer needing a transaction, usually for the purpose of managing a particular risk.

▶ Equity forward contracts can be written on individual stocks, specific stock portfolios, or stock indices. Equity forward **contract prices** and values must take into account the fact that the underlying stock, portfolio, or index could pay dividends.

▶ Forward contracts on bonds can be based on zero-coupon bonds or on coupon bonds, as well as portfolios or indices based on zero-coupon bonds or coupon bonds. Zero-coupon bonds pay their return by discounting the face value, often using a 360-day year assumption. Forward contracts on bonds must expire before the bond's maturity. In addition, a forward contract on a bond can be affected by special features of bonds, such as callability and convertibility.

▶ Eurodollar time deposits are dollar loans made by one bank to another. Although the term "Eurodollars" refers to dollar-denominated loans, similar loans exist in other currencies. Eurodollar deposits accrue interest by adding it on to the principal, using a 360-day year assumption. The primary Eurodollar rate is called LIBOR.

▶ LIBOR stands for London Interbank Offer Rate, the rate at which London banks are willing to lend to other London banks. Euribor is the rate on a euro time deposit, a loan made by banks to other banks in Frankfurt in which the currency is the euro.

▶ An FRA is a forward contract in which one party, the long, agrees to pay a fixed interest payment at a future date and receive an interest payment at a rate to be determined at expiration. FRAs are described by a special notation. For example, a 3×6 FRA expires in three months; the underlying is a Eurodollar deposit that begins in three months and ends three months later, or six months from now.

▶ The payment of an FRA at expiration is based on the net difference between the underlying rate and the agreed-upon rate, adjusted by the notional principal and the number of days in the instrument on which the underlying rate is based. The payoff is also discounted, however, to reflect the fact that the underlying rate on which the instrument is based assumes that payment will occur at a later date.

▶ A currency forward contract is a commitment for one party, the long, to buy a currency at a fixed price from the other party, the short, at a specific date. The contract can be settled by actual delivery, or the two parties can choose to settle in cash on the expiration day.

PRACTICE PROBLEMS FOR READING 71

1. The treasurer of Company A expects to receive a cash inflow of $15,000,000 in 90 days. The treasurer expects short-term interest rates to fall during the next 90 days. In order to hedge against this risk, the treasurer decides to use an FRA that expires in 90 days and is based on 90-day LIBOR. The FRA is quoted at 5 percent. At expiration, LIBOR is 4.5 percent. Assume that the notional principal on the contract is $15,000,000.

   A. Indicate whether the treasurer should take a long or short position to hedge interest rate risk.

   B. Using the appropriate terminology, identify the type of FRA used here.

   C. Calculate the gain or loss to Company A as a consequence of entering the FRA.

2. Suppose that a party wanted to enter into an FRA that expires in 42 days and is based on 137-day LIBOR. The dealer quotes a rate of 4.75 percent on this FRA. Assume that at expiration, the 137-day LIBOR is 4 percent and the notional principal is $20,000,000.

   A. What is the term used to describe such nonstandard instruments?

   B. Calculate the FRA payoff on a long position.

3. Assume Sun Microsystems expects to receive €20,000,000 in 90 days. A dealer provides a quote of $0.875 for a currency forward contract to expire in 90 days. Suppose that at the end of 90 days, the rate is $0.90. Assume that settlement is in cash. Calculate the cash flow at expiration if Sun Microsystems enters into a forward contract expiring in 90 days to buy dollars at $0.875.

4⅝ 4

5½ 5½ −

5½ 21³/₁₆ − ⅛

20⅝ 21³/₁₆ − ¹/₁₆

17³/₈ 18⅛ + ⅞

6½ 6½ − ½

7¼ 31/32 − ⅛

15/16

9/16 9/16

7¹⁵/₁₆ 7¹³/₁₆ 7¹⁵/₁₆

2⅝ 2¹¹/₃₂ 2½ +

2¾ 2¼ 2¼

6⅛ 12¹/₁₆ 11⅜ 11¾ +

87 33¾ 33 33⅛ −

602 25⅝ 24⁹/₁₆ 25⅜ +

833 12 11⅝ 11⅞ +

16 10½ 10½ 10⅛ −

78 15⅞ 15¹³/₁₆ 15⅞ +

4508 9¹/₁₆ 8¼ 8⅜ +

430 11¼ 10⅛

FUTURES MARKETS AND CONTRACTS
by Don M. Chance

LEARNING OUTCOMES

The candidate should be able to:

a. describe the characteristics of futures contracts, and distinguish between futures contracts and forward contracts;

b. differentiate between margin in the securities markets and margin in the futures markets, and define initial margin, maintenance margin, variation margin, and settlement price;

c. describe price limits and the process of marking to market, and compute and interpret the margin balance, given the previous day's balance and the change in the futures price;

d. describe how a futures contract can be terminated by a close-out (i.e., offset) at expiration (or prior to expiration), delivery, an equivalent cash settlement, or an exchange-for-physicals;

e. describe the characteristics of the following types of futures contracts: Eurodollar, Treasury bond, stock index, and currency.

INTRODUCTION   1

In Reading 70, we undertook a general overview of derivative markets. In Reading 71, we focused on forward markets. Now we explore futures markets in a similar fashion. Although we shall see a clear similarity between forward and futures contracts, critical distinctions nonetheless exist between the two.

In Reading 70 we learned that, like a forward contract, *a futures contract is an agreement between two parties in which one party, the buyer, agrees to buy from the other party, the seller, an underlying asset or other derivative, at a future date at a price agreed on today.* Unlike a forward contract, however, a futures contract is not a private and customized transaction but rather a public transaction that takes place on an organized futures exchange. In addition, a futures contract is standardized—the exchange, rather than the individual parties, sets the terms and conditions, with the exception of price. As a result, futures contracts have a secondary market, meaning that previously created contracts can be traded. Also, parties to futures contracts are guaranteed against credit losses resulting from the counterparty's inability to pay. A clearinghouse provides this guarantee via a procedure in which it converts gains and losses that accrue on a daily basis into actual cash gains and losses. Futures contracts are regulated at the federal government level; as we noted in Reading 71, forward contracts are essentially unregulated. Futures contracts are created on organized trading facilities referred to as futures exchanges, whereas forward contracts are not created in any specific location but rather initiated between any two parties who wish to enter into such a contract. Finally, each futures exchange has a division or subsidiary called a clearinghouse that performs the specific responsibilities of paying and collecting daily gains and losses as well as guaranteeing to each party the performance of the other.

In a futures transaction, one party, the long, is the buyer and the other party, the short, is the seller. The buyer agrees to buy the underlying at a later date, the expiration, at a price agreed on at the start of the contract. The seller agrees to sell the underlying to the buyer at the expiration, at the price agreed on at the start of the contract. Every day, the futures contract trades in the market and its price changes in response to new information. Buyers benefit from price increases, and sellers benefit from price decreases. On the expiration day, the contract terminates and no further trading takes place. Then, either the buyer takes delivery of the underlying from the seller, or the two parties make an equivalent cash settlement. We shall explore each of these characteristics of futures contracts in more detail. First, however, it is important to take a brief look at how futures markets came into being.

1.1 A Brief History of Futures Markets

Although vestiges of futures markets appear in the Japanese rice markets of the 18th century and perhaps even earlier, the mid-1800s marked the first clear origins of modern futures markets. For example, in the United States in the 1840s, Chicago was becoming a major transportation and distribution center for agricultural commodities. Its central location and access to the Great Lakes gave Chicago a competitive advantage over other U.S. cities. Farmers from the Midwest would harvest their grain and take it to Chicago for sale. Grain production, however, is seasonal. As a result, grain prices would rise sharply just prior to the harvest but then plunge when the grain was brought to the market. Too much grain at one time and too little at another resulted in severe problems. Grain storage facilities in Chicago were inadequate to accommodate the oversupply. Some farmers even dumped their grain in the Chicago River because prices were so low that they could not afford to take their grain to another city to sell.

To address this problem, in 1848 a group of businessmen formed an organization later named the Chicago Board of Trade (CBOT) and created an arrangement called a "to-arrive" contract. These contracts permitted farmers to sell their grain before delivering it. In other words, farmers could harvest the grain and enter into a contract to deliver it at a much later date at a price already agreed on. This transaction allowed the farmer to hold the grain in storage at some other location besides Chicago. On the other side of these contracts were the businessmen who had formed the Chicago Board of Trade.

It soon became apparent that trading in these to-arrive contracts was more important and useful than trading in the grain itself. Soon the contracts began trading in a type of secondary market, which allowed buyers and sellers to discharge their obligations by passing them on, for a price, to other parties. With the addition of the clearinghouse in the 1920s, which provided a guarantee against default, modern futures markets firmly established their place in the financial world. It was left to other exchanges, such as today's Chicago Mercantile Exchange, the New York Mercantile Exchange, Eurex, and the London International Financial Futures Exchange, to develop and become, along with the Chicago Board of Trade, the global leaders in futures markets.

We shall now explore the important features of futures contracts in more detail.

1.2 Public Standardized Transactions

A private transaction is not generally reported in the news or to any price-reporting service. Forward contracts are private contracts. Just as in most legal contracts, the parties do not publicly report that they have engaged in a contract. In contrast, a futures transaction is reported to the futures exchange, the clearinghouse, and at least one regulatory agency. The price is recorded and available from price reporting services and even on the Internet.[1]

We noted that a futures transaction is not customized. Recall from Reading 71 that in a forward contract, the two parties establish all of the terms of the contract, including the identity of the underlying, the expiration date, and the manner in which the contract is settled (cash or actual delivery) as well as the price. The terms are customized to meet the needs of both parties. In a futures contract, the price is the only term established by the two parties; the exchange establishes all other terms. Moreover, the terms that are established by the exchange are standardized, meaning that the exchange selects a number of choices for underlyings, expiration dates, and a variety of other contract-specific items. These standardized terms are well known to all parties. If a party wishes to trade a futures contract, it must accept these terms. The only alternative would be to create a similar but customized contract on the forward market.

With respect to the underlying, for example, a given asset has a variety of specifications and grades. Consider a futures contract on U.S. Treasury bonds. There are many different Treasury bonds with a variety of characteristics. The futures exchange must decide which Treasury bond or group of bonds the contract covers. One of the most actively traded **commodity futures** contracts is oil, but there are many different types of oil.[2] To which type of oil does the contract apply? The exchange decides at the time it designs the contract.

The parties to a forward contract set its expiration at whatever date they want. For a futures contract, the exchange establishes a set of expiration dates.

---

[1] The information reported to the general public does not disclose the identity of the parties to transactions but only that a transaction took place at a particular price.

[2] Some of the main types are Saudi Arabian light crude, Brent crude, and West Texas intermediate crude.

The first specification of the expiration is the month. An exchange might establish that a given futures contract expires only in the months of March, June, September, and December. The second specification determines how far the expirations go out into the future. For example, in January of a given year, there may be expirations of March, June, September, and December. Expirations might also be available for March, June, September, and December of the following year, and perhaps some months of the year after that. The exchange decides which expiration months are appropriate for trading, based on which expirations they believe would be actively traded. Treasury bond futures have expirations going out only about a year. Eurodollar futures, however, have expirations that go out about 10 years.[3] The third specification of the expiration is the specific day of expiration. Many, but not all, contracts expire some time during the third week of the expiration month.

The exchange determines a number of other contract characteristics, including the contract size. For example, one Eurodollar futures contract covers $1 million of a Eurodollar time deposit. One U.S. Treasury bond futures contract covers $100,000 face value of Treasury bonds. One futures contract on crude oil covers 1,000 barrels. The exchange also decides on the price quotation unit. For example, Treasury bond futures are quoted in points and 32nds of par of 100. Hence, you will see a price like 104 21/32, which means 104.65625. With a contract size of $100,000, the actual price is $104,656.25.

The exchange also determines what hours of the day trading takes place and at what physical location on the exchange the contract will be traded. Many futures exchanges have a trading floor, which contains octagonal-shaped pits. A contract is assigned to a certain pit. Traders enter the pits and express their willingness to buy and sell by calling out and/or indicating by hand signals their bids and offers. Some exchanges have electronic trading, which means that trading takes place on computer terminals, generally located in companies' offices. Some exchanges have both floor trading and electronic trading; some have only one or the other.

1.3 Homogenization and Liquidity

By creating contracts with generally accepted terms, the exchange standardizes the instrument. In contrast, forward contracts are quite heterogeneous because they are customized. Standardizing the instrument makes it more acceptable to a broader group of participants, with the advantage being that the instrument can then more easily trade in a type of secondary market. Indeed, the ability to sell a previously purchased contract or purchase a previously sold contract is one of the important features of futures contracts. A futures contract is therefore said to have liquidity in contrast to a forward contract, which does not generally trade after it has been created.[4] This ability to trade a previously opened contract allows participants in this market to offset the position before expiration, thereby obtaining exposure to price movements in the underlying without the actual requirement of holding the position to expiration. We shall discuss this characteristic further when we describe futures trading in Section 2.

---

[3] You may be wondering why some Eurodollar futures contracts have such long expirations. Dealers in swaps and forward rate agreements use Eurodollar futures to hedge their positions. Many of those over-the-counter contracts have very long expirations.

[4] The notion of liquidity here is only that a market exists for futures contracts, but this does not imply a high degree of liquidity. There may be little trading in a given contract, and the bid–ask spread can be high. In contrast, some forward markets can be very liquid, allowing forward contracts to be offset.

1.4 The Clearinghouse, Daily Settlement, and Performance Guarantee

Another important distinction between futures and forwards is that the futures exchange guarantees to each party the performance of the other party, through a mechanism known as the clearinghouse. This guarantee means that if one party makes money on the transaction, it does not have to worry about whether it will collect the money from the other party because the clearinghouse ensures it will be paid. In contrast, each party to a forward contract assumes the risk that the other party will default.

An important and distinguishing feature of futures contracts is that the gains and losses on each party's position are credited and charged on a daily basis. This procedure, called **daily settlement** or **marking to market**, essentially results in paper gains and losses being converted to cash gains and losses each day. It is also equivalent to terminating a contract at the end of each day and reopening it the next day at that settlement price. In some sense, a futures contract is like a strategy of opening up a forward contract, closing it one day later, opening up a new contract, closing it one day later, and continuing in that manner until expiration. The exact manner in which the daily settlement works will be covered in more detail later in Section 3.

1.5 Regulation

In most countries, futures contracts are regulated at the federal government level. State and regional laws may also apply. In the United States, the Commodity Futures Trading Commission regulates the futures market. In the United Kingdom, the Securities and Futures Authority regulates both the securities and futures markets.

Federal regulation of futures markets generally arises out of a concern to protect the general public and other futures market participants, as well as through a recognition that futures markets affect all financial markets and the economy. Regulations cover such matters as ensuring that prices are reported accurately and in a timely manner, that markets are not manipulated, that professionals who offer their services to the public are qualified and honest, and that disputes are resolved. In the United States, the government has delegated some of these responsibilities to an organization called the National Futures Association (NFA). An industry self-regulatory body, the NFA was created with the objective of having the industry regulate itself and reduce the federal government's burden.

FUTURES TRADING   2

In this section, we look more closely at how futures contracts are traded. As noted above, futures contracts trade on a futures exchange either in a pit or on a screen or electronic terminal.

We briefly mentioned pit trading, also known as floor-based trading, in Section 1.2. Pit trading is a very physical activity. Traders stand in the pit and shout out their orders in the form of prices they are willing to pay or accept. They also use hand signals to indicate their bids and offers.[5] They engage in

---

[5] Hand signals facilitate trading with someone who is too far away in the pit for verbal communication.

transactions with other traders in the pits by simply agreeing on a price and number of contracts to trade. The activity is fast, furious, exciting, and stressful. The average pit trader is quite young, owing to the physical demands of the job and the toll it takes on body and mind. In recent years, more trading has come off of the exchange floor to electronic screens or terminals. In electronic or screen-based trading, exchange members enter their bids and offers into a computer system, which then displays this information and allows a trader to consummate a trade electronically. In the United States, pit trading is dominant, owing to its long history and tradition. Exchange members who trade on the floor enjoy pit trading and have resisted heavily the advent of electronic trading. Nonetheless, the exchanges have had to respond to market demands to offer electronic trading. In the United States, both pit trading and electronic trading are used, but in other countries, electronic trading is beginning to drive pit trading out of business.[6]

A person who enters into a futures contract establishes either a long position or a short position. Similar to forward contracts, long positions are agreements to buy the underlying at the expiration at a price agreed on at the start. Short positions are agreements to sell the underlying at a future date at a price agreed on at the start. When the position is established, each party deposits a small amount of money, typically called the margin, with the clearinghouse. Then, as briefly described in Section 1.4, the contract is marked to market, whereby the gains are distributed to and the losses collected from each party. We cover this marking-to-market process in more detail in the next section. For now, however, we focus only on the opening and closing of the position.

A party that has opened a long position collects profits or incurs losses on a daily basis. At some point in the life of the contract prior to expiration, that party may wish to re-enter the market and close out the position. This process, called **offsetting**, is the same as selling a previously purchased stock or buying back a stock to close a short position. The holder of a long futures position simply goes back into the market and offers the identical contract for sale. The holder of a short position goes back into the market and offers to buy the identical contract. It should be noted that when a party offsets a position, it does not necessary do so with the same counterparty to the original contract. In fact, rarely would a contract be offset with the same counterparty. Because of the ability to offset, futures contracts are said to be fungible, which means that any futures contract with any counterparty can be offset by an equivalent futures contract with another counterparty. Fungibility is assured by the fact that the clearinghouse inserts itself in the middle of each contract and, therefore, becomes the counterparty to each party.

For example, suppose in early January a futures trader purchases an S&P 500 stock index futures contract expiring in March. Through 15 February, the trader has incurred some gains and losses from the daily settlement and decides that she wants to close the position out. She then goes back into the market and offers for sale the March S&P 500 futures. Once she finds a buyer to take the position, she has a long and short position in the same contract. The clearinghouse considers that she no longer has a position in that contract and has no remaining exposure, nor any obligation to make or take delivery at expiration. Had she initially gone short the March futures, she might re-enter the market in February offering to buy it. Once she finds a seller to take the opposite position, she becomes long and short the same contract and is considered to have offset the contract and therefore have no net position.

---

[6] For example, in France electronic trading was introduced while pit trading continued. Within two weeks, all of the volume had migrated to electronic trading and pit trading was terminated.

THE CLEARINGHOUSE, MARGINS, AND PRICE LIMITS

As briefly noted in the previous section, when a trader takes a long or short position in a futures, he must first deposit sufficient funds in a margin account. This amount of money is traditionally called the margin, a term derived from the stock market practice in which an investor borrows a portion of the money required to purchase a certain amount of stock.

Margin in the stock market is quite different from margin in the futures market. In the stock market, "margin" means that a loan is made. The loan enables the investor to reduce the amount of his own money required to purchase the securities, thereby generating leverage or gearing, as it is sometimes known. If the stock goes up, the percentage gain to the investor is amplified. If the stock goes down, however, the percentage loss is also amplified. The borrowed money must eventually be repaid with interest. The margin percentage equals the market value of the stock minus the market value of the debt divided by the market value of the stock—in other words, the investor's own equity as a percentage of the value of the stock. For example, in the United States, regulations permit an investor to borrow up to 50 percent of the initial value of the stock. This percentage is called the initial margin requirement. On any day thereafter, the equity or percentage ownership in the account, measured as the market value of the securities minus the amount borrowed, can be less than 50 percent but must be at least a percentage known as the maintenance margin requirement. A typical **maintenance margin requirement** is 25 to 30 percent.

In the futures market, by contrast, the word **margin** is commonly used to describe the amount of money that must be put into an account by a party opening up a futures position, but the term is misleading. When a transaction is initiated, a futures trader puts up a certain amount of money to meet the **initial margin requirement**; however, the remaining money is not borrowed. The amount of money deposited is more like a down payment for the commitment to purchase the underlying at a later date. Alternatively, one can view this deposit as a form of good faith money, collateral, or a performance bond: The money helps ensure that the party fulfills his or her obligation.[7] Moreover, both the buyer and the seller of a futures contract must deposit margin.

In securities markets, margin requirements are normally set by federal regulators. In the United States, maintenance margin requirements are set by the securities exchanges and the NASD. In futures markets, margin requirements are set by the clearinghouses. In further contrast to margin practices in securities markets, futures margins are traditionally expressed in dollar terms and not as a percentage of the futures price. For ease of comparison, however, we often speak of the futures margin in terms of its relationship to the futures price. In futures markets, the initial margin requirement is typically much lower than the initial margin requirement in the stock market. In fact, futures margins are usually less than 10 percent of the futures price.[8] Futures clearinghouses set their margin requirements by studying historical price movements. They then establish minimum margin levels by taking into account normal price movements and the fact that accounts are marked to market daily. The clearinghouses thus collect and

---

[7] In fact, the Chicago Mercantile Exchange uses the term "performance bond" instead of "margin." Most other exchanges use the term "margin."

[8] For example, the margin requirement of the Eurodollar futures contract at the Chicago Mercantile Exchange has been less than one-tenth of one percent of the futures price. An exception to this requirement, however, is individual stock futures, which in the United States have margin requirements comparable to those of the stock market.

disburse margin money every day. Moreover, they are permitted to do so more often than daily, and on some occasions they have used that privilege. By carefully setting margin requirements and collecting margin money every day, clearinghouses are able to control the risk of default.

In spite of the differences in margin practices for futures and securities markets, the effect of leverage is similar for both. By putting up a small amount of money, the trader's gains and losses are magnified. Given the tremendously low margin requirements of futures markets, however, the magnitude of the leverage effect is much greater in futures markets. We shall see how this works as we examine the process of the daily settlement.

As previously noted, each day the clearinghouse conducts an activity known as the daily settlement, also called marking to market. This practice results in the conversion of gains and losses on paper into actual gains and losses. As margin account balances change, holders of futures positions must maintain balances above a level called the **maintenance margin requirement**. The maintenance margin requirement is lower than the initial margin requirement. On any day in which the amount of money in the margin account at the end of the day falls below the maintenance margin requirement, the trader must deposit sufficient funds to bring the balance back up to the initial margin requirement. Alternatively, the trader can simply close out the position but is responsible for any further losses incurred if the price changes before a closing transaction can be made.

To provide a fair mark-to-market process, the clearinghouse must designate the official price for determining daily gains and losses. This price is called the **settlement price** and represents an average of the final few trades of the day. It would appear that the closing price of the day would serve as the settlement price, but the closing price is a single value that can potentially be biased high or low or perhaps even manipulated by an unscrupulous trader. Hence, the clearinghouse takes an average of all trades during the closing period (as defined by each exchange).

Exhibit 1 provides an example of the marking-to-market process that occurs over a period of six trading days. We start with the assumption that the futures price is $100 when the transaction opens, the initial margin requirement is $5, and the maintenance margin requirement is $3. In Panel A, the trader takes a long position of 10 contracts on Day 0, depositing $50 ($5 times 10 contracts) as indicated in Column 3. At the end of the day, his ending balance is $50.[9] Although the trader can withdraw any funds in excess of the initial margin requirement, we shall assume that he does not do so.[10]

The ending balance on Day 0 is then carried forward to the beginning balance on Day 1. On Day 1, the futures price moves down to 99.20, as indicated in Column 4 of Panel A. The futures price change, Column 5, is −0.80 (99.20 − 100). This amount is then multiplied by the number of contracts to obtain the number in Column 6 of −0.80 × 10 = −$8. The ending balance, Column 7, is the beginning balance plus the gain or loss. The ending balance on Day 1 of $42 is above the maintenance margin requirement of $30, so no funds need to be deposited on Day 2.

---

[9] Technically, we are assuming that the position was opened at the settlement price on Day 0. If the position is opened earlier during the day, it would be marked to the settlement price at the end of the day.

[10] Virtually all professional traders are able to deposit interest-earning assets, although many other account holders are required to deposit cash. If the deposit earns interest, there is no opportunity cost and no obvious necessity to withdraw the money to invest elsewhere.

EXHIBIT 1 Mark-to-Market Example

Initial futures price = $100, Initial margin requirement = $5, Maintenance margin requirement = $3

Panel A. *Holder of Long Position of 10 Contracts*

Day (1)	Beginning Balance (2)	Funds Deposited (3)	Settlement Price (4)	Futures Price Change (5)	Gain/ Loss (6)	Ending Balance (7)
0	0	50	100.00			50
1	50	0	99.20	−0.80	−8	42
2	42	0	96.00	−3.20	−32	10
3	10	40	101.00	5.00	50	100
4	100	0	103.50	2.50	25	125
5	125	0	103.00	−0.50	−5	120
6	120	0	104.00	1.00	10	130

Panel B. *Holder of Short Position of 10 Contracts*

Day (1)	Beginning Balance (2)	Funds Deposited (3)	Settlement Price (4)	Futures Price Change (5)	Gain/ Loss (6)	Ending Balance (7)
0	0	50	100.00			50
1	50	0	99.20	−0.80	8	58
2	58	0	96.00	−3.20	32	90
3	90	0	101.00	5.00	−50	40
4	40	0	103.50	2.50	−25	15
5	15	35	103.00	−0.50	5	55
6	55	0	104.00	1.00	−10	45

On Day 2 the settlement price goes down to $96. Based on a price decrease of $3.20 per contract and 10 contracts, the loss is $32, lowering the ending balance to $10. This amount is $20 below the maintenance margin requirement. Thus, the trader will get a margin call the following morning and must deposit $40 to bring the balance up to the initial margin level of $50. This deposit is shown in Column 3 on Day 3.

Here, we must emphasize two important points. First, additional margin that must be deposited is the amount sufficient to bring the ending balance up to the initial margin requirement, not the maintenance margin requirement.[11] This additional margin is called the **variation margin**. In addition, the amount that must be deposited the following day is determined regardless of the price change the following day, which might bring the ending balance well above the initial margin requirement, as it does here, or even well below the maintenance margin requirement. Thus, another margin call could occur. Also note that

[11] In the stock market, one must deposit only the amount necessary to bring the balance up to the maintenance margin requirement.

when the trader closes the position, the account is marked to market to the final price at which the transaction occurs, not the settlement price that day.

Over the six-day period, the trader in this example deposited $90. The account balance at the end of the sixth day is $130—nearly a 50 percent return over six days; not bad. But look at Panel B, which shows the position of a holder of 10 short contracts over that same period. Note that the short gains when prices decrease and loses when prices increase. Here the ending balance falls below the maintenance margin requirement on Day 4, and the short must deposit $35 on Day 5. At the end of Day 6, the short has deposited $85 and the balance is $45, a loss of $40 or nearly 50 percent, which is the same $40 the long made. Both cases illustrate the leverage effect that magnifies gains and losses.

When establishing a futures position, it is important to know the price level that would trigger a margin call. In this case, it does not matter how many contracts one has. The price change would need to fall for a long position (or rise for a short position) by the difference between the initial and maintenance margin requirements. In this example, the difference between the initial and maintenance margin requirements is \$5 − \$3 = \$2. Thus, the price would need to fall from $100 to $98 for a long position (or rise from $100 to $102 for a short position) to trigger a margin call.

As described here, when a trader receives a margin call, he is required to deposit funds sufficient to bring the account balance back up to the initial margin level. Alternatively, the trader can choose to simply close out the position as soon as possible. For example, consider the position of the long at the end of the second day when the margin balance is $10. This amount is $20 below the maintenance level, and he is required to deposit $40 to bring the balance up to the initial margin level. If he would prefer not to deposit the additional funds, he can close out the position as soon as possible the following day. Suppose, however, that the price is moving quickly at the opening on Day 3. If the price falls from $96 to $95, he has lost $10 more, wiping out the margin account balance. In fact, if it fell any further, he would have a negative margin account balance. He is still responsible for these losses. Thus, the trader could lose more than the amount of money he has placed in the margin account. The total amount of money he could lose is limited to the price per contract at which he bought, $100, times the number of contracts, 10, or $1,000. Such a loss would occur if the price fell to zero, although this is not likely. This potential loss may not seem like a lot, but it is certainly large relative to the initial margin requirement of $50. For the holder of the short position, there is no upper limit on the price and the potential loss is theoretically infinite.

EXAMPLE 1

Consider a futures contract in which the current futures price is $82. The initial margin requirement is $5, and the maintenance margin requirement is $2. You go long 20 contracts and meet all margin calls but do not withdraw any excess margin. Assume that on the first day, the contract is established at the settlement price, so there is no mark-to-market gain or loss on that day.

A. Complete the table below and provide an explanation of any funds deposited.

Day	Beginning Balance	Funds Deposited	Futures Price	Price Change	Gain/Loss	Ending Balance
0			82			
1			84			
2			78			
3			73			
4			79			
5			82			
6			84			

B. Determine the price level that would trigger a margin call.

Solutions:

A.

Day	Beginning Balance	Funds Deposited	Futures Price	Price Change	Gain/Loss	Ending Balance
0	0	100	82			100
1	100	0	84	2	40	140
2	140	0	78	−6	−120	20
3	20	80	73	−5	−100	0
4	0	100	79	6	120	220
5	220	0	82	3	60	280
6	280	0	84	2	40	320

On Day 0, you deposit $100 because the initial margin requirement is $5 per contract and you go long 20 contracts. At the end of Day 2, the balance is down to $20, which is $20 below the $40 maintenance margin requirement ($2 per contract times 20 contracts). You must deposit enough money to bring the balance up to the initial margin requirement of $100 ($5 per contract times 20 contracts). So on Day 3, you deposit $80. The price change on Day 3 causes a gain/loss of −$100, leaving you with a balance of $0 at the end of Day 3. On Day 4, you must deposit $100 to return the balance to the initial margin level.

B. A price decrease to $79 would trigger a margin call. This calculation is based on the fact that the difference between the initial margin requirement and the maintenance margin requirement is $3. If the futures price starts at $82, it can fall by $3 to $79 before it triggers a margin call.

Some futures contracts impose limits on the price change that can occur from one day to the next. Appropriately, these are called **price limits**. These limits are usually set as an absolute change over the previous day. Using the example above, suppose the price limit was $4. This would mean that each day, no transaction could take place higher than the previous settlement price plus $4 or lower than the previous settlement price minus $4. So the next day's settlement price cannot go beyond the price limit and thus no transaction can take place beyond the limits.

If the price at which a transaction would be made exceeds the limits, then price essentially freezes at one of the limits, which is called a **limit move**. If the price is stuck at the upper limit, it is called **limit up**; if stuck at the lower limit, it is called **limit down**. If a transaction cannot take place because the price would be beyond the limits, this situation is called **locked limit**. By the end of the day, unless the price has moved back within the limits, the settlement price will then be at one of the limits. The following day, the new range of acceptable prices is based on the settlement price plus or minus limits. The exchanges have different rules that provide for expansion or contraction of price limits under some circumstances. In addition, not all contracts have price limits.

Finally, we note that the exchanges have the power to mark contracts to market whenever they deem it necessary. Thus, they can do so during the trading day rather than wait until the end of the day. They sometimes do so when abnormally large market moves occur.

The daily settlement procedure is designed to collect losses and distribute gains in such a manner that losses are paid before becoming large enough to impose a serious risk of default. Recall that the clearinghouse guarantees to each party that it need not worry about collecting from the counterparty. The clearinghouse essentially positions itself in the middle of each contract, becoming the short counterparty to the long and the long counterparty to the short. The clearinghouse collects funds from the parties incurring losses in this daily settlement procedure and distributes them to the parties incurring gains. By doing so each day, the clearinghouse ensures that losses cannot build up. Of course, this process offers no guarantee that counterparties will not default. Some defaults do occur, but the counterparty is defaulting to the clearinghouse, which has never failed to pay off the opposite party. In the unlikely event that the clearinghouse were unable to pay, it would turn to a reserve fund or to the exchange, or it would levy a tax on exchange members to cover losses.

4   DELIVERY AND CASH SETTLEMENT

As previously described, a futures trader can close out a position before expiration. If the trader holds a long position, she can simply enter into a position to go short the same futures contract. From the clearinghouse's perspective, the trader holds both a long and short position in the same contract. These positions are considered to offset and, therefore, there is no open position in place. Most futures contracts are offset before expiration. Those that remain in place are subject to either delivery or a final cash settlement. Here we explore this process, which determines how a futures contract terminates at expiration.

When the exchange designs a futures contract, it specifies whether the contract will terminate with delivery or cash settlement. If the contract terminates in delivery, the clearinghouse selects a counterparty, usually the holder of the oldest long contract, to accept delivery. The holder of the short position then delivers the underlying to the holder of the long position, who pays the short the necessary cash for the underlying. Suppose, for example, that two days before expiration, a party goes long one futures contract at a price of $50. The following day (the day **before expiration**), the settlement price is $52. The trader's margin account is then marked to market by crediting it with a gain of $2. Then suppose that the next day the contract expires with the settlement price at $53. As the end of the trading day draws near, the trader has two choices. She can attempt to close out the position by selling the futures contract. The margin account would then be marked to market at the price at which she sells. If she sells close enough to the expiration, the price she sold at would be very close to the final settlement price of $53. Doing so would add $1 to her margin account balance.

The other choice is to leave the position open at the end of the trading day. Then she would have to take delivery. If that occurred, she would be required to take possession of the asset and pay the short the settlement price of the previous day. Doing so would be equivalent to paying $52 and receiving the asset. She could then sell the asset for its price of $53, netting a $1 gain, which is equivalent to the final $1 credited to her margin account if she had terminated the position at the settlement price of $53, as described above.[12]

An alternative settlement procedure, which we described in Reading 71 on forward contracts, is cash settlement. The exchange designates certain futures contracts as cash-settled contracts. If the contract used in this example were cash settled, then the trader would not need to close out the position close to the end of the expiration day. She could simply leave the position open. When the contract expires, her margin account would be marked to market for a gain on the final day of $1. Cash settlement contracts have some advantages over delivery contracts, particularly with respect to significant savings in transaction costs.[13]

Exhibit 2 illustrates the equivalence of these three forms of delivery. Note, however, that because of the transaction costs of delivery, parties clearly prefer a

EXHIBIT 2	Closeout versus Physical Delivery versus Cash Settlement

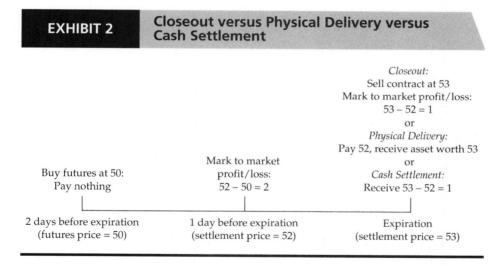

Closeout:
Sell contract at 53
Mark to market profit/loss:
53 − 52 = 1
or
Physical Delivery:
Pay 52, receive asset worth 53
or
Cash Settlement:
Receive 53 − 52 = 1

Buy futures at 50:
Pay nothing

Mark to market profit/loss:
52 − 50 = 2

2 days before expiration
(futures price = 50)

1 day before expiration
(settlement price = 52)

Expiration
(settlement price = 53)

---

[12] The reason she pays the settlement price of the previous day is because on the previous day when her account was marked to market, she essentially created a new futures position at a price of $52. Thus, she committed to purchase the asset at expiration, just one day later, at a price of $52. The next day when the contract expires, it is then appropriate that she buy the underlying for $52.

[13] Nonetheless, cash settlement has been somewhat controversial in the United States. If a contract is designated as cash settlement, it implies that the buyer of the contract never intended to actually take possession of the underlying asset. Some legislators and regulators feel that this design is against the spirit of the law, which views a futures contract as a commitment to buy the asset at a later date. Even though parties often offset futures contracts prior to expiration, the possibility of actual delivery is still present in contracts other than those settled by cash. This controversy, however, is relatively minor and has caused no serious problems or debates in recent years.

closeout or cash settlement over physical delivery, particularly when the underlying asset is a physical commodity.

Contracts designated for delivery have a variety of features that can complicate delivery. In most cases, delivery does not occur immediately after expiration but takes place over several days. In addition, many contracts permit the short to choose when delivery takes place. For many contracts, delivery can be made any business day of the month. The delivery period usually includes the days following the last trading day of the month, which is usually in the third week of the month.

In addition, the short often has other choices regarding delivery, a major one being exactly which underlying asset is delivered. For example, a futures contract on U.S. Treasury bonds trading at the Chicago Board of Trade permits the short to deliver any of a number of U.S. Treasury bonds.[14] The wheat futures contract at the Chicago Board of Trade permits delivery of any of several types of wheat. Futures contracts calling for physical delivery of commodities often permit delivery at different locations. A given commodity delivered to one location is not the same as that commodity delivered to another because of the costs involved in transporting the commodity. The short holds the sole right to make decisions about what, when, and where to deliver, and the right to make these decisions can be extremely valuable. The right to make a decision concerning these aspects of delivery is called a **delivery option**.

Some futures contracts that call for delivery require delivery of the actual asset, and some use only a book entry. For example, in this day and age, no one physically handles U.S. Treasury bonds in the form of pieces of paper. Bonds are transferred electronically over the Federal Reserve's wire system. Other contracts, such as oil or wheat, do actually involve the physical transfer of the asset. Physical delivery is more common when the underlying is a physical commodity, whereas book entry is more common when the underlying is a financial asset.

Futures market participants use one additional delivery procedure, which is called **exchange for physicals (EFP)**. In an EFP transaction, the long and short arrange an alternative delivery procedure. For example, the Chicago Board of Trade's wheat futures contracts require delivery on certain dates at certain locations either in Chicago or in a few other specified locations in the Midwest. If the long and short agree, they could effect delivery by having the short deliver the wheat to the long in, for example, Omaha. The two parties would then report to the Chicago Board of Trade that they had settled their contract outside of the exchange's normal delivery procedures, which would be satisfactory to the exchange.

5 FUTURES EXCHANGES

A futures exchange is a legal corporate entity whose shareholders are its members. The members own memberships, more commonly called **seats**. Exchange members have the privilege of executing transactions on the exchange. Each member acts as either a **floor trader** or a **broker**. Floor traders are typically called **locals**; brokers are typically called **futures commission merchants (FCMs)**. Locals are market makers, standing ready to buy and sell by quoting a bid and an ask

---

[14] We shall cover this feature in more detail in Section 6.2.

price. They are the primary providers of liquidity to the market. FCMs execute transactions for other parties off the exchange.

The locals on the exchange floor typically trade according to one of several distinct styles. The most common is called scalping. A **scalper** offers to buy or sell futures contracts, holding the position for only a brief period of time, perhaps just seconds. Scalpers attempt to profit by buying at the bid price and selling at the higher ask price. A **day trader** holds a position open somewhat longer but closes all positions at the end of the day.[15] A **position trader** holds positions open overnight. Day traders and position traders are quite distinct from scalpers in that they attempt to profit from the anticipated direction of the market; scalpers are trying simply to buy at the bid and sell at the ask.

Recall that futures exchanges have trading either on the floor or off the floor on electronic terminals, or in some cases, both. As previously described, floor trading in the United States takes place in pits, which are octagonal, multi-tiered areas where floor traders stand and conduct transactions. Traders wear jackets of specific colors and badges to indicate such information as what type of trader (FCM or local) they are and whom they represent.[16] As noted, to indicate a willingness to trade, a trader shouts and uses a set of standard hand signals. A trade is consummated by two traders agreeing on a price and a number of contracts. These traders might not actually say anything to each other; they may simply use a combination of hand signals and/or eye contact to agree on a transaction. When a transaction is agreed on, the traders fill out small paper forms and turn them over to clerks, who then see that the transactions are entered into the system and reported.

Each trader is required to have an account at a clearing firm. The clearing firms are the actual members of the clearinghouse. The clearinghouse deals only with the clearing firms, which then deal with their individual and institutional customers.

In electronic trading, the principles remain essentially the same but the traders do not stand in the pits. In fact, they do not see each other at all. They sit at computer terminals, which enable them to see the bids and offers of other traders. Transactions are executed by the click of a computer mouse or an entry from a keyboard.

Exhibit 3 lists the world's 20 leading futures exchanges in 2001, ranked by trading volume. Recall from Reading 70 that trading volume can be a misleading measure of the size of futures markets; nonetheless, it is the measure primarily used. The structure of global futures exchanges has changed considerably in recent years. Exchanges in the United States, primarily the Chicago Board of Trade and the Chicago Mercantile Exchange, were clearly the world leaders in the past. Note that the volume leader now, however, is Eurex, the combined German–Swiss exchange. Eurex has been so successful partly because of its decision to be an all-electronic futures exchange, whereas the Chicago exchanges are still primarily pit-trading exchanges. Note the popularity of futures trading in Japan; four of the 20 leading exchanges are Japanese.

---

[15] The term "day trader" has been around the futures market for a long time but has recently acquired a new meaning in the broader financial markets. The term is now used to describe individual investors who trade stocks, often over the Internet, during the day for a living or as a hobby. In fact, the term has even been used in a somewhat pejorative manner, in that day traders are often thought of as naïve investors speculating wildly with money they can ill afford to lose.

[16] For example, an FCM or local could be trading for himself or could represent a company.

EXHIBIT 3	The World's 20 Leading Futures Exchanges

Exchange and Location	Volume in 2001 (Number of Contracts)
Eurex (Germany and Switzerland)	435,141,707
Chicago Mercantile Exchange (United States)	315,971,885
Chicago Board of Trade (United States)	209,988,002
London International Financial Futures and Options Exchange (United Kingdom)	161,522,775
Bolsa de Mercadorias & Futuros (Brazil)	94,174,452
New York Mercantile Exchange (United States)	85,039,984
Tokyo Commodity Exchange (Japan)	56,538,245
London Metal Exchange (United Kingdom)	56,224,495
Paris Bourse SA (France)	42,042,673
Sydney Futures Exchange (Australia)	34,075,508
Korea Stock Exchange (Korea)	31,502,184
Singapore Exchange (Singapore)	30,606,546
Central Japan Commodity Exchange (Japan)	27,846,712
International Petroleum Exchange (United Kingdom)	26,098,207
OM Stockholm Exchange (Sweden)	23,408,198
Tokyo Grain Exchange (Japan)	22,707,808
New York Board of Trade (United States)	14,034,168
MEFF Renta Variable (Spain)	13,108,293
Tokyo Stock Exchange (Japan)	12,465,433
South African Futures Exchange (South Africa)	11,868,242

Source: Futures Industry, January/February 2002.

6 TYPES OF FUTURES CONTRACTS

The different types of futures contracts are generally divided into two main groups: commodity futures and financial futures. Commodity futures cover traditional agricultural, metal, and petroleum products. Financial futures include stocks, bonds, and currencies. Exhibit 4 gives a broad overview of the most active types of futures contracts traded on global futures exchanges. These contracts are those covered by the *Wall Street Journal* on the date indicated.

Our primary focus in this book is on financial and currency futures contracts. Within the financials group, our main interest is on interest rate and bond futures, stock index futures, and currency futures. We may occasionally make reference to a commodity futures contract, but that will primarily be for illustrative purposes. In the following subsections, we introduce the primary contracts we shall focus on. These are U.S. contracts, but they resemble most types of futures contracts found on exchanges throughout the world. Full contract specifications for these and other contracts are available on the websites of the futures exchanges, which are easy to locate with most Internet search engines.

EXHIBIT 4	Most-Active Global Futures Contracts as Covered by the *Wall Street Journal*, 18 June 2002

Commodity Futures

Corn (CBOT)	Treasury Bonds (CBOT)	Euro (CME)
Oats (CBOT)	Treasury Notes (CBOT)	Euro–Sterling (NYBOT)
Soybeans (CBOT)	10-Year Agency Notes (CBOT)	Euro–U.S. Dollar (NYBOT)
Soybean Meal (CBOT)	10-Year Interest Rate Swaps (CBOT)	Euro–Yen (NYBOT)
Soybean Oil (CBOT)	2-Year Agency Notes (CBOT)	Dow Jones Industrial Average (CBOT)
Wheat (CBOT, KCBT, MGE)	5-Year Treasury Notes (CBOT)	Mini Dow Jones Industrial Average (CBOT)
Canola (WPG)	2-Year Treasury Notes (CBOT)	S&P 500 Index (CME)
Barley (WPG)	Federal Funds (CBOT)	Mini S&P 500 Index (CME)
Feeder Cattle (CME)	Municipal Bond Index (CBOT)	S&P Midcap 400 Index (CME)
Live Cattle (CME)	Treasury Bills (CME)	Nikkei 225 (CME)
Lean Hogs (CME)	1-Month LIBOR (CME)	Nasdaq 100 Index (CME)
Pork Bellies (CME)	Eurodollar (CME)	Mini Nasdaq Index (CME)
Milk (CME)	Euroyen (CME, SGX)	Goldman Sachs Commodity Index (CME)
Lumber (CME)	Short Sterling (LIFFE)	Russell 1000 Index (CME)
Cocoa (NYBOT)	Long Gilt (LIFFE)	Russell 2000 Index (CME)
Coffee (NYBOT)	3-Month Euribor (LIFFE)	NYSE Composite Index (NYBOT)
World Sugar (NYBOT)	3-Month Euroswiss (LIFFE)	U.S. Dollar Index (NYBOT)
Domestic Sugar (NYBOT)	Canadian Bankers Acceptance (ME)	Share Price Index (SFE)
Cotton (NYBOT)	10-Year Canadian Government Bond (ME)	CAC 40 Stock Index (MATIF)
Orange Juice (NYBOT)	10-Year Euro Notional Bond (MATIF)	Xetra Dax (EUREX)
Copper (NYMEX)	3-Month Euribor (MATIF)	FTSE 200 Index (LIFFE)
Gold (NYMEX)	3-Year Commonwealth T-Bonds (SFE)	Dow Jones Euro Stoxx 50 Index (EUREX)
Platinum (NYMEX)	5-Year German Euro Government Bond (EUREX)	Dow Jones Stoxx 50 Index (EUREX)
Palladium (NYMEX)	10-Year German Euro Government Bond (EUREX)	
Silver (NYMEX)	2-Year German Euro Government Bond (EUREX)	
Crude Oil (NYMEX)	Japanese Yen (CME)	
No. 2 Heating Oil (NYMEX)	Canadian Dollar (CME)	
Unleaded Gasoline (NYMEX)	British Pound (CME)	
Natural Gas (NYMEX)	Swiss Franc (CME)	
Brent Crude Oil (IPEX)	Australian Dollar (CME)	
Gas Oil (IPEX)	Mexican Peso (CME)	

Financial Futures

Exchange codes: CBOT (Chicago Board of Trade), CME (Chicago Mercantile Exchange), LIFFE (London International Financial Futures Exchange), WPG (Winnipeg Grain Exchange), EUREX (Eurex), NYBOT (New York Board of Trade), IPEX (International Petroleum Exchange), MATIF (Marché a Terme International de France), ME (Montreal Exchange), MGE (Minneapolis Grain Exchange), SFE (Sydney Futures Exchange), SGX (Singapore Exchange), KCBT (Kansas City Board of Trade), NYMEX (New York Mercantile Exchange).
Note: These are not the only global futures contracts but are those covered in the Wall Street Journal on the date given and represent the most active contracts at that time.

6.1 Short-Term Interest Rate Futures Contracts

The primary short-term interest rate futures contracts are those on U.S. Treasury bills and Eurodollars on the Chicago Mercantile Exchange.

6.1.1 Treasury Bill Futures

The Treasury bill contract, launched in 1976, was the first interest rate futures contract. It is based on a 90-day U.S. Treasury bill, one of the most important U.S. government debt instruments (described in Reading 71, Section 3.2.1). The Treasury bill, or T-bill, is a discount instrument, meaning that its price equals the face value minus a discount representing interest. The discount equals the face value multiplied by the quoted rate times the days to maturity divided by 360. Thus, using the example from Reading 71, if a 180-day T-bill is selling at a discount of 4 percent, its price per \$1 par is $1 - 0.04(180/360) = 0.98$. An investor who buys the bill and holds it to maturity would receive \$1 at maturity, netting a gain of \$0.02.

The futures contract is based on a 90-day \$1,000,000 U.S. Treasury bill. Thus, on any given day, the contract trades with the understanding that a 90-day T-bill will be delivered at expiration. While the contract is trading, its price is quoted as 100 minus the rate quoted as a percent priced into the contract by the futures market. This value, 100 − Rate, is known as the IMM Index; IMM stands for International Monetary Market, a division of the Chicago Mercantile Exchange. The IMM Index is a reported and publicly available price; however, it is not the actual futures price, which is

$$100 - (\text{Rate}/100)(90/360)$$

For example, suppose on a given day the rate priced into the contract is 6.25 percent. Then the quoted price will be $100 - 6.25 = 93.75$. The actual futures price would be

$$\$1,000,000[1 - 0.0625(90/360)] = \$984,375$$

Recall, however, that except for the small margin deposit, a futures transaction does not require any cash to be paid up front. As trading takes place, the rate fluctuates with market interest rates and the associated IMM Index price changes accordingly. The actual futures price, as calculated above, also fluctuates according to the above formula, but interestingly, that price is not very important. The same information can be captured more easily by referencing the IMM Index than by calculating the actual price.

Suppose, for example, that a trader had his account marked to market to the above price, 6.25 in terms of the rate, 93.75 in terms of the IMM Index, and \$984,375 in terms of the actual futures price. Now suppose the rate goes to 6.50, an increase of 0.25 or 25 basis points. The IMM Index declines to 93.50, and the actual futures price drops to

$$\$1,000,000[1 - 0.065(90/360)] = \$983,750$$

Thus, the actual futures price decreased by $\$984,375 - \$983,750 = \$625$. A trader who is long would have a loss of \$625; a trader who is short would have a gain of \$625.

This \$625 gain or loss can be arrived at more directly, however, by simply noting that each basis point move is equivalent to \$25.[17] This special design of the contract makes it easy for floor traders to do the necessary arithmetic in their heads. For example, if floor traders observe the IMM Index move from 93.75 to 93.50, they immediately know that it has moved down 25 basis points and that 25 basis points times \$25 per basis point is a loss of \$625. The minimum **tick** size is one-half basis point or \$12.50.

T-bill futures contracts have expirations of the current month, the next month, and the next four months of March, June, September, and December. Because of the small trading volume, however, only the closest expiration has much trading volume, and even that one is only lightly traded. T-bill futures expire specifically on the Monday of the week of the third Wednesday each month and settle in cash rather than physical delivery of the T-bill, as described in Section 4.

As important as Treasury bills are in U.S. financial markets, however, today this futures contract is barely active. The Eurodollar contract is considered much more important because it reflects the interest rate on a dollar borrowed by a high-quality private borrower. The rates on T-bills are considered too heavily influenced by U.S. government policies, budget deficits, government funding plans, politics, and Federal Reserve monetary policy. Although unquestionably Eurodollar rates are affected by those factors, market participants consider them much less directly influenced. But in spite of this relative inactivity, T-bill futures are useful instruments for illustrating certain principles of futures market pricing and trading. Accordingly, we shall use them on some occasions. For now, however, we turn to the Eurodollar futures contract.

6.1.2 Eurodollar Futures

Recall that in Reading 71, we devoted a good bit of effort to understanding Eurodollar forward contracts, known as FRAs. These contracts pay off based on LIBOR on a given day. The Eurodollar futures contract of the Chicago Mercantile Exchange is based on \$1 million notional principal of 90-day Eurodollars. Specifically, the underlying is the rate on a 90-day dollar-denominated time deposit issued by a bank in London. As we described in Reading 71, this deposit is called a Eurodollar time deposit, and the rate is referred to as LIBOR (London Interbank Offer Rate). On a given day, the futures contract trades based on the understanding that at expiration, the official Eurodollar rate, as compiled by the British Bankers Association (BBA), will be the rate at which the final settlement of the contract is made. While the contract is trading, its price is quoted as 100 minus the rate priced into the contract by futures traders. Like its counterpart in the T-bill futures market, this value, $100 - \text{Rate}$, is also known as the IMM Index.

As in the T-bill futures market, on a given day, if the rate priced into the contract is 5.25 percent, the quoted price will be $100 - 5.25 = 94.75$. With each contract based on \$1 million notional principal of Eurodollars, the actual futures price is

$$\$1,000,000[1 - 0.0525(90/360)] = \$986,875$$

Like the T-bill contract, the actual futures price moves \$25 for every basis point move in the rate or IMM Index price.

---

[17] Expressed mathematically, $\$1,000,000[0.0001(90/360)] = \$25$. In other words, any move in the last digit of the rate (a basis point) affects the actual futures price by \$25.

As with all futures contracts, the price fluctuates on a daily basis and margin accounts are marked to market according to the exchange's official settlement price. At expiration, the final settlement price is the official rate quoted on a 90-day Eurodollar time deposit by the BBA. That rate determines the final settlement. Eurodollar futures contracts do not permit actual delivery of a Eurodollar time deposit; rather, they settle in cash, as described in Section 4.

The Eurodollar futures contract is one of the most active in the world. Because its rate is based on LIBOR, it is widely used by dealers in swaps, FRAs, and interest rate options to hedge their positions taken in dollar-denominated over-the-counter interest rate derivatives. Such derivatives usually use LIBOR as the underlying rate.

It is important to note, however, that there is a critical distinction between the manner in which the interest calculation is built into the Eurodollar futures contract and the manner in which interest is imputed on actual Eurodollar time deposits. Recall from Reading 71 that when a bank borrows $1 million at a rate of 5 percent for 90 days, the amount it will owe in 90 days is

$$\$1,000,000[1 + 0.05(90/360)] = \$1,012,500$$

Interest on Eurodollar time deposits is computed on an add-on basis to the principal. As described in this section, however, it appears that in computing the futures price, interest is deducted from the principal so that a bank borrowing $1,000,000 at a rate of 5 percent would receive

$$\$1,000,000[1 - 0.05(90/360)] = \$987,500$$

and would pay back $1,000,000. This procedure is referred to as discount interest and is used in the T-bill market.

The discount interest computation associated with Eurodollar futures is merely a convenience contrived by the futures exchange to facilitate quoting prices in a manner already familiar to its traders, who were previously trading T-bill futures.

The minimum tick size for Eurodollar futures is 1 basis point or $25. The available expirations are the next two months plus March, June, September, and December. The expirations go out about 10 years, a reflection of their use by over-the-counter derivatives dealers to hedge their positions in long-term interest rate derivatives. Eurodollar futures expire on the second business day on which London banks are open before the third Wednesday of the month and terminate with a cash settlement.

6.2 Intermediate- and Long-Term Interest Rate Futures Contracts

In U.S. markets, the primary interest-rate-related instruments of intermediate and long maturities are U.S. Treasury notes and bonds. The U.S. government issues both instruments: Treasury notes have an original maturity of 2 to 10 years, and Treasury bonds have an original maturity of more than 10 years. Futures contracts on these instruments are very actively traded on the Chicago Board of Trade. For the most part, there are no real differences in the contract characteristics for Treasury note and Treasury bond futures; the underlying bonds differ slightly, but the futures contracts are qualitatively the same. We shall focus here on one of the most active instruments, the U.S. Treasury bond futures contract.

The contract is based on the delivery of a U.S. Treasury bond with any coupon but with a maturity of at least 15 years. If the deliverable bond is callable, it cannot be callable for at least 15 years from the delivery date.[18] These specifications mean that there are potentially a large number of deliverable bonds, which is exactly the way the Chicago Board of Trade, the Federal Reserve, and the U.S. Treasury want it. They do not want a potential run on a single issue that might distort prices. By having multiple deliverable issues, however, the contract must be structured with some fairly complicated procedures to adjust for the fact that the short can deliver whatever bond he chooses from among the eligible bonds. This choice gives the short a potentially valuable option and puts the long at a disadvantage. Moreover, it complicates pricing the contract, because the identity of the underlying bond is not clear. Although when referring to a futures contract on a 90-day Eurodollar time deposit we are relatively clear about the underlying instrument, a futures contract on a long-term Treasury bond does not allow us the same clarity.

To reduce the confusion, the exchange declares a standard or hypothetical version of the deliverable bond. This hypothetical deliverable bond has a 6 percent coupon. When a trader holding a short position at expiration delivers a bond with a coupon greater (less) than 6 percent, she receives an upward (a downward) adjustment to the price paid for the bond by the long. The adjustment is done by means of a device called the **conversion factor**. In brief, the conversion factor is the price of a $1.00 par bond with a coupon and maturity equal to those of the deliverable bond and a yield of 6 percent. Thus, if the short delivers a bond with a coupon greater (less) than 6 percent, the conversion factor exceeds (is less than) 1.0.[19] The amount the long pays the short is the futures price at expiration multiplied by the conversion factor. Thus, delivery of a bond with coupon greater (less) than the standard amount, 6 percent, results in the short receiving an upward (a downward) adjustment to the amount received. A number of other technical considerations are also involved in determining the delivery price.[20]

The conversion factor system is designed to put all bonds on equal footing. Ideally, application of the conversion factor would result in the short finding no preference for delivery of any one bond over any other. That is not the case, however, because the complex relationships between bond prices cannot be reduced to a simple linear adjustment, such as the conversion factor method. As a result, some bonds are cheaper to deliver than others. When making the delivery decision, the short compares the cost of buying a given bond on the open market with the amount she would receive upon delivery of that bond. The former will always exceed the latter; otherwise, a clear arbitrage opportunity would be available. The most attractive bond for delivery would be the one in which the amount received for delivering the bond is largest relative to the amount paid on the open market for the bond. The bond that minimizes this loss is referred to as the **cheapest-to-deliver** bond.

At any time during the life of a Treasury bond futures contract, traders can identify the cheapest-to-deliver bond. Determining the amount received at delivery is straightforward; it equals the current futures price times the conversion

---

[18] The U.S. government no longer issues callable bonds but has done so in the past.

[19] This statement is true regardless of the maturity of the deliverable bond. Any bond with a coupon in excess of its yield is worth more than its par value.

[20] For example, the actual procedure for delivery of U.S. Treasury bonds is a three-day process starting with the short notifying the exchange of intention to make delivery. Delivery actually occurs several days later. In addition, as is the custom in U.S. bond markets, the quoted price does not include the accrued interest. Accordingly, an adjustment must be made.

factor for a given bond. To determine the amount the bond would cost at expiration, one calculates the forward price of the bond, positioned at the delivery date. Of course, this is just a forward computation; circumstances could change by the expiration date. But this forward calculation gives a picture of circumstances as they currently stand and identifies which bond is currently the **cheapest to deliver**. That bond is then considered the bond most likely to be delivered. Recall that one problem with this futures contract is that the identity of the underlying bond is unclear. Traders traditionally treat the cheapest to deliver as the bond that underlies the contract. As time passes and interest rates change, however, the cheapest-to-deliver bond can change. Thus, the bond underlying the futures contract can change, adding an element of uncertainty to the pricing and trading of this contract.

With this complexity associated with the U.S. Treasury bond futures contract, one might suspect that it is less actively traded. In fact, the opposite is true: Complexity creates extraordinary opportunities for gain for those who understand what is going on and can identify the cheapest bond to deliver.

The Chicago Board of Trade's U.S. Treasury bond futures contract covers $100,000 par value of U.S. Treasury bonds. The expiration months are March, June, September, and December. They expire on the seventh business day preceding the last business day of the month and call for actual delivery, through the Federal Reserve's wire system, of the Treasury bond. Prices are quoted in points and 32nds, meaning that you will see prices like 98 18/32, which equals 98.5625. For a contract covering $100,000 par value, for example, the price is $98,562.50. The minimum tick size is 1/32, which is $31.25.

In addition to the futures contract on the long-term government bond, there are also very similar futures contracts on intermediate-term government bonds. The Chicago Board of Trade's contracts on 2-, 5-, and 10-year Treasury notes are very actively traded and are almost identical to its long-term bond contract, except for the exact specification of the underlying instrument. Intermediate and long-term government bonds are important instruments in every country's financial markets. They give the best indication of the long-term default-free interest rate and are often viewed as a **benchmark bond** for various comparisons in financial markets.[21] Accordingly, futures contracts on such bonds play an important role in a country's financial markets and are almost always among the most actively traded contracts in futures markets around the world.

If the underlying instrument is not widely available and not actively traded, the viability of a futures contract on it becomes questionable. The reduction seen in U.S. government debt in the late 1990s has led to a reduction in the supply of intermediate and long-term government bonds, and some concern has arisen over this fact. In the United States, some efforts have been made to promote the long-term debt of Fannie Mae and Freddie Mac as substitute benchmark bonds.[22] It remains to be seen whether such efforts will be necessary and, if so, whether they will succeed.

---

[21] For example, the default risk of a corporate bond is often measured as the difference between the corporate bond yield and the yield on a Treasury bond or note of comparable maturity. Fixed rates on interest rate swaps are usually quoted as a spread over the rate on a Treasury bond or note of comparable maturity.

[22] Fannie Mae is the Federal National Mortgage Association, and Freddie Mac is the Federal Home Loan Mortgage Corporation. These institutions are formerly U.S. government agencies that issued debt to raise funds to buy and sell mortgages and mortgage-backed securities. These institutions are now publicly traded corporations but are considered to have extremely low default risk because of their critical importance in U.S. mortgage markets. It is believed that an implicit Federal government guarantee is associated with their debt. Nonetheless, it seems unlikely that the debt of these institutions could take over that of the U.S. government as a benchmark. The Chicago Board of Trade has offered futures contracts on the bonds of these organizations, but the contracts have not traded actively.

6.3 Stock Index Futures Contracts

One of the most successful types of futures contracts of all time is the class of futures on stock indices. Probably the most successful has been the Chicago Mercantile Exchange's contract on the Standard and Poor's 500 Stock Index. Called the S&P 500 Stock Index futures, this contract premiered in 1982 and has benefited from the widespread acceptance of the S&P 500 Index as a stock market benchmark. The contract is quoted in terms of a price on the same order of magnitude as the S&P 500 itself. For example, if the S&P 500 Index is at 1183, a two-month futures contract might be quoted at a price of, say, 1187.

The contract implicitly contains a multiplier, which is (appropriately) multiplied by the quoted futures price to produce the actual futures price. The multiplier for the S&P 500 futures is $250. Thus, when you hear of a futures price of 1187, the actual price is 1187($250) = $296,750.

S&P 500 futures expirations are March, June, September, and December and go out about two years, although trading is active only in the nearest two to three expirations. With occasional exceptions, the contracts expire on the Thursday preceding the third Friday of the month. Given the impracticality of delivering a portfolio of the 500 stocks in the index combined according to their relative weights in the index, the contract is structured to provide for cash settlement at expiration.

The S&P 500 is not the only active stock index futures contract. In fact, the Chicago Mercantile Exchange has a smaller version of the S&P 500 contract, called the Mini S&P 500, which has a multiplier of $50 and trades only electronically. Other widely traded contracts in the United States are on the Dow Jones Industrials, the S&P Midcap 400, and the Nasdaq 100. Virtually every developed country has a stock index futures contract based on the leading equities of that country. Well-known stock index futures contracts around the world include the United Kingdom's FTSE 100 (pronounced "Footsie 100"), Japan's Nikkei 225, France's CAC 40, and Germany's DAX 30.

6.4 Currency Futures Contracts

In Reading 71 we described forward contracts on foreign currencies. There are also futures contracts on foreign currencies. Although the forward market for foreign currencies is much more widely used, the futures market is still quite active. In fact, currency futures were the first futures contracts not based on physical commodities. Thus, they are sometimes referred to as the first financial futures contracts, and their initial success paved the way for the later introduction of interest rate and stock index futures.

Compared with forward contracts on currencies, currency futures contracts are much smaller in size. In the United States, these contracts trade at the Chicago Mercantile Exchange with a small amount of trading at the New York Board of Trade. In addition there is some trading on exchanges outside the United States. The characteristics we describe below refer to the Chicago Mercantile Exchange's contract.

In the United States, the primary currencies on which trading occurs are the euro, Canadian dollar, Swiss franc, Japanese yen, British pound, Mexican peso, and Australian dollar. Each contract has a designated size and a quotation unit. For example, the euro contract covers €125,000 and is quoted in dollars per euro. A futures price such as $0.8555 is stated in dollars and converts to a contract price of

$$125,000($0.8555) = $106,937.50$$

The Japanese yen futures price is structured somewhat differently. Because of the large number of yen per dollar, the contract covers ¥12,500,000 and is quoted without two zeroes that ordinarily precede the price. For example, a price might be stated as 0.8205, but this actually represents a price of 0.008205, which converts to a contract price of

$$12,500,000(0.008205) = \$102,562.50$$

Alternatively, a quoted price of 0.8205 can be viewed as $1/0.008205 = $ ¥121.88 per dollar.

Currency futures contracts expire in the months of March, June, September, and December. The specific expiration is the second business day before the third Wednesday of the month. Currency futures contracts call for actual delivery, through book entry, of the underlying currency.

We have briefly examined the different types of futures contracts of interest to us. Of course there are a variety of similar instruments trading on futures exchanges around the world. The purpose of this book, however, is not to provide institutional details, which can be obtained at the Web sites of the world's futures exchanges, but rather to enhance your understanding of the important principles necessary to function in the world of derivatives.

SUMMARY

▶ Futures contracts are standardized instruments that trade on a futures exchange, have a secondary market, and are guaranteed against default by means of a daily settling of gains and losses. Forward contracts are customized instruments that are not guaranteed against default and are created anywhere off of an exchange.

▶ Modern futures markets primarily originated in Chicago out of a need for grain farmers and buyers to be able to transact for delivery at future dates for grain that would, in the interim, be placed in storage.

▶ Futures transactions are standardized and conducted in a public market, are homogeneous, have a secondary market giving them an element of liquidity, and have a clearinghouse, which collects margins and settles gains and losses daily to provide a guarantee against default. Futures markets are also regulated at the federal government level.

▶ Margin in the securities markets is the deposit of money, the margin, and a loan for the remainder of the funds required to purchase a stock or bond. Margin in the futures markets is much smaller and does not involve a loan. Futures margin is more like a performance bond or down payment.

▶ Futures trading occurs on a futures exchange, which involves trading either in a physical location called a pit or via a computer terminal off of the floor of the futures exchange as part of an electronic trading system. In either case, a party to a futures contract goes long, committing to buy the underlying asset at an agreed-upon price, or short, committing to sell the underlying asset at an agreed-upon price.

▶ A futures trader who has established a position can re-enter the market and close out the position by doing the opposite transaction (sell if the original position was long or buy if the original position was short). The party has offset the position, no longer has a contract outstanding, and has no further obligation.

▶ Initial margin is the amount of money in a margin account on the day of a transaction or when a margin call is made. Maintenance margin is the amount of money in a margin account on any day other than when the initial margin applies. Minimum requirements exist for the initial and maintenance margins, with the initial margin requirement normally being less than 10 percent of the futures price and the maintenance margin requirement being smaller than the initial margin requirement. Variation margin is the amount of money that must be deposited into the account to bring the balance up to the required level. The settlement price is an average of the last few trades of the day and is used to determine the gains and losses marked to the parties' accounts.

▶ The futures clearinghouse engages in a practice called marking to market, also known as the daily settlement, in which gains and losses on a futures position are credited and charged to the trader's margin account on a daily basis. Thus, profits are available for withdrawal and losses must be paid quickly before they build up and pose a risk that the party will be unable to cover large losses.

▶ The margin balance at the end of the day is determined by taking the previous balance and accounting for any gains or losses from the day's activity, based on the settlement price, as well as any money added or withdrawn.

► Price limits are restrictions on the price of a futures trade and are based on a range relative to the previous day's settlement price. No trade can take place outside of the price limits. A limit move is when the price at which two parties would like to trade is at or beyond the price limit. Limit up is when the market price would be at or above the upper limit. Limit down is when the market price would be at or below the lower limit. Locked limit occurs when a trade cannot take place because the price would be above the limit up or below the limit down prices.

► A futures contract can be terminated by entering into an offsetting position very shortly before the end of the expiration day. If the position is still open when the contract expires, the trader must take delivery (if long) or make delivery (if short), unless the contract requires that an equivalent cash settlement be used in lieu of delivery. In addition, two participants can agree to alternative delivery terms, an arrangement called exchange for physicals.

► Delivery options are features associated with a futures contract that permit the short some flexibility in what to deliver, where to deliver it, and when in the expiration month to make delivery.

► Scalpers are futures traders who take positions for very short periods of time and attempt to profit by buying at the bid price and selling at the ask price. Day traders close out all positions by the end of the day. Position traders leave their positions open overnight and potentially longer.

► Treasury bill futures are contracts in which the underlying is $1,000,000 of a U.S. Treasury bill. Eurodollar futures are contracts in which the underlying is $1,000,000 of a Eurodollar time deposit. Treasury bond futures are contracts in which the underlying is $100,000 of a U.S. Treasury bond with a minimum 15-year maturity. Stock index futures are contracts in which the underlying is a well-known stock index, such as the S&P 500 or FTSE 100. Currency futures are contracts in which the underlying is a foreign currency.

PRACTICE PROBLEMS FOR READING 72

1. A. In February, Dave Parsons purchased a June futures contract on the Nasdaq 100 Index. He decides to close out his position in April. Describe how he would do so.

  B. Peggy Smith is a futures trader. In early August, she took a short position in an S&P 500 Index futures contract expiring in September. After a week, she decides to close out her position. Describe how she would do so.

2. A gold futures contract requires the long trader to buy 100 troy ounces of gold. The initial margin requirement is $2,000, and the maintenance margin requirement is $1,500.

  A. Matthew Evans goes long one June gold futures contract at the futures price of $320 per troy ounce. When could Evans receive a maintenance margin call?

  B. Chris Tosca sells one August gold futures contract at a futures price of $323 per ounce. When could Tosca receive a maintenance margin call?

3. A copper futures contract requires the long trader to buy 25,000 lbs of copper. A trader buys one November copper futures contract at a price of $0.75/lb. Theoretically, what is the maximum loss this trader could have? Another trader sells one November copper futures contract. Theoretically, what is the maximum loss this trader with a short position could have?

4. Consider a hypothetical futures contract in which the current price is $212. The initial margin requirement is $10, and the maintenance margin requirement is $8. You go long 20 contracts and meet all margin calls but do not withdraw any excess margin.

  A. When could there be a margin call?

  B. Complete the table below and explain any funds deposited. Assume that the contract is purchased at the settlement price of that day so there is no mark-to-market profit or loss on the day of purchase.

Day	Beginning Balance	Funds Deposited	Futures Price	Price Change	Gain/Loss	Ending Balance
0			212			
1			211			
2			214			
3			209			
4			210			
5			204			
6			202			

  C. How much are your total gains or losses by the end of day 6?

5. Sarah Moore has taken a short position in one Chicago Board of Trade Treasury bond futures contract with a face value of $100,000 at the price of 96 6/32. The initial margin requirement is $2,700, and the maintenance margin requirement is $2,000. Moore would meet all margin calls but would not withdraw any excess margin.

   A. Complete the table below and provide an explanation of any funds deposited. Assume that the contract is purchased at the settlement price of that day, so there is no mark-to-market profit or loss on the day of purchase.

Day	Beginning Balance	Funds Deposited	Futures Price	Price Change	Gain/Loss	Ending Balance
0			96-06			
1			96-31			
2			97-22			
3			97-18			
4			97-24			
5			98-04			
6			97-31			

   B. How much are Moore's total gains or losses by the end of day 6?

6. A. The IMM index price in yesterday's newspaper for a September Eurodollar futures contract is 95.23. What is the actual price of this contract?

   B. The IMM index price in today's newspaper for the contract mentioned above is 95.25. How much is the change in the actual futures price of the contract since the previous day?

7. Are these two statements about a futures clearinghouse, respectively, correct?

   Statement 1:   "A clearinghouse in futures contracts allows for the offsetting of contracts prior to delivery."

   Statement 2:   "A clearinghouse in futures contracts collects initial margin (performance bonds) from both the long and short sides in the contract."

	Statement 1	Statement 2
A.	No	No
B.	No	Yes
C.	Yes	No
D.	Yes	Yes

8. A trader enters into a short position of 20 futures contracts at an initial futures price of $85.00. Initial margin, per contract, is $7.50. Maintenance margin, per contract, is $7.00. Each contract is for one unit of the underlying asset. Over the next three days, the contract settles at $86.00, $84.25, and $85.50. Assuming the trader does not withdraw any funds from his/her margin account during the period, but does post variation margin sufficient to meet any maintenance margin calls, the balance in the margin account will be

A. $150.00 at initiation and $140.00 at settlement on Day 3.
B. $150.00 at initiation and $150.00 at settlement on Day 3.
C. $150.00 at initiation and $165.00 at settlement on Day 3.
D. $140.00 at initiation and $150.00 at settlement on Day 3.

9. Are the following two statements correct regarding futures contracts that are designed to be settled by delivery?

Statement 1:   "The long initiates the delivery process."
Statement 2:   "For many such contracts, delivery can take place any business day during the delivery month."

	Statement 1	Statement 2
A.	No	No
B.	No	Yes
C.	Yes	No
D.	Yes	Yes

4⅝ 4

5½ – ⅝

5½ 5½ –

20⅝ 21³⁄₁₆ – ⅛

17⅜ **18⅛** + ⅞

6½ **6½** – ½

7¼ 6½ 31/32 – ⅛

15/16 9/16

9/16 9/16

7¹⁵⁄₁₆ 7¹³⁄₁₆ 7¹⁵⁄₁₆

2⅝ 2¹¹⁄₃₂ **2½** +

2¾ 2¼ 2¼

616 12¼₆ 11⅜ 11¾ +

87 33¾ 33 33¼ –

602 25⅝ 24⁹⁄₁₆ 25⅛ +

833 12 11⅝ 11⅞ +

16 10½ 10½ 10⅛ –

78 15⅞ 15¹³⁄₁₆ 15⅞ –

4508 9¹⁄₁₆ 8¼ 8⅛ +

430 11¼ 10⅛ 10

OPTION MARKETS AND CONTRACTS
by Don M. Chance

LEARNING OUTCOMES

The candidate should be able to:

a. define European option, American option, and moneyness, and differentiate between exchange-traded options and over-the-counter options;

b. identify the types of options in terms of the underlying instruments;

c. compare and contrast interest rate options to forward rate agreements (FRAs);

d. define interest rate caps, floors, and collars;

e. compute and interpret option payoffs, and explain how interest rate option payoffs differ from the payoffs of other types of options;

f. define intrinsic value and time value, and explain their relationship;

g. determine the minimum and maximum values of European options and American options;

h. calculate and interpret the lowest prices of European and American calls and puts based on the rules for minimum values and lower bounds;

i. explain how option prices are affected by the exercise price and the time to expiration;

j. explain put-call parity for European options, and relate put-call parity to arbitrage and the construction of synthetic options;

k. contrast American options with European options in terms of the lower bounds on option prices and the possibility of early exercise;

l. explain how cash flows on the underlying asset affect put-call parity and the lower bounds of option prices;

m. indicate the directional effect of an interest rate change or volatility change on an option's price.

Analysis of Derivatives for the CFA® Program, by Don M. Chance. Copyright © 2003 by AIMR. Reprinted with permission.

the long defaulting—the credit risk in an option is unilateral. Only the buyer faces credit risk because only the seller can default. As we discuss later, in exchange-listed options, the clearinghouse guarantees payment to the buyer.

2.2 Some Examples of Options

Consider some call and put options on Sun Microsystems (SUNW). The date is 13 June and Sun is selling for $16.25. Exhibit 1 gives information on the closing prices of four options, ones expiring in July and October and ones with exercise prices of 15.00 and 17.50. The July options expire on 20 July and the October options expire on 18 October. In the parlance of the profession, these are referred to as the July 15 calls, July 17.50 calls, October 15 calls, and October 17.50 calls, with similar terminology for the puts. These particular options are American style.

EXHIBIT 1	Closing Prices of Selected Options on SUNW, 13 June			
Exercise Price	**July Calls**	**October Calls**	**July Puts**	**October Puts**
15.00	2.35	3.30	0.90	1.85
17.50	1.00	2.15	2.15	3.20

Note: Stock price is $16.25; July options expire on 20 July; October options expire on 18 October.

Consider the July 15 call. This option permits the holder to buy SUNW at a price of $15 a share any time through 20 July. To obtain this option, one would pay a price of $2.35. Therefore, a writer received $2.35 on 13 June and must be ready to sell SUNW to the buyer for $15 during the period through 20 July. Currently, SUNW trades above $15 a share, but as we shall see in more detail later, the option holder has no reason to exercise the option right now.[3] To justify purchase of the call, the buyer must be anticipating that SUNW will increase in price before the option expires. The seller of the call must be anticipating that SUNW will not rise sufficiently in price before the option expires.

Note that the option buyer could purchase a call expiring in July but permitting the purchase of SUNW at a price of $17.50. This price is more than the $15.00 exercise price, but as a result, the option, which sells for $1.00, is considerably cheaper. The cheaper price comes from the fact that the July 17.50 call is less likely to be exercised, because the stock has a higher hurdle to clear. A buyer is not willing to pay as much and a seller is more willing to take less for an option that is less likely to be exercised.

Alternatively, the option buyer could choose to purchase an October call instead of a July call. For any exercise price, however, the October calls would be more expensive than the July calls because they allow a longer period for the stock to make the move that the buyer wants. October options are more likely to

---

[3] The buyer paid $2.35 for the option. If he exercised it right now, he would pay $15.00 for the stock, which is worth only $16.25. Thus, he would have effectively paid $17.35 (the cost of the option of $2.35 plus the exercise price of $15) for a stock worth $16.25. Even if he had purchased the option previously at a much lower price, the current option price of $2.35 is the opportunity cost of exercising the option—that is, he can always sell the option for $2.35. Therefore, if he exercised the option, he would be throwing away the $2.35 he could receive if he sold it.

be exercised than July options; therefore, a buyer would be willing to pay more and the seller would demand more for the October calls.

Suppose the buyer expects the stock price to go down. In that case, he might buy a put. Consider the October 17.50 put, which would cost the buyer $3.20. This option would allow the holder to sell SUNW at a price of $17.50 any time up through 18 October.[4] He has no reason to exercise the option right now, because it would mean he would be buying the option for $3.20 and selling a stock worth $16.25 for $17.50. In effect, the option holder would part with $19.45 (the cost of the option of $3.20 plus the value of the stock of $16.25) and obtain only $17.50.[5] The buyer of a put obviously must be anticipating that the stock will fall before the expiration day.

If he wanted a cheaper option than the October 17.50 put, he could buy the October 15 put, which would cost only $1.85 but would allow him to sell the stock for only $15.00 a share. The October 15 put is less likely to be exercised than the October 17.50, because the stock price must fall below a lower hurdle. Thus, the buyer is not willing to pay as much and the seller is willing to take less.

For either exercise price, purchase of a July put instead of an October put would be much cheaper but would allow less time for the stock to make the downward move necessary for the transaction to be worthwhile. The July put is cheaper than the October put; the buyer is not willing to pay as much and the seller is willing to take less because the option is less likely to be exercised.

In observing these option prices, we have obtained our first taste of some principles involved in pricing options.

> *Call options have a lower premium the higher the exercise price.*
> *Put options have a lower premium the lower the exercise price.*
> *Both call and put options are cheaper the shorter the time to expiration.*[6]

These results should be intuitive, but later in this reading we show unequivocally why they must be true.

2.3 The Concept of Moneyness of an Option

An important concept in the study of options is the notion of an option's **moneyness**, which refers to the relationship between the price of the underlying and the exercise price.

We use the terms **in-the-money**, **out-of-the-money**, and **at-the-money**. We explain the concept in Exhibit 2 with examples from the SUNW options. Note that **in-the-money options** are those in which exercising the option would produce a cash inflow that exceeds the cash outflow. Thus, calls are in-the-money when the value of the underlying exceeds the exercise price. Puts are in-the-money when the exercise price exceeds the value of the underlying. In our example, there are no at-the-money SUNW options, which would require that the stock value equal the exercise price; however, an **.** can effectively be viewed as an **out-of-the-money option**, because its exercise would not bring in more money than is paid out.

---

[4] Even if the option holder did not own the stock, he could use the option to sell the stock short.

[5] Again, even if the option were purchased in the past at a much lower price, the $3.20 current value of the option is an opportunity cost. Exercise of the option is equivalent to throwing away the opportunity cost.

[6] There is an exception to the rule that put options are cheaper the shorter the time to expiration. This statement is always true for American options but not always for European options. We explore this point later.

EXHIBIT 2	Moneyness of an Option		
In-the-Money		**Out-of-the-Money**	
Option	Justification	Option	Justification
July 15 call	16.25 > 15.00	July 17.50 call	16.25 < 17.50
October 15 call	16.25 > 15.00	October 17.50 call	16.25 < 17.50
July 17.50 put	17.50 > 16.25	July 15 put	15.00 < 16.25
October 17.50 put	17.50 > 16.25	October 15 put	15.00 < 16.25

Notes: Sun Microsystems options on 13 June; stock price is 16.25. See Exhibit 1 for more details. There are no options with an exercise price of 16.25, so no options are at-the-money.

As explained above, *one would not necessarily exercise an in-the-money option, but one would never exercise an out-of-the-money option.*

We now move on to explore how options markets are organized.

3   THE STRUCTURE OF GLOBAL OPTIONS MARKETS

Although no one knows exactly how options first got started, contracts similar to options have been around for thousands of years. In fact, insurance is a form of an option. The insurance buyer pays the insurance writer a premium and receives a type of guarantee that covers losses. This transaction is similar to a put option, which provides coverage of a portion of losses on the underlying and is often used by holders of the underlying. The first true options markets were over-the-counter options markets in the United States in the 19th century.

3.1 Over-the-Counter Options Markets

In the United States, customized over-the-counter options markets were in existence in the early part of the 20th century and lasted well into the 1970s. An organization called the Put and Call Brokers and Dealers Association consisted of a group of firms that served as brokers and dealers. As brokers, they attempted to match buyers of options with sellers, thereby earning a commission. As dealers, they offered to take either side of the option transaction, usually laying off (hedging) the risk in another transaction. Most of these transactions were retail, meaning that the general public were their customers.

As we discuss in Section 3.2, the creation of the Chicago Board Options Exchange was a revolutionary event, but it effectively killed the Put and Call Brokers and Dealers Association. Subsequently, the increasing use of swaps facilitated a rebirth of the customized over-the-counter options market. **Currency options**, a natural extension to currency swaps, were in much demand. Later, interest rate options emerged as a natural outgrowth of interest rate swaps. Soon bond, equity, and index options were trading in a vibrant over-the-counter market. In contrast to the previous over-the-counter options market, however, the current one emerged as a largely wholesale market. Transactions are usually made with institutions and corporations and are rarely conducted directly with individuals. This market is much like the forward market described in Reading 71, with dealers offering to take either the long or short position in options and hedging that risk with transactions in other options or derivatives. There are no guarantees that the seller will perform; hence, the buyer faces credit risk. As such, option buyers must scrutinize sellers' credit risk and may require some risk reduction measures, such as collateral.

As previously noted, customized options have *all* of their terms—such as price, exercise price, time to expiration, identification of the underlying, settlement or delivery terms, size of the contract, and so on—determined by the two parties.

Like forward markets, over-the-counter options markets are essentially unregulated. In most countries, participating firms, such as banks and securities firms, are regulated by the appropriate authorities, but there is usually no particular regulatory body for the over-the-counter options markets. In some countries, however, there are regulatory bodies for these markets.

Exhibit 3 provides information on the leading dealers in over-the-counter currency and interest rate options as determined by *Risk* magazine in its annual surveys of banks and investment banks and also end users.

EXHIBIT 3	*Risk* Magazine Surveys of Banks, Investment Banks, and Corporate End Users to Determine the Top Three Dealers in Over-the-Counter Currency and Interest Rate Options

	Respondents	
Currencies	**Banks and Investment Banks**	**Corporate End Users**
Currency Options		
$/€	UBS Warburg	Citigroup
	Citigroup/Deutsche Bank	Royal Bank of Scotland
		Deutsche Bank
$/¥	UBS Warburg	Citigroup
	Credit Suisse First Boston	JP Morgan Chase
	JP Morgan Chase/Royal Bank of Scotland	UBS Warburg
$/£	Royal Bank of Scotland	Royal Bank of Scotland
	UBS Warburg	Citigroup
	Citigroup	Hong Kong Shanghai Banking Corp.
$/SF	UBS Warburg	UBS Warburg
	Credit Suisse First Boston	Credit Suisse First Boston
	Citigroup	Citigroup
Interest Rate Options		
$	JP Morgan Chase	JP Morgan Chase
	Deutsche Bank	Citigroup

(Exhibit continued on next page …)

EXHIBIT 3	(continued)

	Respondents	
Currencies	Banks and Investment Banks	Corporate End Users
Interest Rate Options		
	Bank of America	Deutsche Bank/ Lehman Brothers
€	JP Morgan Chase	JP Morgan Chase
	Credit Suisse First Boston/ Morgan Stanley	Citigroup UBS Warburg
¥	JP Morgan Chase/ Deutsche Bank	UBS Warburg
	Bank of America	Barclays Capital
		Citigroup
£	Barclays Capital	Royal Bank of Scotland
	Societe Generale Groupe	Citigroup
	Bank of America/Royal Bank of Scotland	Hong Kong Shanghai Banking Corp.
SF	UBS Warburg	UBS Warburg
	JP Morgan Chase	JP Morgan
	Credit Suisse First Boston	Goldman Sachs

Notes: $ = U.S. dollar, € = euro, ¥ = Japanese yen, £ = U.K. pound sterling, SF = Swiss franc.

Source: Risk, September 2002, pp. 30–67 for Banks and Investment Banking dealer respondents, and June 2002, pp. 24–34 for Corporate End User respondents.

Results for Corporate End Users for Interest Rate Options are from *Risk,* July 2001, pp. 38–46. *Risk* omitted this category from its 2002 survey.

3.2 Exchange Listed Options Markets

As briefly noted above, the Chicago Board Options Exchange was formed in 1973. Created as an extension of the Chicago Board of Trade, it became the first organization to offer a market for standardized options. In the United States, standardized options also trade on the Amex–Nasdaq, the Philadelphia Stock Exchange, and the Pacific Stock Exchange.[7] On a worldwide basis, standardized options are widely traded on such exchanges as LIFFE (the London International Financial Futures and Options Exchange) in London, Eurex in Frankfurt, and most other foreign exchanges. Exhibit 4 shows the 20 largest options exchanges in the world. Note, perhaps surprisingly, that the leading options exchange is in Korea.

---

[7] You may wonder why the New York Stock Exchange is not mentioned. Standardized options did trade on the NYSE at one time but were not successful, and the right to trade these options was sold to another exchange.

EXHIBIT 4	World's 20 Largest Options Exchanges
Exchange and Location	**Volume in 2001**
Korea Stock Exchange (Korea)	854,791,792
Chicago Board Options Exchange (United States)	306,667,851
MONEP (France)	285,667,686
Eurex (Germany and Switzerland)	239,016,516
American Stock Exchange (United States)	205,103,884
Pacific Stock Exchange (United States)	102,701,752
Philadelphia Stock Exchange (United States)	101,373,433
Chicago Mercantile Exchange (United States)	95,740,352
Amsterdam Exchange (Netherlands)	66,400,654
LIFFE (United Kingdom)	54,225,652
Chicago Board of Trade (United States)	50,345,068
OM Stockholm (Sweden)	39,327,619
South African Futures Exchange (South Africa)	24,307,477
MEFF Renta Variable (Spain)	23,628,446
New York Mercantile Exchange (United States)	17,985,109
Korea Futures Exchange (Korea)	11,468,991
Italian Derivatives Exchange (Italy)	11,045,804
Osaka Securities Exchange (Japan)	6,991,908
Bourse de Montreal (Canada)	5,372,930
Hong Kong Futures Exchange (China)	4,718,880

Note: Volume given is in number of contracts.
Source: Data supplied by *Futures Industry* magazine.

As described in Reading 72 on futures, the exchange fixes all terms of standardized instruments except the price. Thus, the exchange establishes the expiration dates and exercise prices as well as the minimum price quotation unit. The exchange also determines whether the option is European or American, whether the exercise is cash settlement or delivery of the underlying, and the contract size. In the United States, an option contract on an individual stock covers 100 shares of stock. Terminology such as "one option" is often used to refer to one option contract, which is really a set of options on 100 shares of stock. Index option sizes are stated in terms of a multiplier, indicating that the contract covers a hypothetical number of shares, as though the index were an individual stock. Similar specifications apply for options on other types of underlyings.

The exchange generally allows trading in exercise prices that surround the current stock price. As the stock price moves, options with exercise prices around the new stock price are usually added. The majority of trading occurs in options that are close to being at-the-money. Options that are far in-the-money or far out-of-the-money, called **deep-in-the-money** and **deep-out-of-the-money** options, are usually not very actively traded and are often not even listed for trading.

Most exchange-listed options have fairly short-term expirations, usually the current month, the next month, and perhaps one or two other months. Most of the trading takes place for the two shortest expirations. Some exchanges list options with expirations of several years, which have come to be called LEAPS, for **long-term equity anticipatory securities**. These options are fairly actively purchased, but most investors tend to buy and hold them and do not trade them as often as they do the shorter-term options.

The exchanges also determine on which companies they will list options for trading. Although specific requirements do exist, generally the exchange will list the options of any company for which it feels the options would be actively traded. The company has no voice in the matter. Options of a company can be listed on more than one exchange in a given country.

In Reading 72, we described the manner in which futures are traded. The procedure is very similar for exchange-listed options. Some exchanges have pit trading, whereby parties meet in the pit and arrange a transaction. Some exchanges use electronic trading, in which transactions are conducted through computers. In either case, the transactions are guaranteed by the clearinghouse. In the United States, the clearinghouse is an independent company called the Options Clearing Corporation or OCC. The OCC guarantees to the buyer that the clearinghouse will step in and fulfill the obligation if the seller reneges at exercise.

When the buyer purchases the option, the premium, which one might think would go to the seller, instead goes to the clearinghouse, which maintains it in a margin account. In addition, the seller must post some margin money, which is based on a formula that reflects whether the seller has a position that hedges the risk and whether the option is in- or out-of-the-money. If the price moves against the seller, the clearinghouse will force the seller to put up additional margin money. Although defaults are rare, the clearinghouse has always been successful in paying when the seller defaults. Thus, exchange-listed options are effectively free of credit risk.

Because of the standardization of option terms and participants' general acceptance of these terms, exchange-listed options can be bought and sold at any time prior to expiration. Thus, a party who buys or sells an option can re-enter the market before the option expires and offset the position with a sale or a purchase of the identical option. From the clearinghouse's perspective, the positions cancel.

As in futures markets, traders on the options exchange are generally either market makers or brokers. Some slight technical distinctions exist between different types of market makers in different options markets, but the differences are minor and do not concern us here. Like futures traders, option market makers attempt to profit by scalping (holding positions very short term) to earn the bid–ask spread and sometimes holding positions longer, perhaps closing them overnight or leaving them open for days or more.

When an option expires, the holder decides whether or not to exercise it. When the option is expiring, there are no further gains to waiting, so in-the-money options are always exercised, assuming they are in-the-money by more than the transaction cost of buying or selling the underlying or arranging a cash settlement when exercising. Using our example of the SUNW options, if at expiration the stock is at 16, the calls with an exercise price of 15 would be exercised. Most exchange-listed stock options call for actual delivery of the stock. Thus, the seller delivers the stock and the buyer pays the seller, through the clearinghouse, $15 per share. If the exchange specifies that the contract is cash settled, the seller simply pays the buyer $1. For puts requiring delivery, the buyer tenders the stock and receives the exercise price from the seller. If the option is out-of-the-money, it simply expires unexercised and is removed from the books. If the put is cash settled, the writer pays the buyer the equivalent cash amount.

Some nonstandardized exchange-traded options exist in the United States. In an attempt to compete with the over-the-counter options market, some exchanges permit some options to be individually customized and traded on the exchange, thereby benefiting from the advantages of the clearinghouse's credit guarantee. These options are primarily available only in large sizes and tend to be traded only by large institutional investors.

Like futures markets, exchange-listed options markets are typically regulated at the federal level. In the United States, federal regulation of options markets is the responsibility of the Securities and Exchange Commission; similar regulatory structures exist in other countries.

TYPES OF OPTIONS 4

Almost anything with a random outcome can have an option on it. Note that by using the word *anything*, we are implying that the underlying does not even need to be an asset. In this section, we shall discover the different types of options, identified by the nature of the underlying. Our focus in this book is on financial options, but it is important, nonetheless, to gain some awareness of other types of options.

4.1 Financial Options

Financial options are options in which the underlying is a financial asset, interest rate, or a currency.

4.1.1 Stock Options

Options on individual stocks, also called **equity options**, are among the most popular. Exchange-listed options are available on most widely traded stocks and an option on any stock can potentially be created on the over-the-counter market. We have already given examples of stock options in an earlier section; we now move on to index options.

4.1.2 Index Options

Stock market indices are well known, not only in the investment community but also among many individuals who are not even directly investing in the market. Because a stock index is just an artificial portfolio of stocks, it is reasonable to expect that one could create an option on a stock index. Indeed, we have already covered forward and futures contracts on stock indices; options are no more difficult in structure.

For example, consider options on the S&P 500 Index, which trade on the Chicago Board Options Exchange and have a designated index contract multiplier of 100. On 13 June of a given year, the S&P 500 closed at 1241.60. A call option with an exercise price of $1,250 expiring on 20 July was selling for $28. The option is European style and settles in cash. The underlying, the S&P 500, is treated as though it were a share of stock worth $1,241.60, which can be bought, using the call option, for $1,250 on 20 July. At expiration, if the option is in-the-money, the buyer exercises it and the writer pays the buyer the $250 contract multiplier times the difference between the index value at expiration and $1,250.

In the United States, there are also options on the Dow Jones Industrial Average, the Nasdaq, and various other indices. There are nearly always options on the best-known stock indices in most countries.

Just as there are options on stocks, there are also options on bonds.

buy into it or what someone would receive to sell out of it. A forward or futures contract has zero value at the start of the contract, but the value turns positive or negative as prices or rates change. A contract that has positive value to one party and negative value to the counterparty can turn around and have negative value to the former and positive value to the latter as prices or rates change. The forward or futures price is the price that the parties agree will be paid on the future date to buy and sell the underlying.

With options, these concepts are different. An option has a positive value at the start. The buyer must pay money and the seller receives money to initiate the contract. Prior to expiration, the option always has positive value to the buyer and negative value to the seller. In a forward or futures contract, the two parties agree on the fixed price the buyer will pay the seller. This fixed price is set such that the buyer and seller do not exchange any money. The corresponding fixed price at which a call holder can buy the underlying or a put holder can sell the underlying is the exercise price. It, too, is negotiated between buyer and seller but still results in the buyer paying the seller money up front in the form of an option premium or price.[12]

Thus, what we called the forward or futures price corresponds more to the exercise price of an option. The option price *is* the option value: With a few exceptions that will be clearly noted, in this reading we do not distinguish between the option price and value.

In this section of the reading, we examine the principles of option pricing. These principles are characteristics of option prices that are governed by the rationality of investors.

Before we begin, it is important to remind the reader that we assume all participants in the market behave in a rational manner such that they do not throw away money and that they take advantage of arbitrage opportunities. As such, we assume that markets are sufficiently competitive that no arbitrage opportunities exist.

Let us start by developing the notation, which is very similar to what we have used previously. Note that time 0 is today and time T is the expiration.

S_0, S_T = price of the underlying asset at time 0 (today) and time T (expiration)

X = exercise price

r = risk-free rate

T = time to expiration, equal to number of days to expiration divided by 365

c_0, c_T = price of European call today and at expiration

C_0, C_T = price of American call today and at expiration

p_0, p_T = price of European put today and at expiration

P_0, P_T = price of American put today and at expiration

On occasion, we will introduce some variations of the above as well as some new notation. For example, we start off with no cash flows on the underlying, but we shall discuss the effects of cash flows on the underlying in Section 5.7.

5.1 Payoff Values

The easiest time to determine an option's value is at expiration. At that point, there is no future. Only the present matters. An option's value at expiration is

---

[12] For a call, there is no finite exercise price that drives the option price to zero. For a put, the unrealistic example of a zero exercise price would make the put price be zero.

called its **payoff**. We introduced this material briefly in our basic descriptions of types of options; now we cover it in more depth.

At expiration, a call option is worth either zero or the difference between the underlying price and the exercise price, whichever is greater:

$$c_T = Max(0, S_T - X)$$
$$C_T = Max(0, S_T - X)$$

(73-3)

Note that at expiration, a European option and an American option have the same payoff because they are equivalent instruments at that point.

The expression $Max(0, S_T - X)$ means to take the greater of zero or $S_T - X$. Suppose the underlying price exceeds the exercise price, $S_T > X$. In this case, the option is expiring in-the-money and the option is worth $S_T - X$. Suppose that at the instant of expiration, it is possible to buy the option for less than $S_T - X$. Then one could buy the option, immediately exercise it, and immediately sell the underlying. Doing so would cost c_T (or C_T) for the option and X to buy the underlying but would bring in S_T for the sale of the underlying. If c_T (or C_T) $< S_T - X$, this transaction would net an immediate risk-free profit. The collective actions of all investors doing this would force the option price up to $S_T - X$. The price could not go higher than $S_T - X$, because all that the option holder would end up with an instant later when the option expires is $S_T - X$. If $S_T < X$, meaning that the call is expiring out-of-the-money, the formula says the option should be worth zero. It cannot sell for less than zero because that would mean that the option seller would have to pay the option buyer. A buyer would not pay more than zero, because the option will expire an instant later with no value.

At expiration, a put option is worth either zero or the difference between the exercise price and the underlying price, whichever is greater:

$$p_T = Max(0, X - S_T)$$
$$P_T = Max(0, X - S_T)$$

(73-4)

Suppose $S_T < X$, meaning that the put is expiring in-the-money. At the instant of expiration, suppose the put is selling for less than $X - S_T$. Then an investor buys the put for p_T (or P_T) and the underlying for S_T and exercises the put, receiving X. If p_T (or P_T) $< X - S_T$, this transaction will net an immediate risk-free profit. The combined actions of participants doing this will force the put price up to $X - S_T$. It cannot go any higher, because the put buyer will end up an instant later with only $X - S_T$ and would not pay more than this. If $S_T > X$, meaning that the put is expiring out-of the-money, it is worth zero. It cannot be worth less than zero because the option seller would have to pay the option buyer. It cannot be worth more than zero because the buyer would not pay for a position that, an instant later, will be worth nothing.

These important results are summarized along with an example in Exhibit 5. The payoff diagrams for the short positions are also shown and are obtained as the negative of the long positions. For the special case of $S_T = X$, meaning that both call and put are expiring at-the-money, we can effectively treat the option as out-of-the-money because it is worth zero at expiration.

The value $Max(0, S_T - X)$ for calls or $Max(0, X - S_T)$ for puts is also called the option's **intrinsic value** or **exercise value**. We shall use the former terminology. Intrinsic value is what the option is worth to exercise it based on current conditions. In this section, we have talked only about the option at expiration. Prior to expiration, an option will normally sell for more than its intrinsic value.[13] The difference between the market price of the option and its intrinsic value is called its **time value**

---

[13] We shall later see an exception to this statement for European puts, but for now take it as the truth.

or **speculative value**. We shall use the former terminology. The time value reflects the potential for the option's intrinsic value at expiration to be greater than its current intrinsic value. At expiration, of course, the time value is zero.

There is no question that everyone agrees on the option's intrinsic value; after all, it is based on the current stock price and exercise price. It is the time value that we have more difficulty estimating. So remembering that Option price = Intrinsic value + Time value, let us move forward and attempt to determine the value of an option today, prior to expiration.

EXHIBIT 5	**Option Values at Expiration (Payoffs)**		
		Example (X = 50)	
Option	**Value**	$S_T = 52$	$S_T = 48$
European call	$c_T = Max(0, S_T - X)$	$c_T = Max(0, 52 - 50) = 2$	$c_T = Max(0, 48 - 50) = 0$
American call	$C_T = Max(0, S_T - X)$	$C_T = Max(0, 52 - 50) = 2$	$C_T = Max(0, 48 - 50) = 0$
European put	$p_T = Max(0, X - S_T)$	$p_T = Max(0, 50 - 52) = 0$	$p_T = Max(0, 50 - 48) = 2$
American put	$P_T = Max(0, X - S_T)$	$P_T = Max(0, 50 - 52) = 0$	$P_T = Max(0, 50 - 48) = 2$

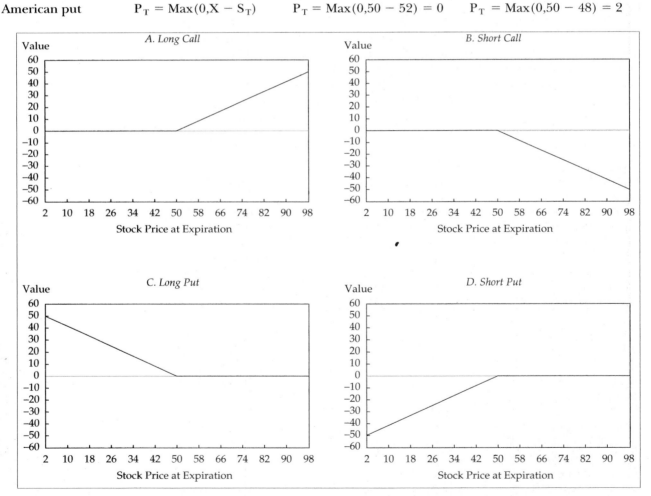

Notes: **Results for the European and American calls correspond to Graph A. Results for Graph B are the negative of Graph A. Results for the European and American puts correspond to Graph C, and results for Graph D are the negative of Graph C.**

EXAMPLE 1

For Parts A through E, determine the payoffs of calls and puts under the conditions given.

A. The underlying is a stock index and is at 5,601.19 when the options expire. The multiplier is 500. The exercise price is

   i. 5,500
   ii. 6,000

B. The underlying is a bond and is at $1.035 per $1 par when the options expire. The contract is on $100,000 face value of bonds. The exercise price is
   i. $1.00
   ii. $1.05

C. The underlying is a 90-day interest rate and is at 9 percent when the options expire. The notional principal is $50 million. The exercise rate is
   i. 8 percent
   ii. 10.5 percent

D. The underlying is the Swiss franc and is at $0.775 when the options expire. The options are on SF500,000. The exercise price is
   i. $0.75
   ii. $0.81

E. The underlying is a futures contract and is at 110.5 when the options expire. The options are on a futures contract covering $1 million of the underlying. These prices are percentages of par. The exercise price is
   i. 110
   ii. 115

For Parts F and G, determine the payoffs of the strategies indicated and describe the payoff graph.

F. The underlying is a stock priced at $40. A call option with an exercise price of $40 is selling for $7. You buy the stock and sell the call. At expiration, the stock price is
   i. $52
   ii. $38

G. The underlying is a stock priced at $60. A put option with an exercise price of $60 is priced at $5. You buy the stock and buy the put. At expiration, the stock price is
   i. $68
   ii. $50

Solutions:

A. **i.** Calls: $\text{Max}(0, 5601.19 - 5500) \times 500 = 50,595$
   Puts: $\text{Max}(0, 5500 - 5601.19) \times 500 = 0$
   ii. Calls: $\text{Max}(0, 5601.19 - 6000) \times 500 = 0$
   Puts: $\text{Max}(0, 6000 - 5601.19) \times 500 = 199,405$

B. **i.** Calls: $\text{Max}(0, 1.035 - 1.00) \times \$100,000 = \$3,500$
   Puts: $\text{Max}(0, 1.00 - 1.035) \times \$100,000 = \$0$

ii. Calls: $\text{Max}(0, 1.035 - 1.05) \times \$100{,}000 = \$0$
Puts: $\text{Max}(0, 1.05 - 1.035) \times \$100{,}000 = \$1{,}500$

C. **i.** Calls: $\text{Max}(0, 0.09 - 0.08) \times (90/360) \times \$50{,}000{,}000 = \$125{,}000$
Puts: $\text{Max}(0, 0.08 - 0.09) \times (90/360) \times \$50{,}000{,}000 = \$0$

ii. Calls: $\text{Max}(0, 0.09 - 0.105) \times (90/360) \times \$50{,}000{,}000 = \$0$
Puts: $\text{Max}(0, 0.105 - 0.09) \times (90/360) \times \$50{,}000{,}000 = \$187{,}500$

D. **i.** Calls: $\text{Max}(0, 0.775 - 0.75) \times \text{SF}500{,}000 = \$12{,}500$
Puts: $\text{Max}(0, 0.75 - 0.775) \times \text{SF}500{,}000 = \$0$

ii. Calls: $\text{Max}(0, 0.775 - 0.81) \times \text{SF}500{,}000 = \$0$
Puts: $\text{Max}(0, 0.81 - 0.775) \times \text{SF}500{,}000 = \$17{,}500$

E. **i.** Calls: $\text{Max}(0, 110.5 - 110) \times (1/100) \times \$1{,}000{,}000 = \$5{,}000$
Puts: $\text{Max}(0, 110 - 110.5) \times (1/100) \times \$1{,}000{,}000 = \$0$

ii. Calls: $\text{Max}(0, 110.5 - 115) \times (1/100) \times \$1{,}000{,}000 = \$0$
Puts: $\text{Max}(0, 115 - 110.5) \times (1/100) \times \$1{,}000{,}000 = \$45{,}000$

F. **i.** $52 - \text{Max}(0, 52 - 40) = 40$
ii. $38 - \text{Max}(0, 38 - 40) = 38$

For any value of the stock price at expiration of 40 or above, the payoff is constant at 40. For stock price values below 40 at expiration, the payoff declines with the stock price. The graph would look similar to the short put in Panel D of Exhibit 5. This strategy is known as a covered call and is discussed in Reading 75.

G. **i.** $68 + \text{Max}(0, 60 - 68) = 68$
ii. $50 + \text{Max}(0, 60 - 50) = 60$

For any value of the stock price at expiration of 60 or below, the payoff is constant at 60. For stock price values above 60 at expiration, the payoff increases with the stock price at expiration. The graph will look similar to the long call in Panel A of Exhibit 5. This strategy is known as a protective put and is covered later in this reading and in Reading 75.

5.2 Boundary Conditions

We start by examining some simple results that establish minimum and maximum values for options prior to expiration.

5.2.1 Minimum and Maximum Values

The first and perhaps most obvious result is one we have already alluded to: *The minimum value of any option is zero.* We state this formally as

$$c_0 \geq 0,\ C_0 \geq 0$$
$$p_0 \geq 0,\ P_0 \geq 0$$

(73-5)

No option can sell for less than zero, for in that case the writer would have to pay the buyer.

Now consider the maximum value of an option. It differs somewhat depending on whether the option is a call or a put and whether it is European or American. *The maximum value of a call is the current value of the underlying:*

$$c_0 \leq S_0,\ C_0 \leq S_0$$

(73-6)

A call is a means of buying the underlying. It would not make sense to pay more for the right to buy the underlying than the value of the underlying itself.

For a put, it makes a difference whether the put is European or American. One way to see the maximum value for puts is to consider the best possible outcome for the put holder. The best outcome is that the underlying goes to a value of zero. Then the put holder could sell a worthless asset for X. For an American put, the holder could sell it immediately and capture a value of X. For a European put, the holder would have to wait until expiration; consequently, we must discount X from the expiration day to the present. Thus, *the maximum value of a European put is the present value of the exercise price. The maximum value of an American put is the exercise price,*

$$p_0 \leq X/(1+r)^T, P_0 \leq X \qquad \textbf{(73-7)}$$

where r is the risk-free interest rate and T is the time to expiration. These results for the maximums and minimums for calls and puts are summarized in Exhibit 6, which also includes a numerical example.

EXHIBIT 6	Minimum and Maximum Values of Options		
Option	**Minimum Value**	**Maximum Value**	**Example ($S_0 = 52$, X = 50, r = 5%, T = 1/2 year)**
European call	$c_0 \geq 0$	$c_0 \leq S_0$	$0 \leq c_0 \leq 52$
American call	$C_0 \geq 0$	$C_0 \leq S_0$	$0 \leq C_0 \leq 52$
European put	$p_0 \geq 0$	$p_0 \leq X/(1+r)^T$	$0 \leq p_0 \leq 48.80 \; [48.80 = 50/(1.05)^{0.5}]$
American put	$P_0 \geq 0$	$P_0 \leq X$	$0 \leq P_0 \leq 50$

5.2.2 Lower Bounds

The results we established in Section 5.2.1 do not put much in the way of restrictions on the option price. They tell us that the price is somewhere between zero and the maximum, which is either the underlying price, the exercise price, or the present value of the exercise price—a fairly wide range of possibilities. Fortunately, we can tighten the range up a little on the low side: We can establish a **lower bound** on the option price.

For American options, which are exercisable immediately, we can state that the lower bound of an American option price is its current intrinsic value:[14]

$$C_0 \geq Max(0, S_0 - X)$$
$$P_0 \geq Max(0, X - S_0) \qquad \textbf{(73-8)}$$

The reason these results hold today is the same reason we have already shown for why they must hold at expiration. If the option is in-the-money and is selling for less than its intrinsic value, it can be bought and exercised to net an immediate

---

[14] Normally we have italicized sentences containing important results. This one, however, is a little different: We are stating it temporarily. We shall soon show that we can override one of these results with a lower bound that is higher and, therefore, is a better lower bound.

risk-free profit.[15] The collective actions of market participants doing this will force the American option price up to at least the intrinsic value.

Unfortunately, we cannot make such a statement about European options—but we can show that the lower bound is either zero or the current underlying price minus the present value of the exercise price, whichever is greater. They cannot be exercised early; thus, there is no way for market participants to exercise an option selling for too little with respect to its intrinsic value. Fortunately, however, there is a way to establish a lower bound for European options. We can combine options with risk-free bonds and the underlying in such a way that a lower bound for the option price emerges.

First, we need the ability to buy and sell a risk-free bond with a face value equal to the exercise price and current value equal to the present value of the exercise price. This procedure is simple but perhaps not obvious. If the exercise price is X (say, 100), we buy a bond with a face value of X (100) maturing on the option expiration day. The current value of that bond is the present value of X, which is $X/(1 + r)^T$. So we buy the bond today for $X/(1 + r)^T$ and hold it until it matures on the option expiration day, at which time it will pay off X. We assume that we can buy or sell (issue) this type of bond. Note that this transaction involves borrowing or lending an amount of money equal to the present value of the exercise price with repayment of the full exercise price.

Exhibit 7 illustrates the construction of a special combination of instruments. We buy the European call and the risk-free bond and sell short the underlying asset. Recall that short selling involves borrowing the asset and selling it. At expiration, we shall buy back the asset. In order to illustrate the logic behind the lower bound for a European call in the simplest way, we assume that we can sell short without any restrictions.

EXHIBIT 7	A Lower Bound Combination for European Calls		
		Value at Expiration	
Transaction	Current Value	ST ≤ X	ST > X
Buy call	c_0	0	$S_T - X$
Sell short underlying	$-S_0$	$-S_T$	$-S_T$
Buy bond	$X/(1 + r)^T$	X	X
Total	$c_0 - S_0 + X/(1 + r)^T$	$X - S_T \geq 0$	0

In Exhibit 7 the two right-hand columns contain the value of each instrument when the option expires. The rightmost column is the case of the call expiring in-the-money, in which case it is worth $S_T - X$. In the other column, the out-of-the-money case, the call is worth zero. The underlying is worth $-S_T$ (the negative of its current value) in either case, reflecting the fact that we buy it back

---

[15] Consider, for example, an in-the-money call selling for less than $S_0 - X$. One can buy the call for C_0, exercise it, paying X, and sell the underlying netting a gain of $S_0 - X - C_0$. This value is positive and represents an immediate risk-free gain. If the option is an in-the-money put selling for less than $X - S_0$, one can buy the put for P_0, buy the underlying for S_0, and exercise the put to receive X, thereby netting an immediate risk-free gain of $X - S_0 - P_0$.

to cover the short position. The bond is worth X in both cases. The sum of all the positions is positive when the option expires out-of-the-money and zero when the option expires in-the-money. Therefore, in no case does this combination of instruments have a negative value. That means that we never have to pay out any money at expiration. We are guaranteed at least no loss at expiration and possibly something positive.

If there is a possibility of a positive outcome from the combination and if we know we shall never have to pay anything out from holding a combination of instruments, the cost of that combination must be positive—it must cost us something to enter into the position. We cannot take in money to enter into the position. In that case, we would be receiving money up front and never having to pay anything out. The cost of entering the position is shown in the second column, labeled the "Current Value." Because that value must be positive, we therefore require that $c_0 - S_0 + X/(1 + r)^T \geq 0$. Rearranging this equation, we obtain $c_0 \geq S_0 - X/(1 + r)^T$. Now we have a statement about the minimum value of the option, which can serve as a lower bound. This result is solid, because if the call is selling for less than $S_0 - X/(1 + r)^T$, an investor can buy the call, sell short the underlying, and buy the bond. Doing so would bring in money up front and, as we see in Exhibit 7, an investor would not have to pay out any money at expiration and might even get a little more money. Because other investors would do the same, the call price would be forced up until it is at least $S_0 - X/(1 + r)^T$.

But we can improve on this result. Suppose $S_0 - X/(1 + r)^T$ is negative. Then we are stating that the call price is greater than a negative number. But we already know that the call price cannot be negative. So we can now say that

$$c_0 \geq \text{Max}[0, S_0 - X/(1 + r)^T]$$

In other words, *the lower bound on a European call price is either zero or the underlying price minus the present value of the exercise price, whichever is greater.* Notice how this lower bound differs from the minimum value for the American call, $\text{Max}(0, S_0 - X)$. For the European call, we must wait to pay the exercise price and obtain the underlying. Therefore, the expression contains the current underlying value—the present value of its future value—as well as the present value of the exercise price. For the American call, we do not have to wait until expiration; therefore, the expression reflects the potential to immediately receive the underlying price minus the exercise price. We shall have more to say, however, about the relationship between these two values.

To illustrate the lower bound, let X = 50, r = 0.05, and T = 0.5. If the current underlying price is 45, then the lower bound for the European call is

$$\text{Max}[0, 45 - 50/(1.05)^{0.5}] = \text{Max}(0, 45 - 48.80) = \text{Max}(0, -3.80) = 0$$

All this calculation tells us is that the call must be worth no less than zero, which we already knew. If the current underlying price is 54, however, the lower bound for the European call is

$$\text{Max}(0, 54 - 48.80) = \text{Max}(0, 5.20) = 5.20$$

which tells us that the call must be worth no less than 5.20. With European puts, we can also see that the lower bound differs from the lower bound on American puts in this same use of the present value of the exercise price.

Exhibit 8 constructs a similar type of portfolio for European puts. Here, however, we buy the put and the underlying and borrow by issuing the zero-coupon bond. The payoff of each instrument is indicated in the two rightmost

EXHIBIT 8	A Lower Bound Combination for European Puts		
		Value at Expiration	
Transaction	Current Value	$S_T < X$	$S_T \geq X$
Buy put	p_0	$X - S_T$	0
Buy underlying	S_0	S_T	S_T
Issue bond	$-X/(1 + r)^T$	$-X$	$-X$
Total	$p_0 + S_0 - X/(1 + r)^T$	0	$S_T - X \geq 0$

columns. Note that the total payoff is never less than zero. Consequently, the initial value of the combination must not be less than zero. Therefore, $p_0 + S_0 - X/(1 + r)^T \geq 0$. Isolating the put price gives us $p_0 \geq X/(1 + r)^T - S_0$. But suppose that $X/(1 + r)^T - S_0$ is negative. Then, the put price must be greater than a negative number. We know that the put price must be no less than zero. So we can now formally say that

$$p_0 \geq \text{Max}[0, X/(1 + r)^T - S_0]$$

In other words, *the lower bound of a European put is the greater of either zero or the present value of the exercise price minus the underlying price.* For the American put, recall that the expression was $\text{Max}(0, X - S_0)$. So for the European put, we adjust this value to the present value of the exercise price. The present value of the asset price is already adjusted to S_0.

Using the same example we did for calls, let $X = 50$, $r = 0.05$, and $T = 0.5$. If the current underlying price is 45, then the lower bound for the European put is

$$\text{Max}(0, 50/(1.05)^{0.5} - 45) = \text{Max}(0, 48.80 - 45) = \text{Max}(0, 3.80) = 3.80$$

If the current underlying price is 54, however, the lower bound is

$$\text{Max}(0, 48.80 - 54) = \text{Max}(0, -5.20) = 0$$

At this point let us reconsider what we have found. The lower bound for a European call is $\text{Max}[0, S_0 - X/(1 + r)^T]$. We also observed that an American call must be worth at least $\text{Max}(0, S_0 - X)$. But except at expiration, the European lower bound is greater than the minimum value of the American call.[16] We could not, however, expect an American call to be worth less than a European call. Thus the lower bound of the European call holds for American calls as well. Hence, we can conclude that

$$\begin{aligned} c_0 &\geq \text{Max}[0, S_0 - X/(1 + r)^T] \\ C_0 &\geq \text{Max}[0, S_0 - X/(1 + r)^T] \end{aligned} \qquad \text{(73-9)}$$

For European puts, the lower bound is $\text{Max}[0, X/(1 + r)^T - S_0]$. For American puts, the minimum price is $\text{Max}(0, X - S_0)$. The European lower bound is lower than the minimum price of the American put, so the American put lower bound is not changed to the European lower bound, the way we did for calls. Hence,

---

[16] We discuss this point more formally and in the context of whether it is ever worthwhile to exercise an American call early in Section 5.6.

$$p_0 \geq \text{Max}[0, X/(1 + r)^T - S_0]$$
$$P_0 \geq \text{Max}(0, X - S_0)$$

(73-10)

These results tell us the lowest possible price for European and American options.

Recall that we previously referred to an option price as having an intrinsic value and a time value. For American options, the intrinsic value is the value if exercised, $\text{Max}(0, S_0 - X)$ for calls and $\text{Max}(0, X - S_0)$ for puts. The remainder of the option price is the time value. For European options, the notion of a time value is somewhat murky, because it first requires recognition of an intrinsic value. Because a European option cannot be exercised until expiration, in a sense, all of the value of a European option is time value. The notion of an intrinsic value and its complement, a time value, is therefore inappropriate for European options, though the concepts are commonly applied to European options. Fortunately, understanding European options does not require that we separate intrinsic value from time value. We shall include them together as they make up the option price.

EXAMPLE 2

Consider call and put options expiring in 42 days, in which the underlying is at 72 and the risk-free rate is 4.5 percent. The underlying makes no cash payments during the life of the options.

A. Find the lower bounds for European calls and puts with exercise prices of 70 and 75.

B. Find the lower bounds for American calls and puts with exercise prices of 70 and 75.

Solutions:

A. 70 call: $\text{Max}[0, 72 - 70/(1.045)^{0.1151}] = \text{Max}(0, 2.35) = 2.35$
75 call: $\text{Max}[0, 72 - 75/(1.045)^{0.1151}] = \text{Max}(0, -2.62) = 0$
70 put: $\text{Max}[0, 70/(1.045)^{0.1151} - 72] = \text{Max}(0, -2.35) = 0$
75 put: $\text{Max}[0, 75/(1.045)^{0.1151} - 72] = \text{Max}(0, 2.62) = 2.62$

B. 70 call: $\text{Max}[0, 72 - 70/(1.045)^{0.1151}] = \text{Max}(0, 2.35) = 2.35$
75 call: $\text{Max}[0, 72 - 75/(1.045)^{0.1151}] = \text{Max}(0, -2.62) = 0$
70 put: $\text{Max}(0, 70 - 72) = 0$
75 put: $\text{Max}(0, 75 - 72) = 3$

5.3 The Effect of a Difference in Exercise Price

Now consider two options on the same underlying with the same expiration day but different exercise prices. Generally, the higher the exercise price, the lower the value of a call and the higher the price of a put. To see this, let the two exercise prices be X_1 and X_2, with X_1 being the smaller. Let $c_0(X_1)$ be the price of a European call with exercise price X_1 and $c_0(X_2)$ be the price of a European call with exercise price X_2. We refer to these as the X_1 call and the X_2 call. In Exhibit 9, we construct a combination in which we buy the X_1 call and sell the X_2 call.

EXHIBIT 9	Portfolio Combination for European Calls Illustrating the Effect of Differences in Exercise Prices				

Transaction	Current Value	Value at Expiration		
		$S_T \leq X_1$	$X_1 < S_T < X_2$	$S_T \geq X_2$
Buy call ($X = X_1$)	$c_0(X_1)$	0	$S_T - X_1$	$S_T - X_1$
Sell call ($X = X_2$)	$-c_0(X_2)$	0	0	$-(S_T - X_2)$
Total	$c_0(X_1) - c_0(X_2)$	0	$S_T - X_1 > 0$	$X_2 - X_1 > 0$

Note first that the three outcomes are all non-negative. This fact establishes that the current value of the combination, $c_0(X_1) - c_0(X_2)$ has to be non-negative. We have to pay out at least as much for the X_1 call as we take in for the X_2 call; otherwise, we would get money up front, have the possibility of a positive value at expiration, and never have to pay any money out. Thus, because $c_0(X_1) - c_0(X_2) \geq 0$, we restate this result as

$$c_0(X_1) \geq c_0(X_2)$$

This expression is equivalent to the statement that *a call option with a higher exercise price cannot have a higher value than one with a lower exercise price*. The option with the higher exercise price has a higher hurdle to get over; therefore, the buyer is not willing to pay as much for it. Even though we demonstrated this result with European calls, it is also true for American calls. Thus,[17]

$$C_0(X_1) \geq C_0(X_2)$$

In Exhibit 10 we construct a similar portfolio for puts, except that we buy the X_2 put (the one with the higher exercise price) and sell the X_1 put (the one with the lower exercise price).

EXHIBIT 10	Portfolio Combination for European Puts Illustrating the Effect of Differences in Exercise Prices				

Transaction	Current Value	Value at Expiration		
		$ST \leq X1$	$X1 < ST < X2$	$ST \geq X2$
Buy put ($X = X_2$)	$p_0(X_2)$	$X_2 - S_T$	$X_2 - S_T$	0
Sell put ($X = X_1$)	$-p_0(X_1)$	$-(X_1 - S_T)$	0	0
Total	$p_0(X_2) - p_0(X_1)$	$X_2 - X_1 > 0$	$X_2 - S_T > 0$	0

---

[17] It is possible to use the results from this table to establish a limit on the difference between the prices of these two options, but we shall not do so here.

Observe that the value of this combination is never negative at expiration; therefore, it must be non-negative today. Hence, $p_0(X_2) - p_0(X_1) \geq 0$. We restate this result as

$$p_0(X_2) \geq p_0(X_1)$$

Thus, *the value of a European put with a higher exercise price must be at least as great as the value of a European put with a lower exercise price.* These results also hold for American puts. Therefore,

$$P_0(X_2) \geq P_0(X_1)$$

Even though it is technically possible for calls and puts with different exercise prices to have the same price, *generally we can say that the higher the exercise price, the lower the price of a call and the higher the price of a put.* For example, refer back to Exhibit 1 and observe how the most expensive calls and least expensive puts have the lower exercise prices.

5.4 The Effect of a Difference in Time to Expiration

Option prices are also affected by the time to expiration of the option. Intuitively, one might expect that the longer the time to expiration, the more valuable the option. A longer-term option has more time for the underlying to make a favorable move. In addition, if the option is in-the-money by the end of a given period of time, it has a better chance of moving even further in-the-money over a longer period of time. If the additional time gives it a better chance of moving out-of-the-money or further out-of-the-money, the limitation of losses to the amount of the option premium means that the disadvantage of the longer time is no greater. In most cases, a longer time to expiration is beneficial for an option. We will see that longer-term American and European calls and longer-term American puts are worth no less than their shorter-term counterparts.

First let us consider each of the four types of options: European calls, American calls, European puts, and American puts. We shall introduce options otherwise identical except that one has a longer time to expiration than the other. The one expiring earlier has an expiration of T_1 and the one expiring later has an expiration of T_2. The prices of the options are $c_0(T_1)$ and $c_0(T_2)$ for the European calls, $C_0(T_1)$ and $C_0(T_2)$ for the American calls, $p_0(T_1)$ and $p_0(T_2)$ for the European puts, and $P_0(T_1)$ and $P_0(T_2)$ for the American puts.

When the shorter-term call expires, the European call is worth $Max(0, S_{T_1} - X)$, but we have already shown that the longer-term European call is worth *at least* $Max(0, S_{T_1} - X/(1 + r)^{(T_2-T_1)})$, which is at least as great as this amount.[18] Thus, the longer-term European call is worth at least the value of the shorter-term European call. These results are not altered if the call is American. When the shorter-term American call expires, it is worth $Max(0, S_{T_1} - X)$. The longer-term American call must be worth at least the value of the European call, so it is worth *at least* $Max[0, S - X/(1 + r)^{T_2-T_1}]$. Thus, the longer-term call, European or American, is worth no less than the shorter-term call when the shorter-term call expires. Because this statement is always true, the longer-term call, European or American, is worth no less than the shorter-term call at any time prior to expiration. Thus,

$$c_0(T_2) \geq c_0(T_1)$$
$$C_0(T_2) \geq C_0(T_1)$$

(73-11)

---

[18] Technically, we showed this calculation using a time to expiration of T, but here the time to expiration is $T_2 - T_1$.

Notice that these statements do not mean that the longer-term call is always worth more; it means that the longer-term call can be worth no less. With the exception of the rare case in which both calls are so far out-of-the-money or in-the-money that the additional time is of no value, the longer-term call will be worth more.

For European puts, we have a slight problem. For calls, the longer term gives additional time for a favorable move in the underlying to occur. For puts, this is also true, but there is one disadvantage to waiting the additional time. When a put is exercised, the holder receives money. The lost interest on the money is a disadvantage of the additional time. For calls, there is no lost interest. In fact, a call holder earns additional interest on the money by paying out the exercise price later. Therefore, it is not always true that additional time is beneficial to the holder of a European put. It is true, however, that the additional time is beneficial to the holder of an American put. An American put can always be exercised; there is no penalty for waiting. Thus, we have

$$p_0(T_2) \text{ can be either greater or less than } p_0(T_1)$$
$$P_0(T_2) \geq P_0(T_1)$$

(73-12)

So for European puts, either the longer-term or the shorter-term option can be worth more. The longer-term European put will tend to be worth more when volatility is greater and interest rates are lower.

Referring back to Exhibit 1, observe that the longer-term put and call options are more expensive than the shorter-term ones. As noted, we might observe an exception to this rule for European puts, but these are all American options.

5.5 Put–Call Parity

So far we have been working with puts and calls separately. To see how their prices must be consistent with each other and to explore common option strategies, let us combine puts and calls with each other or with a risk-free bond. We shall put together some combinations that produce equivalent results.

5.5.1 Fiduciary Calls and Protective Puts

First we consider an option strategy referred to as a **fiduciary call**. It consists of a European call and a risk-free bond, just like the ones we have been using, that matures on the option expiration day and has a face value equal to the exercise price of the call. The upper part of the table in Exhibit 11 shows the payoffs at expiration of the fiduciary call. We see that if the price of the underlying is below X at expiration, the call expires worthless and the bond is worth X. If the price of the underlying is above X at expiration, the call expires and is worth S_T (the underlying price) $- X$. So at expiration, the fiduciary call will end up worth X or S_T, whichever is greater.

EXHIBIT 11	Portfolio Combinations for Equivalent Packages of Puts and Calls

		Value at Expiration	
Transaction	Current Value	$S_T \leq X$	$S_T > X$
Fiduciary Call			
Buy call	c_0	0	$S_T - X$

(Exhibit continued on next page ...)

EXHIBIT 11	(continued)

Transaction	Current Value	Value at Expiration $S_T \leq X$	Value at Expiration $S_T > X$
Buy bond	$X/(1 + r)^T$	X	X
Total	$c_0 + X/(1 + r)^T$	X	S_T
Protective Put			
Buy put	p_0	$X - S_T$	0
Buy underlying asset	S_0	S_T	S_T
Total	$p_0 + S_0$	X	S_T

Value of Fiduciary Call and
Protective Put at Expiration

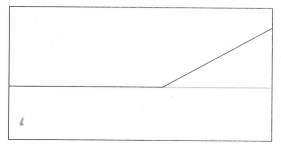

Stock Price at Expiration

This type of combination is called a fiduciary call because it allows protection against downside losses and is thus faithful to the notion of preserving capital.

Now we construct a strategy known as a **protective put**, which consists of a European put and the underlying asset. If the price of the underlying is below X at expiration, the put expires and is worth $X - S_T$ and the underlying is worth S_T. If the price of the underlying is above X at expiration, the put expires with no value and the underlying is worth S_T. So at expiration, the protective put is worth X or S_T, whichever is greater. The lower part of the table in Exhibit 11 shows the payoffs at expiration of the protective put.

Thus, the fiduciary call and protective put end up with the same value. They are, therefore, identical combinations. To avoid arbitrage, their values today must be the same. The value of the fiduciary call is the cost of the call, c_0, and the cost of the bond, $X/(1 + r)^T$. The value of the protective put is the cost of the put, p_0, and the cost of the underlying, S_0. Thus,

$$c_0 + X/(1 + r)^T = p_0 + S_0 \qquad \textbf{(73-13)}$$

This equation is called **put–call parity** and is one of the most important results in options. It does not say that puts and calls are equivalent, but it does show an equivalence (parity) of a call/bond portfolio and a put/underlying portfolio.

Put–call parity can be written in a number of other ways. By rearranging the four terms to isolate one term, we can obtain some interesting and important results. For example,

$$c_0 = p_0 + S_0 - X/(1 + r)^T$$

means that a call is equivalent to a long position in the put, a long position in the asset, and a short position in the risk-free bond. The short bond position simply means to borrow by issuing the bond, rather than lend by buying the bond as we did in the fiduciary call portfolio. We can tell from the sign whether we should go long or short. Positive signs mean to go long; negative signs mean to go short.

5.5.2 Synthetics

Because the right-hand side of the above equation is equivalent to a call, we often refer to it as a **synthetic call**. To see that the synthetic call is equivalent to the actual call, look at Exhibit 12:

EXHIBIT 12	Call and Synthetic Call		
		Value at Expiration	
Transaction	**Current Value**	$S_T \leq X$	$S_T > X$
Call			
Buy call	c_0	0	$S_T - X$
Synthetic Call			
Buy put	p_0	$X - S_T$	0
Buy underlying asset	S_0	S_T	S_T
Issue bond	$-X/(1 + r)^T$	$-X$	$-X$
Total	$p_0 + S_0 - X/(1 + r)^T$	0	$S_T - X$

The call produces the value of the underlying minus the exercise price or zero, whichever is greater. The synthetic call does the same thing, but in a different way. When the call expires in-the-money, the synthetic call produces the underlying value minus the payoff on the bond, which is X. When the call expires out-of-the-money, the put covers the loss on the underlying and the exercise price on the put matches the amount of money needed to pay off the bond.

Similarly, we can isolate the put as follows:

$$p_0 = c_0 - S_0 + X/(1 + r)^T$$

which says that a put is equivalent to a long call, a short position in the underlying, and a long position in the bond. Because the left-hand side is a put, it follows that the right-hand side is a **synthetic put**. The equivalence of the put and synthetic put is shown in Exhibit 13.

As you can well imagine, there are numerous other combinations that can be constructed. Exhibit 14 shows a number of the more important combinations. There are two primary reasons that it is important to understand synthetic positions in option pricing. Synthetic positions enable us to price options, because they produce the same results as options and have known prices. Synthetic positions also tell how to exploit mispricing of options relative to their underlying assets. Note that we

EXHIBIT 13	Put and Synthetic Put

		Value at Expiration	
Transaction	Current Value	$S_T \le X$	$S_T > X$
Put			
Buy put	p_0	$X - S_T$	0
Synthetic Put			
Buy call	c_0	0	$S_T - X$
Short underlying asset	$-S_0$	$-S_T$	$-S_T$
Buy bond	$X/(1+r)^T$	X	X
Total	$c_0 - S_0 + X/(1+r)^T$	$X - S_T$	0

EXHIBIT 14	Alternative Equivalent Combinations of Calls, Puts, the Underlying, and Risk-Free Bonds

Strategy	Consisting of	Worth	Equates to	Strategy	Consisting of	Worth
Fiduciary call	Long call + Long bond	$c_0 + X/(1+r)^T$	=	Protective put	Long put + Long underlying	$p_0 + S_0$
Long call	Long call	c_0	=	Synthetic call	Long put + Long underlying + Short bond	$p_0 + S_0 - X/(1+r)^T$
Long put	Long put	p_0	=	Synthetic put	Long call + Short underlying + Long bond	$c_0 - S_0 + X/(1+r)^T$
Long underlying	Long underlying	S_0	=	Synthetic underlying	Long call + Long bond + Short put	$c_0 + X/(1+r)^T - p_0$
Long bond	Long bond	$X/(1+r)^T$	=	Synthetic bond	Long put + Long underlying + Short call	$p_0 + S_0 - c_0$

can not only synthesize a call or a put, but we can also synthesize the underlying or the bond. As complex as it might seem to do this, it is really quite easy. First, we learn that *a fiduciary call is a call plus a risk-free bond maturing on the option expiration day with a face value equal to the exercise price of the option.* Then we learn that *a protective put is the underlying plus a put.* Then we learn the basic put–call parity equation: *A fiduciary call is equivalent to a protective put:*

$$c_0 + X/(1+r)^T = p_0 + S_0$$

Learn the put–call parity equation this way, because it is the easiest form to remember and has no minus signs.

Next, we decide which instrument we want to synthesize. We use simple algebra to isolate that instrument, with a plus sign, on one side of the equation, moving all other instruments to the other side. We then see what instruments are on the other side, taking plus signs as long positions and minus signs as short positions. Finally, to check our results, we should construct a table like Exhibits 11 or 12, with the expiration payoffs of the instrument we wish to synthesize compared with the expiration payoffs of the equivalent combination of instruments. We then check to determine that the expiration payoffs are the same.

5.5.3 An Arbitrage Opportunity

In this section we examine the arbitrage strategies that will push prices to put–call parity. Suppose that in the market, prices do not conform to put–call parity. This is a situation in which price does not equal value. Recalling our basic equation, $c_0 + X/(1 + r)^T = p_0 + S_0$, we should insert values into the equation and see if the equality holds. If it does not, then obviously one side is greater than the other. We can view one side as overpriced and the other as underpriced, which suggests an arbitrage opportunity. To exploit this mispricing, we buy the underpriced combination and sell the overpriced combination.

Consider the following example involving call options with an exercise price of $100 expiring in half a year ($T = 0.5$). The risk-free rate is 10 percent. The call is priced at $7.50, and the put is priced at $4.25. The underlying price is $99.

The left-hand side of the basic put–call parity equation is $c_0 + X/(1 + r)^T = 7.50 + 100/(1.10)^{0.5} = 7.50 + 95.35 = 102.85$. The right-hand side is $p_0 + S_0 = 4.25 + 99 = 103.25$. So the right-hand side is greater than the left-hand side. This means that the protective put is overpriced. Equivalently, we could view this as the fiduciary call being underpriced. Either way will lead us to the correct strategy to exploit the mispricing.

We sell the overpriced combination, the protective put. This means that we sell the put and sell short the underlying. Doing so will generate a cash inflow of $103.25. We buy the fiduciary call, paying out $102.85. This series of transactions nets a cash inflow of $103.25 − $102.85 = $0.40. Now, let us see what happens at expiration.

> *The options expire with the underlying above 100:*
>   The bond matures, paying $100.
>   Use the $100 to exercise the call, receiving the underlying.
>   Deliver the underlying to cover the short sale.
>   The put expires with no value.
>   Net effect: No money in or out.
> *The options expire with the underlying below 100:*
>   The bond matures, paying $100.
>   The put expires in-the-money; use the $100 to buy the underlying.
>   Use the underlying to cover the short sale.
>   The call expires with no value.
>   Net effect: No money in or out.

So we receive $0.40 up front and do not have to pay anything out. The position is perfectly hedged and represents an arbitrage profit. The combined effects of other investors performing this transaction will result in the value of the protective put going down and/or the value of the covered call going up until the two strategies are equivalent in value. Of course, it is possible that transaction costs might consume any profit, so small discrepancies will not be exploited.

It is important to note that regardless of which put–call parity equation we use, we will arrive at the same strategy. For example, in the above problem, the synthetic put (a long call, a short position in the underlying, and a long bond) is worth $\$7.50 - \$99 + \$95.35 = \$3.85$. The actual put is worth $\$4.25$. Thus, we would conclude that we should sell the actual put and buy the synthetic put. To buy the synthetic put, we would buy the call, short the underlying, and buy the bond—precisely the strategy we used to exploit this price discrepancy.

In all of these examples based on put–call parity, we used only European options. Put–call parity using American options is considerably more complicated. The resulting parity equation is a complex combination of inequalities. Thus, we cannot say that a given combination exactly equals another; we can say only that one combination is more valuable than another. Exploitation of any such mispricing is somewhat more complicated, and we shall not explore it here.

EXAMPLE 3

European put and call options with an exercise price of 45 expire in 115 days. The underlying is priced at 48 and makes no cash payments during the life of the options. The risk-free rate is 4.5 percent. The put is selling for 3.75, and the call is selling for 8.00.

A. Identify the mispricing by comparing the price of the actual call with the price of the synthetic call.

B. Based on your answer in Part A, demonstrate how an arbitrage transaction is executed.

Solutions:

A. Using put–call parity, the following formula applies:

$$c_0 = p_0 + S_0 - X/(1 + r)^T$$

The time to expiration is $T = 115/365 = 0.3151$. Substituting values into the right-hand side:

$$c_0 = 3.75 + 48 - 45/(1.045)^{0.3151} = 7.37$$

Hence, the synthetic call is worth 7.37, but the actual call is selling for 8.00 and is, therefore, overpriced.

B. Sell the call for 8.00 and buy the synthetic call for 7.37. To buy the synthetic call, buy the put for 3.75, buy the underlying for 48.00, and issue a zero-coupon bond paying 45.00 at expiration. The bond will bring in $45.00/(1.045)^{0.3151} = 44.38$ today. This transaction will bring in $8.00 - 7.37 = 0.63$.

At expiration, the following payoffs will occur:

	$S_T < 45$	$S_T \geq 45$
Short call	0	$-(S_T - 45)$
Long put	$45 - S_T$	0
Underlying	S_T	S_T
Bond	-45	-45
Total	0	0

Thus there will be no cash in or out at expiration. The transaction will net a risk-free gain of $8.00 - 7.37 = 0.63$ up front.

5.6 American Options, Lower Bounds, and Early Exercise

As we have noted, American options can be exercised early and in this section we specify cases in which early exercise can have value. Because early exercise is never mandatory, the right to exercise early may be worth something but could never hurt the option holder. Consequently, the prices of American options must be no less than the prices of European options:

$$C_0 \geq c_0$$
$$P_0 \geq p_0$$

(73-14)

Recall that we already used this result in establishing the minimum price from the lower bounds and intrinsic value results in Section 5.2.2. Now, however, our concern is understanding the conditions under which early exercise of an American option might occur.

Suppose today, time 0, we are considering exercising early an in-the-money American call. If we exercise, we pay X and receive an asset worth S_0. But we already determined that a European call is worth at least $S_0 - X/(1 + r)^T$—that is, the underlying price minus the present value of the exercise price, which is more than $S_0 - X$. Because we just argued that the American call must be worth no less than the European call, it therefore must also be worth at least $S_0 - X/(1 + r)^T$. This means that the value we could obtain by selling it to someone else is more than the value we could obtain by exercising it. Thus, there is no reason to exercise the call early.

Some people fail to see the logic behind not exercising early. Exercising a call early simply gives the money to the call writer and throws away the right to decide at expiration if you want the underlying. It is like renewing a magazine subscription before the current subscription expires. Not only do you lose the interest on the money, you also lose the right to decide later if you want to renew. Without offering an early exercise incentive, the American call would have a price equal to the European call price. Thus, we must look at another case to see the value of the early exercise option.

If the underlying makes a cash payment, there may be reason to exercise early. If the underlying is a stock and pays a dividend, there may be sufficient reason to exercise just before the stock goes ex-dividend. By exercising, the option holder throws away the time value but captures the dividend. We shall skip the technical details of how this decision is made and conclude by stating that

► *When the underlying makes no cash payments, $C_0 = c_0$.*

► *When the underlying makes cash payments during the life of the option, early exercise can be worthwhile and C_0 can thus be higher than c_0.*

We emphasize the word *can*. It is possible that the dividend is not high enough to justify early exercise.

For puts, there is nearly always a possibility of early exercise. Consider the most obvious case, an investor holding an American put on a bankrupt company. The stock is worth zero. It cannot go any lower. Thus, the put holder would exercise immediately. As long as there is a possibility of bankruptcy, the American put will be worth more than the European put. But in fact, bankruptcy is not required for early exercise. The stock price must be very low, although we cannot say exactly how low without resorting to an analysis using option pricing models. Suffice it to say that *the American put is nearly always worth more than the European put: $P_0 > p_0$.*

5.7 The Effect of Cash Flows on the Underlying Asset

Both the lower bounds on puts and calls and the put–call parity relationship must be modified to account for cash flows on the underlying asset. In Readings 71 and 72, we discussed situations in which the underlying has cash flows. Stocks pay dividends, bonds pay interest, foreign currencies pay interest, and commodities have carrying costs. As we have done in the previous readings, we shall assume that these cash flows are either known or can be expressed as a percentage of the asset price. Moreover, as we did previously, we can remove the present value of those cash flows from the price of the underlying and use this adjusted underlying price in the results we have obtained above.

We can specify these cash flows in the form of the accumulated value at T of all cash flows incurred on the underlying over the life of the derivative contract. When the underlying is a stock, we specify these cash flows more precisely in the form of dividends, using the notation $FV(D,0,T)$ as the future value, or alternatively $PV(D,0,T)$ as the present value, of these dividends. When the underlying is a bond, we use the notation $FV(CI,0,T)$ or $PV(CI,0,T)$, where CI stands for "coupon interest." When the cash flows can be specified in terms of a yield or rate, we use the notation δ where $S_0/(1 + \delta)^T$ is the underlying price reduced by the present value of the cash flows. Using continuous compounding, the rate can be specified as dc so that $S_0 e^{-\delta^c T}$ is the underlying price reduced by the present value of the dividends. For our purposes in this reading on options, let us just write this specification as $PV(CF,0,T)$, which represents the present value of the cash flows on the underlying over the life of the options. Therefore, we can restate the lower bounds for European options as

$$c_0 \geq \text{Max}\{0,[S_0 - PV(CF,0,T)] - X/(1 + r)^T\}$$
$$p_0 \geq \text{Max}\{0,X/(1 + r)^T - [S_0 - PV(CF,0,T)]\}$$

and put–call parity as

$$c_0 + X/(1 + r)^T = p_0 + [S_0 - PV(CF,0,T)]$$

which reflects the fact that, as we said, we simply reduce the underlying price by the present value of its cash flows over the life of the option.

5.8 The Effect of Interest Rates and Volatility

It is important to know that interest rates and volatility exert an influence on option prices. *When interest rates are higher, call option prices are higher and put option prices are lower.* This effect is not obvious and strains the intuition somewhat. When investors buy call options instead of the underlying, they are effectively buying an indirect leveraged position in the underlying. When interest rates are higher, buying the call instead of a direct leveraged position in the underlying is more attractive. Moreover, by using call options, investors save more money by not paying for the underlying until a later date. For put options, however, higher interest rates are disadvantageous. When interest rates are higher, investors lose more interest while waiting to sell the underlying when using puts. Thus, the opportunity cost of waiting is higher when interest rates are higher. Although these points may not seem completely clear, fortunately they are not critical. Except when the underlying is a bond or interest rate, interest rates do not have a very strong effect on option prices.

Volatility, however, has an extremely strong effect on option prices. *Higher volatility increases call and put option prices because it increases possible upside values and increases possible downside values of the underlying.* The upside effect helps calls and does not hurt puts. The downside effect does not hurt calls and helps puts. The reason calls are not hurt on the downside and puts are not hurt on the upside is that when options are out-of-the-money, it does not matter if they end up more out-of-the-money. But when options are in-the-money, it does matter if they end up more in-the-money.

Volatility is a critical variable in pricing options. It is the only variable that affects option prices that is not directly observable either in the option contract or in the market. It must be estimated.

5.9 Option Price Sensitivities

Option price sensitivity measures have Greek names:

- ▶ *Delta* is the sensitivity of the option price to a change in the price of the underlying.
- ▶ *Gamma* is a measure of how well the delta sensitivity measure will approximate the option price's response to a change in the price of the underlying.
- ▶ *Rho* is the sensitivity of the option price to the risk-free rate.
- ▶ *Theta* is the rate at which the **time value decays** as the option approaches expiration.
- ▶ *Vega* is the sensitivity of the option price to volatility.

SUMMARY

► Options are rights to buy or sell an underlying at a fixed price, the exercise price, for a period of time. The right to buy is a call; the right to sell is a put. Options have a definite expiration date. Using the option to buy or sell is the action of exercising it. The buyer or holder of an option pays a price to the seller or writer for the right to buy (a call) or sell (a put) the underlying instrument. The writer of an option has the corresponding potential obligation to sell or buy the underlying.

► European options can be exercised only at expiration; American options can be exercised at any time prior to expiration. Moneyness refers to the characteristic that an option has positive intrinsic value. The payoff is the value of the option at expiration. An option's intrinsic value is the value that can be captured if the option is exercised. Time value is the component of an option's price that reflects the uncertainty of what will happen in the future to the price of the underlying.

► Options can be traded as standardized instruments on an options exchange, where they are protected from default on the part of the writer, or as customized instruments on the over-the-counter market, where they are subject to the possibility of the writer defaulting. Because the buyer pays a price at the start and does not have to do anything else, the buyer cannot default.

► The underlying instruments for options are individual stocks, stock indices, bonds, interest rates, currencies, futures, commodities, and even such random factors as the weather. In addition, a class of options called real options is associated with the flexibility in capital investment projects.

► Like FRAs, which are forward contracts in which the underlying is an interest rate, interest rate options are options in which the underlying is an interest rate. However, FRAs are commitments to make one interest payment and receive another, whereas interest rate options are rights to make one interest payment and receive another.

► Option payoffs, which are the values of options when they expire, are determined by the greater of zero or the difference between underlying price and exercise price, if a call, or the greater of zero or the difference between exercise price and underlying price, if a put. For interest rate options, the exercise price is a specified rate and the underlying price is a variable interest rate.

► Interest rate options exist in the form of caps, which are call options on interest rates, and floors, which are put options on interest rates. Caps consist of a series of call options, called caplets, on an underlying rate, with each option expiring at a different time. Floors consist of a series of put options, called floorlets, on an underlying rate, with each option expiring at a different time.

► The minimum value of European and American calls and puts is zero. The maximum value of European and American calls is the underlying price. The maximum value of a European put is the present value of the exercise price. The maximum value of an American put is the exercise price.

► The lower bound of a European call is established by constructing a portfolio consisting of a long call and risk-free bond and a short position in the underlying asset. This combination produces a non-negative value at expiration, so its current value must be non-negative. For this situation to occur, the call price has to be worth at least the underlying price minus the present value of the exercise price. The lower bound of a European put is established by constructing a portfolio consisting of a long put, a long position in the underlying, and the issuance of a zero-coupon bond. This combination produces a non-negative value at expiration so its current value must be non-negative. For this to occur, the put price has to be at least as much as the present value of the exercise price minus the underlying price. For both calls and puts, if this lower bound is negative, we invoke the rule that an option price can be no lower than zero.

▶ The lowest price of a European call is referred to as the lower bound. The lowest price of an American call is also the lower bound of a European call. The lowest price of a European put is also referred to as the lower bound. The lowest price of an American put, however, is its intrinsic value.

▶ Buying a call with a given exercise price and selling an otherwise identical call with a higher exercise price creates a combination that always pays off with a non-negative value. Therefore, its current value must be non-negative. For this to occur, the call with the lower exercise price must be worth at least as much as the other call. A similar argument holds for puts, except that one would buy the put with the higher exercise price. This line of reasoning shows that the put with the higher exercise price must be worth at least as much as the one with the lower exercise price.

▶ A longer-term European or American call must be worth at least as much as a corresponding shorter-term European or American call. A longer-term American put must be worth at least as much as a shorter-term American put. A longer-term European put, however, can be worth more or less than a shorter-term European put.

▶ A fiduciary call, consisting of a European call and a zero-coupon bond, produces the same payoff as a protective put, consisting of the underlying and a European put. Therefore, their current values must be the same. For this equivalence to occur, the call price plus bond price must equal the underlying price plus put price. This relationship is called put–call parity and can be used to identify combinations of instruments that synthesize another instrument by rearranging the equation to isolate the instrument you are trying to create. Long positions are indicated by positive signs, and short positions are indicated by negative signs. One can create a synthetic call, a synthetic put, a synthetic underlying, and a synthetic bond, as well as synthetic short positions in these instruments for the purpose of exploiting mispricing in these instruments.

▶ Put–call parity violations exist when one side of the equation does not equal the other. An arbitrageur buys the lower-priced side and sells the higher-priced side, thereby earning the difference in price, and the positions offset at expiration. The combined actions of many arbitrageurs performing this set of transactions would increase the demand and price for the underpriced instruments and decrease the demand and price for the overpriced instruments, until the put–call parity relationship is upheld.

▶ American option prices must always be no less than those of otherwise equivalent European options. American call options, however, are never exercised early unless there is a cash flow on the underlying, so they can sell for the same as their European counterparts in the absence of such a cash flow. American put options nearly always have a possibility of early exercise, so they ordinarily sell for more than their European counterparts.

▶ Cash flows on the underlying affect an option's boundary conditions and put–call parity by lowering the underlying price by the present value of the cash flows over the life of the option.

▶ A higher interest rate increases a call option's price and decreases a put option's price.

APPENDIX 73A

Cumulative Probabilities for a Standard Normal Distribution
$P(X \le x) = N(x)$ for $x \ge 0$ or $1 - N(-x)$ for $x < 0$

x	0	0.01	0.02	0.03	0.04	0.05	0.06	0.07	0.08	0.09
0.00	0.5000	0.5040	0.5080	0.5120	0.5160	0.5199	0.5239	0.5279	0.5319	0.5359
0.10	0.5398	0.5438	0.5478	0.5517	0.5557	0.5596	0.5636	0.5675	0.5714	0.5753
0.20	0.5793	0.5832	0.5871	0.5910	0.5948	0.5987	0.6026	0.6064	0.6103	0.6141
0.30	0.6179	0.6217	0.6255	0.6293	0.6331	0.6368	0.6406	0.6443	0.6480	0.6517
0.40	0.6554	0.6591	0.6628	0.6664	0.6700	0.6736	0.6772	0.6808	0.6844	0.6879
0.50	0.6915	0.6950	0.6985	0.7019	0.7054	0.7088	0.7123	0.7157	0.7190	0.7224
0.60	0.7257	0.7291	0.7324	0.7357	0.7389	0.7422	0.7454	0.7486	0.7517	0.7549
0.70	0.7580	0.7611	0.7642	0.7673	0.7704	0.7734	0.7764	0.7794	0.7823	0.7852
0.80	0.7881	0.7910	0.7939	0.7967	0.7995	0.8023	0.8051	0.8078	0.8106	0.8133
0.90	0.8159	0.8186	0.8212	0.8238	0.8264	0.8289	0.8315	0.8340	0.8365	0.8389
1.00	0.8413	0.8438	0.8461	0.8485	0.8508	0.8531	0.8554	0.8577	0.8599	0.8621
1.10	0.8643	0.8665	0.8686	0.8708	0.8729	0.8749	0.8770	0.8790	0.8810	0.8830
1.20	0.8849	0.8869	0.8888	0.8907	0.8925	0.8944	0.8962	0.8980	0.8997	0.9015
1.30	0.9032	0.9049	0.9066	0.9082	0.9099	0.9115	0.9131	0.9147	0.9162	0.9177
1.40	0.9192	0.9207	0.9222	0.9236	0.9251	0.9265	0.9279	0.9292	0.9306	0.9319
1.50	0.9332	0.9345	0.9357	0.9370	0.9382	0.9394	0.9406	0.9418	0.9429	0.9441
1.60	0.9452	0.9463	0.9474	0.9484	0.9495	0.9505	0.9515	0.9525	0.9535	0.9545
1.70	0.9554	0.9564	0.9573	0.9582	0.9591	0.9599	0.9608	0.9616	0.9625	0.9633
1.80	0.9641	0.9649	0.9656	0.9664	0.9671	0.9678	0.9686	0.9693	0.9699	0.9706
1.90	0.9713	0.9719	0.9726	0.9732	0.9738	0.9744	0.9750	0.9756	0.9761	0.9767
2.00	0.9772	0.9778	0.9783	0.9788	0.9793	0.9798	0.9803	0.9808	0.9812	0.9817
2.10	0.9821	0.9826	0.9830	0.9834	0.9838	0.9842	0.9846	0.9850	0.9854	0.9857
2.20	0.9861	0.9864	0.9868	0.9871	0.9875	0.9878	0.9881	0.9884	0.9887	0.9890
2.30	0.9893	0.9896	0.9898	0.9901	0.9904	0.9906	0.9909	0.9911	0.9913	0.9916
2.40	0.9918	0.9920	0.9922	0.9925	0.9927	0.9929	0.9931	0.9932	0.9934	0.9936
2.50	0.9938	0.9940	0.9941	0.9943	0.9945	0.9946	0.9948	0.9949	0.9951	0.9952
2.60	0.9953	0.9955	0.9956	0.9957	0.9959	0.9960	0.9961	0.9962	0.9963	0.9964
2.70	0.9965	0.9966	0.9967	0.9968	0.9969	0.9970	0.9971	0.9972	0.9973	0.9974
2.80	0.9974	0.9975	0.9976	0.9977	0.9977	0.9978	0.9979	0.9979	0.9980	0.9981
2.90	0.9981	0.9982	0.9982	0.9983	0.9984	0.9984	0.9985	0.9985	0.9986	0.9986
3.00	0.9987	0.9987	0.9987	0.9988	0.9988	0.9989	0.9989	0.9989	0.9990	0.9990

PRACTICE PROBLEMS FOR READING 73

1. **A.** Calculate the payoff at expiration for a call option on the S&P 100 stock index in which the underlying price is 579.32 at expiration, the multiplier is 100, and the exercise price is

   i. 450.

   ii. 650.

   B. Calculate the payoff at expiration for a put option on the S&P 100 in which the underlying is at 579.32 at expiration, the multiplier is 100, and the exercise price is

   i. 450.

   ii. 650.

2. **A.** Calculate the payoff at expiration for a call option on a bond in which the underlying is at $0.95 per $1 par at expiration, the contract is on $100,000 face value bonds, and the exercise price is

   i. $0.85.

   ii. $1.15.

   B. Calculate the payoff at expiration for a put option on a bond in which the underlying is at $0.95 per $1 par at expiration, the contract is on $100,000 face value bonds, and the exercise price is

   i. $0.85.

   ii. $1.15.

3. **A.** Calculate the payoff at expiration for a call option on an interest rate in which the underlying is a 180-day interest rate at 6.53 percent at expiration, the notional principal is $10 million, and the exercise price is

   i. 5 percent.

   ii. 8 percent.

   B. Calculate the payoff at expiration for a put option on an interest rate in which the underlying is a 180-day interest rate at 6.53 percent at expiration, the notional principal is $10 million, and the exercise price is

   i. 5 percent.

   ii. 8 percent.

4. **A.** Calculate the payoff at expiration for a call option on the British pound in which the underlying is at $1.438 at expiration, the options are on 125,000 British pounds, and the exercise price is

   i. $1.35.

   ii. $1.55.

   B. Calculate the payoff at expiration for a put option on the British pound where the underlying is at $1.438 at expiration, the options are on 125,000 British pounds, and the exercise price is

   i. $1.35.

   ii. $1.55.

5. A. Calculate the payoff at expiration for a call option on a futures contract in which the underlying is at 1136.76 at expiration, the options are on a futures contract for $1,000, and the exercise price is

   i. 1130.

   ii. 1140.

B. Calculate the payoff at expiration for a put option on a futures contract in which the underlying is at 1136.76 at expiration, the options are on a futures contract for $1000, and the exercise price is

   i. 1130.

   ii. 1140.

6. Consider a stock index option that expires in 75 days. The stock index is currently at 1240.89 and makes no cash payments during the life of the option. Assume that the stock index has a multiplier of 1. The risk-free rate is 3 percent.

A. Calculate the lowest and highest possible prices for European-style call options on the above stock index with exercise prices of

   i. 1225.

   ii. 1255.

B. Calculate the lowest and highest possible prices for European-style put options on the above stock index with exercise prices of

   i. 1225.

   ii. 1255.

7. A. Consider American-style call and put options on a bond. The options expire in 60 days. The bond is currently at $1.05 per $1 par and makes no cash payments during the life of the option. The risk-free rate is 5.5 percent. Assume that the contract is on $1 face value bonds. Calculate the lowest and highest possible prices for the calls and puts with exercise prices of

   i. $0.95.

   ii. $1.10.

B. Consider European style call and put options on a bond. The options expire in 60 days. The bond is currently at $1.05 per $1 par and makes no cash payments during the life of the option. The risk-free rate is 5.5 percent. Assume that the contract is on $1 face value bonds. Calculate the lowest and highest possible prices for the calls and puts with exercise prices of

   i. $0.95.

   ii. $1.10.

8. You are provided with the following information on put and call options on a stock:

Call price, $c_0 = \$6.64$

Put price, $p_0 = \$2.75$

Exercise price, $X = \$30$

Days to option expiration = 219

Current stock price, $S_0 = \$33.19$

Put–call parity shows the equivalence of a call/bond portfolio (fiduciary call) and a put/underlying portfolio (protective put). Illustrate put–call parity assuming stock prices at expiration (S_T) of $20 and of $40. Assume that the risk-free rate, r, is 4 percent.

4⅝ 4⅞ 3⅜
5½ 5½ − ⅜
5½ 21¾₁₆ − ⅜
20⅝ 21¹³⁄₁₆ ⅞
17⅜ 18⅛ + ⅞
6½ − ½
6½ 6½ − ⅛
7¼ 31⁄32 − ⅛
15⁄16
9⁄16
9⁄16
7¹⁵⁄₁₆ 7¹³⁄₁₆ 7¹⁵⁄₁₆
2⅝ 2¹¹⁄₃₂ 2½ +
2¾ 2¼ 2¼
6 12¹⁄₁₆ 11⅜ 11¾ +
87 33¾ 33 33¼ −
602 25⅝ 24⁹⁄₁₆ 25⅜ +
833 12 11⅝ 11⅞ +
16 10½ 10½ 10⅛ −
78 15⅞ 15¹³⁄₁₆ 15⅞ −
4508 9¹⁄₁₆ 8¼ 8⅞ +
430 11¼ 10⅛
4⅝ 4⅞

SWAP MARKETS AND CONTRACTS
by Don M. Chance

LEARNING OUTCOMES

The candidate should be able to:

a. describe the characteristics of swap contracts and explain how swaps are terminated;

b. define and give examples of currency swaps, plain vanilla interest rate swaps, and equity swaps, and calculate and interpret the payments on each.

INTRODUCTION 1

This reading completes the survey of the main types of derivative instruments. The three preceding readings covered forward contracts, futures contracts, and options. This reading covers swaps. Although swaps were the last of the main types of derivatives to be invented, they are clearly not the least important. In fact, judging by the size of the swap market, they are probably the most important. In Reading 70, we noted that the Bank for International Settlements had estimated the notional principal of the global over-the-counter derivatives market as of 30 June 2001 at $100 trillion. Of that amount, interest rate and currency swaps account for about $61 trillion, with interest rate swaps representing about $57 trillion of that total.[1] Indeed, interest rate swaps have had overwhelming success as a derivative product. They are widely used by corporations, financial institutions, and governments.

In Reading 70, we briefly described the characteristics of swaps, but now we explore this subject in more detail. Recall first that *a swap is an agreement*

---

[1] Equity and commodity swaps account for less than the notional principal of currency swaps.

Analysis of Derivatives for the CFA® Program, by Don M. Chance. Copyright © 2003 by AIMR. Reprinted with permission.

between two parties to exchange a series of future cash flows. For most types of swaps, one party makes payments that are determined by a random outcome, such as an interest rate, a currency rate, an equity return, or a commodity price. These payments are commonly referred to as variable or *floating*. The other party either makes variable or floating payments determined by some other random factor or makes fixed payments. At least one type of swap involves both parties making fixed payments, but the values of those payments vary due to random factors.

In forwards, futures, and options, the terminology of *long* and *short* has been used to describe buyers and sellers. These terms are not used as often in swaps. The preferred terminology usually designates a party as being the floating- (or variable-) rate payer or the fixed-rate payer. Nonetheless, in swaps in which one party receives a floating rate and the other receives a fixed rate, the former is usually said to be long and the latter is said to be short. This usage is in keeping with the fact that parties who go long in other instruments pay a known amount and receive a claim on an unknown amount. In some swaps, however, both sides are floating or variable, and this terminology breaks down.

1.1 Characteristics of Swap Contracts

Although technically a swap can have a single payment, most swaps involve multiple payments. Thus, we refer to a swap as a *series* of payments. In fact, we have already covered a swap with one payment, which is just a forward contract. Hence, a swap is basically a series of forward contracts. With this idea in mind, we can see that a swap is like an agreement to buy something over a period of time. We might be paying a variable price or a price that has already been fixed; we might be paying an uncertain price, or we might already know the price we shall pay.

When a swap is initiated, neither party pays any amount to the other. Therefore, a swap has zero value at the start of the contract. Although it is not absolutely necessary for this condition to be true, swaps are typically done in this fashion. Neither party pays anything up front. There is, however, a technical exception to this point in regard to currency swaps. Each party pays the notional principal to the other, but the amounts exchanged are equivalent, though denominated in two different currencies.

Each date on which the parties make payments is called a **settlement date**, sometimes called a payment date, and the time between settlement dates is called the **settlement period**. On a given settlement date when payments are due, one party makes a payment to the other, which in turn makes a payment to the first party. With the exception of currency swaps and a few variations associated with other types of swaps, both sets of payments are made in the same currency. Consequently, the parties typically agree to exchange only the net amount owed from one party to the other, a practice called **netting**. In currency swaps and a few other special cases, the payments are not made in the same currency; hence, the parties usually make separate payments without netting. Note the implication that swaps are generally settled in cash. It is quite rare for swaps to call for actual physical delivery of an underlying asset.

A swap always has a **termination date**, the date of the final payment. We can think of this date as its expiration date, as we do with other derivatives. The original time to maturity is sometimes called the **tenor** of a swap.

The swap market is almost exclusively an over-the-counter market, so swaps contracts are customized to the parties' specific needs. Several of the leading futures exchanges have created futures contracts on swaps. These contracts allow participants to hedge and speculate on the rates that will prevail in the swap market at future dates. Of course, these contracts are not swaps themselves but, as derivatives of swaps, they can in some ways serve as substitutes for swaps. These futures contracts have been moderately successful, but their volume is insignificant compared with the over-the-counter market for swaps.

As we have discussed in previous readings, over-the-counter instruments are subject to default risk. Default is possible whenever a payment is due. When a series of payments is made, there is default risk potential throughout the life of the contract, depending on the financial condition of the two parties. But default can be somewhat complicated in swaps. Suppose, for example, that on a settlement date, Party A owes Party B a payment of $50,000 and Party B owes Party A a payment of $12,000. Agreeing to net, Party A owes Party B $38,000 for that particular payment. Party A may be illiquid, or perhaps even bankrupt, and unable to make the payment. But it may be the case that the market value of the swap, which reflects the present value of the remaining payments, could be positive from the perspective of Party A and negative from the perspective of Party B. In that case, Party B owes Party A more for the remaining payments.

The handling of default in swaps can be complicated, depending on the contract specifications and the applicable laws under which the contract was written. In most cases, the above situation would be resolved by having A be in default but possessing an asset, the swap, that can be used to help settle its other liabilities.

1.2 Termination of a Swap

As we noted earlier, a swap has a termination or expiration date. Sometimes, however, a party could want to terminate a swap before its formal expiration. This scenario is much like a party selling a bond before it matures or selling an exchange-traded option or futures contract before its expiration. With swaps, early termination can take place in several ways.

As we mentioned briefly, a swap has a market value that can be calculated during its life. If a party holds a swap with a market value of $125,000, for example, it can settle the swap with the counterparty by having the counterparty pay it $125,000 in cash. This payment terminates the transaction for both parties. From the opposite perspective, a party holding a swap with a negative market value can terminate the swap by paying the market value to the counterparty. Terminating a swap in this manner is possible only if the counterparties specify in advance that such a transaction can be made, or if they reach an agreement to do so without having specified in advance. In other words, this feature is not automatically available and must be agreed to by both parties.

Many swaps are terminated early by entering into a separate and offsetting swap. For example, suppose a corporation is engaged in a swap to make fixed payments of 5 percent and receive floating payments based on LIBOR, with the payments made each 15 January and 15 July. Three years remain on the swap. That corporation can offset the swap by entering into an entirely new swap in which it makes payments based on LIBOR and receives a fixed rate with the payments made each 15 January and 15 July for three years. The swap fixed rate is determined by market conditions at the time the swap is initiated. Thus, the fixed rate on the new swap is not likely to match the fixed rate on the old swap, but the effect of this transaction is simply to have the floating payments offset;

TGT might then lock in the conversion rate by entering into a currency swap with notional principal amounts that would allow it to receive a fixed amount of dollars on 15 January and 15 July. There would be no reason to specify an exchange of notional principal. As we previously described, there are four types of currency swaps. Using the original Target–Deutsche Bank swap as an example, the semi-annual payments would be

    A. TGT pays euros at a fixed rate; DB pays dollars at a fixed rate.

    B. TGT pays euros at a fixed rate; DB pays dollars at a floating rate.

    C. TGT pays euros at a floating rate; DB pays dollars at a floating rate.

    D. TGT pays euros at a floating rate; DB pays dollars at a fixed rate.

Or, reversing the flow, TGT could be the payer of dollars and DB could be the payer of euros:

    E. TGT pays dollars at a fixed rate; DB pays euros at a fixed rate.

    F. TGT pays dollars at a fixed rate; DB pays euros at a floating rate.

    G. TGT pays dollars at a floating rate; DB pays euros at a floating rate.

    H. TGT pays dollars at a floating rate; DB pays euros at a fixed rate.

Suppose we combine Swap A with Swap H. With TGT paying euros at a fixed rate and DB paying euros at a fixed rate, the euro payments wash out and the net effect is

    I. TGT pays dollars at a floating rate; DB pays dollars at a fixed rate.

Suppose we combine Swap B with Swap E. Similarly, the euro payments again wash out, and the net effect is

    J. TGT pays dollars at a fixed rate; DB pays dollars at a floating rate.

Suppose we combine Swap C with Swap F. Likewise, the euro floating payments wash out, and the net effect is

    K. TGT pays dollars at a fixed rate; DB pays dollars at a floating rate.

Lastly, suppose we combine Swap D with Swap G. Again, the euro floating payments wash out, and the net effect is

    L. TGT pays dollars at a floating rate; DB pays dollars at a fixed rate.

Of course, the net results of I and L are equivalent, and the net results of J and K are equivalent. What we have shown here, however, is that combinations of currency swaps eliminate the currency flows and leave us with transactions in only one currency. A swap in which both sets of interest payments are made in the same currency is an interest rate swap.

3.2 Interest Rate Swaps

As we discovered in the above paragraph, an interest rate swap can be created as a combination of currency swaps. Of course, no one would create an interest rate swap that way; doing so would require two transactions when only one would suffice. Interest rate swaps evolved into their own market. In fact, the interest rate swap market is much bigger than the currency swap market, as we have seen in the notional principal statistics.

As previously noted, one way to look at an interest rate swap is that it is a currency swap in which both currencies are the same. Consider a swap to pay Currency A fixed and Currency B floating. Currency A could be dollars, and B could be euros. But what if A and B are both dollars, or A and B are both euros? The first case is a dollar-denominated plain vanilla swap; the second is a euro-denominated plain vanilla swap. *A* **plain vanilla swap** *is simply an interest rate swap in which one party pays a fixed rate and the other pays a floating rate, with both sets of payments in the same currency.* In fact, the plain vanilla swap is probably the most common derivative transaction in the global financial system.

Note that because we are paying in the same currency, there is no need to exchange notional principals at the beginning and at the end of an interest rate swap. In addition, the interest payments can be, and nearly always are, netted. If one party owes $X and the other owes $Y, the party owing the greater amount pays the net difference, which greatly reduces the credit risk. Finally, we note that there is no reason to have both sides pay a fixed rate. The two streams of payments would be identical in that case. So in an interest rate swap, either one side always pays fixed and the other side pays floating, or both sides pay floating, but never do both sides pay fixed.[5]

Thus, in a plain vanilla interest rate swap, one party makes interest payments at a fixed rate and the other makes interest payments at a floating rate. Both sets of payments are on the same notional principal and occur on regularly scheduled dates. For each payment, the interest rate is multiplied by a fraction representing the number of days in the settlement period over the number of days in a year. In some cases, the settlement period is computed assuming 30 days in each month; in others, an exact day count is used. Some cases assume a 360-day year; others use 365 days.

Let us now illustrate an interest rate swap. Suppose that on 15 December, General Electric Company (NYSE: GE) borrows money for one year from a bank such as Bank of America (NYSE: BAC). The loan is for $25 million and specifies that GE will make interest payments on a quarterly basis on the 15th of March, June, September, and December for one year at the rate of LIBOR plus 25 basis points. At the end of the year, it will pay back the principal. On the 15th of December, March, June, and September, LIBOR is observed and sets the rate for that quarter. The interest is then paid at the end of the quarter.[6]

GE believes that it is getting a good rate, but fearing a rise in interest rates, it would prefer a fixed-rate loan. It can easily convert the floating-rate loan to a fixed-rate loan by engaging in a swap. Suppose it approaches JP Morgan Chase (NYSE: JPM), a large dealer bank, and requests a quote on a swap to pay a fixed rate and receive LIBOR, with payments on the dates of its loan payments. The bank prices the swap and quotes a fixed rate of 6.2 percent.[7] The fixed payments

---

[5] The case of both sides paying floating is called a **basis swap**.

[6] Again, we assume 90 days in each interest payment period for this example. The exact payment dates are not particularly important for illustrative purposes.

[7] Typically the rate is quoted as a spread over the rate on a U.S. Treasury security with a comparable maturity. Suppose the yield on a two-year Treasury note is 6 percent. Then the swap would be quoted as 20 basis points over the two-year Treasury rate. By quoting the rate in the this manner, GE knows what it is paying over the Treasury rate, a differential called the swap spread. In addition, a quote in this form protects the bank from the rate changing drastically either during the phone conversation or shortly thereafter. Thus, the quote can stay in effect for a reasonable period of time while GE checks out quotes from other dealers.

will be made based on a day count of 90/365, and the floating payments will be made based on 90/360. Current LIBOR is 5.9 percent. Therefore, the first fixed payment, which GE makes to JPM, is $25,000,000(0.062)(90/365) = $382,192. This is also the amount of each remaining fixed payment.

The first floating payment, which JPM makes to GE, is $25,000,000(0.059) (90/360) = $368,750. Of course, the remaining floating payments will not be known until later. Exhibit 4 shows the pattern of cash flows on the swap from GE's perspective.

EXHIBIT 4	Cash Flow to GE on Swap with JPM

To GE	$368,750	$^{a}	$^{a}	$^{a}
	15 Mar	15 Jun	15 Sep	15 Dec
15 Dec				
To JPM	$382,192	$382,192	$382,192	$382,192

^{a}Computed as $25,000,000(L)90/360, where L is LIBOR on the previous settlement date.

EXAMPLE 2

Determine the upcoming payments in a **plain vanilla** interest rate swap in which the notional principal is €70 million. The end user makes semi-annual fixed payments at the rate of 7 percent, and the dealer makes semiannual floating payments at Euribor, which was 6.25 percent on the last settlement period. The floating payments are made on the basis of 180 days in the settlement period and 360 days in a year. The fixed payments are made on the basis of 180 days in the settlement period and 365 days in a year. Payments are netted, so determine which party pays which and what amount.

Solution:
The fixed payments are €70,000,000(0.07)(180/365) = €2,416,438.

The upcoming floating payment is €70,000,000(0.0625)(180/360)
= €2,187,500.

The net payment is that the party paying fixed will pay the party
paying floating €2,416,438 − €2,187,500 = €228,938.

Note in Exhibit 4 that we did not show the notional principal, because it was not exchanged. We could implicitly show that GE received $25 million from JPM and paid $25 million to JPM at the start of the swap. We could also show that the same thing happens at the end. If we look at it that way, it appears as if GE has issued a $25 million fixed-rate bond, which was purchased by JPM, which in turn issued a $25 million floating-rate bond, which was in turn purchased by GE. We say that *it appears* as if this is what happened: In fact, neither party actually issued a bond, but they have generated the cash flows that would occur if GE had issued such a fixed-rate bond, JPM had issued such a floating-rate bond, and each purchased the bond of the other. In other words, we could include the principals on both sides to make each set of cash flows look like a bond, yet the overall cash flows would be the same as on the swap.

So let us say that GE enters into this swap. Exhibit 5 shows the net effect of the swap and the loan. GE pays LIBOR plus 25 basis points to Bank of America on its loan, pays 6.2 percent to JPM, and receives LIBOR from JPM. The net effect is that GE pays $6.2 + 0.25 = 6.45$ percent fixed.

EXHIBIT 5	GE's Conversion of a Floating-Rate Loan to a Fixed-Rate Loan Using an Interest Rate Swap with JPM

Now, JPM is engaged in a swap to pay LIBOR and receive 6.2 percent. It is exposed to the risk of LIBOR increasing. It would, therefore, probably engage in some other type of transaction to offset this risk. One transaction commonly used in this situation is to sell Eurodollar futures. As discussed in Reading 75, Eurodollar futures prices move $25 in value for each basis point move in LIBOR. JPM will determine how sensitive its position is to a move in LIBOR and sell an appropriate number of futures to offset the risk. Note that Bank of America is exposed to LIBOR as well, but in the banking industry, floating-rate loans are often made because the funding that the bank obtained to make the loan was probably already at LIBOR or a comparable floating rate.

It is possible but unlikely that GE could get a fixed-rate loan at a better rate. The swap involves some credit risk: the possibility, however small, that JPM will default. In return for assuming that risk, GE in all likelihood would get a better rate than it would if it borrowed at a fixed rate. JPM is effectively a wholesaler of risk, using its powerful position as one of the world's leading banks to facilitate the buying and selling of risk for companies such as GE. Dealers profit from the spread between the rates they quote to pay and the rates they quote to receive. The swaps market is, however, extremely competitive and the spreads have been squeezed very tight, which makes it very challenging for dealers to make a profit. Of course, this competition is good for end users, because it gives them more attractive rates.

3.3 Equity Swaps

By now, it should be apparent that a swap requires at least one variable rate or price underlying it. So far, that rate has been an interest rate.[8] In an equity swap, the rate is the return on a stock or stock index. This characteristic gives the **equity swap** two features that distinguish it from interest rate and currency swaps.

First, the party making the fixed-rate payment could also have to make a variable payment based on the equity return. Suppose the end user pays the equity payment and receives the fixed payment, i.e., it pays the dealer the return on the S&P 500 Index, and the dealer pays the end user a fixed rate. If the S&P 500 increases, the return is positive and the end user pays that return to the dealer. If the S&P 500 goes down, however, its return is obviously negative. In that case, the end user would pay the dealer the *negative return on the S&P 500*, which means that it would receive that return from the dealer. For example, if the S&P 500 falls by 1 percent, the dealer would pay the end user 1 percent, in addition to the fixed payment the dealer makes in any case. So the dealer, or in general the party receiving the equity return, could end up making *both* a fixed-rate payment and an equity payment.

The second distinguishing feature of an equity swap is that the payment is not known until the end of the settlement period, at which time the return on the stock is known. In an interest rate or currency swap, the floating interest rate is set at the beginning of the period.[9] Therefore, one always knows the amount of the upcoming floating interest payment.[10]

Another important feature of some equity swaps is that the rate of return is often structured to include both dividends and capital gains. In interest rate and currency swaps, capital gains are not paid.[11] Finally, we note that in some equity swaps, the notional principal is indexed to change with the level of the stock, although we will not explore such swaps in this book.[12]

Equity swaps are commonly used by asset managers. Let us consider a situation in which an asset manager might use such a swap. Suppose that the Vanguard Asset Allocation Fund (Nasdaq: VAAPX) is authorized to use swaps. On the last day of December, it would like to sell $100 million in U.S. large-cap equities and invest the proceeds at a fixed rate. It believes that a swap allowing it to pay the total return on the S&P 500, while receiving a fixed rate, would achieve this objective. It would like to hold this position for one year, with payments to be made on the last day of March, June, September, and December. It enters into such a swap with Morgan Stanley (NYSE: MWD).

Specifically, the swap covers a notional principal of $100 million and calls for VAAPX to pay MWD the return on the S&P 500 Total Return Index and for MWD to pay VAAPX a fixed rate on the last day of March, June, September, and December for one year. MWD prices the swap at a fixed rate of 6.5 percent. The

---

[8] Currency swaps also have the element that the exchange rate is variable.

[9] Technically, there are interest rate swaps in which the floating rate is set at the end of the period, at which time the payment is made.

[10] In a currency swap, however, one does not know the exchange rate until the settlement date.

[11] In some kinds of interest rate swaps, the total return on a bond, which includes dividends and capital gains, is paid. This instrument is called a **total return swap** and is a common variety of a **credit derivative**.

[12] Some interest rate swaps also have a notional principal that changes.

fixed payments will be made using an actual day count/365 days convention. There are 90 days between 31 December and 31 March, 91 days between 31 March and 30 June, 92 days between 30 June and 30 September, and 92 days between 30 September and 31 December. Thus, the fixed payments will be

31 March:	$100,000,000(0.065)(90/365) = \$1,602,740$
30 June:	$100,000,000(0.065)(91/365) = \$1,620,548$
30 September:	$100,000,000(0.065)(92/365) = \$1,638,356$
31 December:	$100,000,000(0.065)(92/365) = \$1,638,356$

Exhibit 6 shows the cash flow stream to VAAPX.

Suppose that on the day the swap is initiated, 31 December, the S&P 500 Total Return Index is at 3,517.76. Now suppose that on 31 March, the index is at 3,579.12. The return on the index is

$$\frac{3,579.12}{3,517.76} - 1 = 0.0174$$

EXHIBIT 6	Cash Flows to VAAPX on Equity Swap with MWD

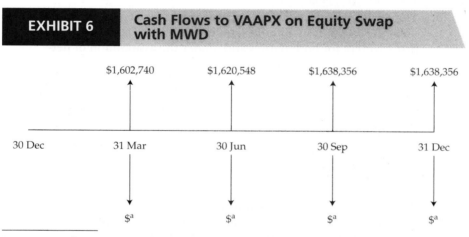

[a] Computed as $100,000,000R$, where R is the return on the S&P 500 Total Return Index from the previous settlement date.

Thus, the return is 1.74 percent. The equity payment that VAAPX would make to MWD would be $100,000,000(0.0174) = \$1,740,000$.

Of course, this amount would not be known until 31 March, and only the difference between this amount and the fixed payment would be paid. Then on 31 March, the index value of 3,579.12 would be the base for the following period. Suppose that on 30 June, the index declines to 3,452.78. Then the return for the second quarter would be

$$\frac{3,452.78}{3,579.12} - 1 = -0.0353$$

Therefore, the loss is 3.53 percent, requiring a payment of $100,000,000(0.0353) = \$3,530,000$.

Because this amount represents a loss on the S&P 500, MWD would make a payment to VAAPX. In addition, MWD would also owe VAAPX the fixed payment of $1,620,548. It is as though VAAPX sold out of its position in stock, thereby

PRACTICE PROBLEMS FOR READING 74

1. A U.S. company enters into a currency swap in which it pays a fixed rate of 5.5 percent in euros and the counterparty pays a fixed rate of 6.75 percent in dollars. The notional principals are $100 million and €116.5 million. Payments are made semiannually and on the basis of 30 days per month and 360 days per year.

   A. Calculate the initial exchange of payments that takes place at the beginning of the swap.

   B. Calculate the semiannual payments.

   C. Calculate the final exchange of payments that takes place at the end of the swap.

2. A British company enters into a currency swap in which it pays a fixed rate of 6 percent in dollars and the counterparty pays a fixed rate of 5 percent in pounds. The notional principals are £75 million and $105 million. Payments are made semiannually and on the basis of 30 days per month and 360 days per year.

   A. Calculate the initial exchange of payments that takes place at the beginning of the swap.

   B. Calculate the semiannual payments.

   C. Calculate the final exchange of payments that takes place at the end of the swap.

3. A U.S. company has entered into an interest rate swap with a dealer in which the notional principal is $50 million. The company will pay a floating rate of LIBOR and receive a fixed rate of 5.75 percent. Interest is paid semiannually, and the current LIBOR is 5.15 percent. Calculate the first payment and indicate which party pays which. Assume that floating-rate payments will be made on the basis of 180/360 and fixed-rate payments will be made on the basis of 180/365.

4. A German company that has issued floating-rate notes now believes that interest rates will rise. It decides to protect itself against this possibility by entering into an interest rate swap with a dealer. In this swap, the notional principal is €25 million and the company will pay a fixed rate of 5.5 percent and receive Euribor. The current Euribor is 5 percent. Calculate the first payment and indicate which party pays which. Assume that floating-rate payments will be made on the basis of 90/360 and fixed-rate payments will be made on the basis of 90/365.

5. An asset manager wishes to reduce his exposure to large-cap stocks and increase his exposure to small-cap stocks. He seeks to do so using an equity swap. He agrees to pay a dealer the return on a large-cap index, and the dealer agrees to pay the manager the return on a small-cap index. For each of the scenarios listed below, calculate the first overall payment and indicate which party makes the payment. Assume that payments are made semiannually. The notional principal is $100 million.

   A. The value of the small-cap index starts off at 689.40, and the large-cap index starts at 1130.20. In six months, the small-cap index is at 625.60 and the large-cap index is at 1251.83.

   B. The value of the small-cap index starts off at 689.40 and the large-cap index starts at 1130.20. In six months, the small-cap index is at 703.23 and the large-cap index is at 1143.56.

6. An asset manager wishes to reduce her exposure to small-cap stocks and increase her exposure to fixed-income securities. She seeks to do so using an equity swap. She agrees to pay a dealer the return on a small-cap index and the dealer agrees to pay the manager a fixed rate of 5.5 percent. For each of the scenarios listed below, calculate the overall payment six months later and indicate which party makes the payment. Assume that payments are made semiannually (180 days per period) and there are 365 days in each year. The notional principal is $50 million.

   A. The value of the small-cap index starts off at 234.10 and six months later is at 238.41.

   B. The value of the small-cap index starts off at 234.10 and six months later is at 241.27.

7. An asset manager wishes to reduce his exposure to fixed-income securities and increase his exposure to large-cap stocks. He seeks to do so using an equity swap. He agrees to pay a dealer a fixed rate of 4.5 percent, and the dealer agrees to pay the manager the return on a large-cap index. For each of the scenarios listed below, calculate the overall payment six months later and indicate which party makes it. Assume that payments are made semi-annually (180 days per period) and there are 365 days in a year. The notional principal is $25 million.

   A. The value of the large-cap index starts off at 578.50 and six months later is at 622.54.

   B. The value of the large-cap index starts off at 578.50 and six months later is at 581.35.

8. The party agreeing to make the fixed-rate payment might also be required to make the variable payment in

2005 exam

   A. an equity swap but not an interest rate swap.

   B. an interest rate swap but not an equity swap.

   C. both an equity swap and an interest rate swap.

   D. neither an equity swap nor an interest rate swap.

9. The formula for calculating the payoff at expiration of a forward rate agreement (FRA) is

$$\text{Notional principal} \left[\frac{(\text{Underlying rate at expiration} - \text{Forward contract rate})\left(\dfrac{\text{Days in underlying rate}}{360}\right)}{1 + \text{Underlying rate at expiration}\left(\dfrac{\text{Days in underlying rate}}{360}\right)} \right]$$

Use the above formula to solve for the payment at expiration for an investor who went long a 3 × 9 FRA with a notional principal of $10,000,000 where the 180–day LIBOR rate at expiration is 4.80% and the forward contract rate was set at 5.20%.

   A. −$588,235

   B. −$19,531

   C. $19,493

   D. $555,556

In this reading, we look at option strategies that are typically used in equity investing, which include standard strategies involving single options and strategies that combine options with the underlying.

Let us begin by reviewing the necessary notation. These symbols are the same ones we have previously used. First recall that time 0 is the time at which the strategy is initiated and time T is the time the option expires, stated as a fraction of a year. Accordingly, the amount of time until expiration is simply $T - 0 = T$, which is (Days to expiration)/365. The other symbols are

c_0, c_T = price of the call option at time 0 and time T
p_0, p_T = price of the put option at time 0 and time T[1]
X = exercise price
S_0, S_T = price of the underlying at time 0 and time T
V_0, V_T = value of the position at time 0 and time T
Π = profit from the transaction: $V_T - V_0$
r = risk-free rate

Some additional notation will be introduced when necessary.

Note that we are going to measure the profit from an option transaction, which is simply the final value of the transaction minus the initial value of the transaction. Profit does not take into account the time value of money or the risk. Although a focus on profit is not completely satisfactory from a theoretical point of view, it is nonetheless instructive, simple, and a common approach to examining options. Our primary objective here is to obtain a general picture of the manner in which option strategies perform. With that in mind, discussing profit offers probably the best trade-off in terms of gaining the necessary knowledge with a minimum of complexity.

In this reading, we assume that the option user has a view regarding potential movements of the underlying. In most cases that view is a prediction of the direction of the underlying, but in some cases it is a prediction of the volatility of the underlying. In all cases, we assume this view is specified over a horizon that corresponds to the option's life or that the option expiration can be tailored to the horizon date. Hence, for the most part, these options should be considered customized, over-the-counter options.[2] Every interest rate option is a customized option.

Because the option expiration corresponds to the horizon date for which a particular view is held, there is no reason to use American options. Accordingly, all

---

[1] As in Reading 73, lower case indicates European options, and upper case indicates American options. In this reading, all options are European.

[2] If the options discussed were exchange-listed options, it would not significantly alter the material in this reading.

options in this reading are European options. Moreover, we shall not consider terminating the strategy early. Putting an option in place and closing the position prior to expiration is certainly a legitimate strategy. It could reflect the arrival of new information over the holding period, but it requires an understanding of more complex issues, such as valuation of the option and the rate at which the option loses its time value. Thus, we shall examine the outcome of a particular strategy over a range of possible values of the underlying only on the expiration day.

OPTION STRATEGIES FOR EQUITY PORTFOLIOS

Many typical illustrations of option strategies use individual stocks, but we shall use options on a stock index, the Nasdaq 100, referred to simply as the Nasdaq. We shall assume that in addition to buying and selling options on the Nasdaq, we can also buy the index, either through construction of the portfolio itself, through an index mutual fund, or an **exchange-traded fund**.[3] We shall simply refer to this instrument as a stock. We are given the following numerical data:

S_0 = 2000, value of the Nasdaq 100 when the strategy is initiated
T = 0.0833, the time to expiration (one month = 1/12)

The options available will be the following:[4]

Exercise Price	Call Price	Put Price
1950	108.43	56.01
2000	81.75	79.25
2050	59.98	107.39

Let us start by examining an initial strategy that is the simplest of all: to buy or sell short the underlying. Panel A of Exhibit 1 illustrates the profit from the transaction of buying a share of stock. We see the obvious result that if you buy the stock and it goes up, you make a profit; if it goes down, you incur a loss. Panel B shows the case of selling short the stock. Recall that this strategy involves borrowing the shares from a broker, selling them at the current price, and then buying them back at a later date. In this case, if you sell short the stock and it goes down, you make a profit. Conversely, if it goes up, you incur a loss. Now we shall move on to strategies involving options, but we shall use the stock strategies again when we combine options with stock.

In this section we examine option strategies in the context of their use in equity portfolios. Although these strategies are perfectly applicable for fixed-income portfolios, corporate borrowing scenarios, or even commodity risk

---

[3] Exchange-traded shares on the Nasdaq 100 are called Nasdaq 100 Trust Shares and QQQs, for their ticker symbol. They are commonly referred to as Qubes, trade on the Amex, and are the most active exchange-traded fund and often the most actively traded of all securities. Options on the Nasdaq 100 are among the most actively traded as well.

[4] These values were obtained using the Black–Scholes–Merton model. By using this model, we know we are working with reasonable values that do not permit arbitrage opportunities.

| **EXHIBIT 1** | **Simple Stock Strategies** |

A. Buy Stock

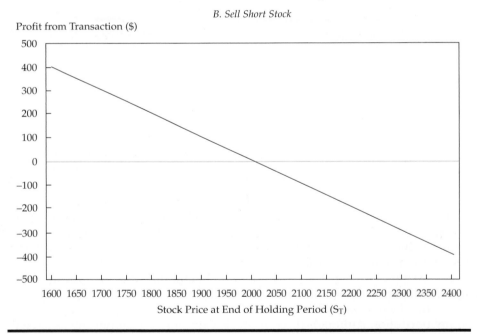

B. Sell Short Stock

management situations, they are generally more easily explained and understood in the context of investing in equities or equity indices.

To analyze an equity option strategy, we first assume that we establish the
position at the current price. We then determine the value of the option at expiration for a specific value of the index at expiration. We calculate the profit as

the value at expiration minus the current price. We then generate a graph to illustrate the value at expiration and profit for a range of index values at expiration. Although the underlying is a stock index, we shall just refer to it as the underlying to keep things as general as possible. We begin by examining the most fundamental option transactions, long and short positions in calls and puts.

2.1 Standard Long and Short Positions

2.1.1 Calls

Consider the purchase of a call option at the price c_0. The value at expiration, c_T, is $c_T = \max(0, S_T - X)$. Broken down into parts,

$$c_T = 0 \qquad \text{if } S_T \leq X$$
$$c_T = S_T - X \qquad \text{if } S_T > X$$

The profit is obtained by subtracting the option premium, which is paid to purchase the option, from the option value at expiration, $\Pi = c_T - c_0$. Broken down into parts,

$$\Pi = -c_0 \qquad \text{if } S_T \leq X$$
$$\Pi = S_T - X - c_0 \qquad \text{if } S_T > X$$

Now consider this example. We buy the call with the exercise price of 2000 for 81.75. Consider values of the index at expiration of 1900 and 2100. For $S_T = 1900$,

$$c_T = \max(0, 1900 - 2000) = 0$$
$$\Pi = 0 - 81.75 = -81.75$$

For $S_T = 2100$,

$$c_T = \max(0, 2100 - 2000) = 100$$
$$\Pi = 100 - 81.75 = 18.25$$

Exhibit 2 illustrates the value at expiration and profit when S_T, the underlying price at expiration, ranges from 1600 to 2400. We see that buying a call results in a limited loss of the premium, 81.75. For an index value at expiration greater than the exercise price of 2000, the value and profit move up one-for-one with the index value, and there is no upper limit.

It is important to identify the breakeven index value at expiration. Recall that the formula for the profit is $\Pi = \max(0, S_T - X) - c_0$. We would like to know the value of S_T for which $\Pi = 0$. We shall call that value S_T^*. It would be nice to be able to solve $\Pi = \max(0, S_T^* - X) - c_0 = 0$ for S_T^*, but that is not directly possible. Instead, we observe that there are two ranges of outcomes, one in which $\Pi = S_T^* - X - c_0$ for $S_T^* > X$, the case of the option expiring in-the-money, and the other in which $\Pi = -c_0$ for $S_T \leq X$, the case of the option expiring out-of-the-money. It is obvious from the equation and by observing Exhibit 2 that in the latter case, there is no possibility of breaking even. In the former case, we see that we can solve for S_T^*. Setting $\Pi = S_T^* - X - c_0 = 0$, we obtain $S_T^* = X + c_0$.

Thus, the breakeven is the exercise price plus the option premium. This result should be intuitive: The value of the underlying at expiration must exceed the exercise price by the amount of the premium to recover the cost of the premium. In this problem, the breakeven is $S_T^* = 2000 + 81.75 = 2081.75$. Observe in Exhibit 2 that the profit line crosses the axis at this value.

In summarizing the strategy, we have the following results for the option buyer:

$c_T = \max(0, S_T - X)$
Value at expiration $= c_T$
Profit: $\Pi = c_T - c_0$
Maximum profit $= \infty$
Maximum loss $= c_0$
Breakeven: $S_T^* = X + c_0$

EXHIBIT 2   **Buy Call**

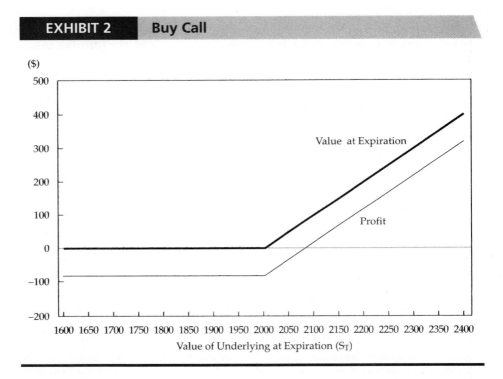

Call options entice naive speculators, but it is important to consider the *likely* gains and losses more than the *potential* gains and losses. For example, in this case, the underlying must go up by about 4.1 percent in one month to cover the cost of the call. This increase equates to an annual rate of almost 50 percent and is an unreasonable expectation by almost any standard. If the underlying does not move at all, the loss is 100 percent of the premium.

For the seller of the call, the results are just the opposite. The sum of the positions of the seller and buyer is zero. Hence, we can take the value and profit results for the buyer and change the signs. The results for the maximum profit and maximum loss are changed accordingly, and the breakeven is the same. Hence, for the option seller,

$$c_T = \max(0, S_T - X)$$

Value at expiration $= -c_T$

Profit: $\Pi = -c_T + c_0$

Maximum profit $= c_0$

Maximum loss $= \infty$

Breakeven: $S_T^* = X + c_0$

Exhibit 3 shows the results for the seller of the call. Note that the value and profit have a fixed maximum. The worst case is an infinite loss. Just as there is no upper limit to the buyer's potential gain, there is no upper limit to how much the seller can lose.

Call options are purchased by investors who are bullish. We now turn to put options, which are purchased by investors who are bearish.

EXHIBIT 3	Sell Call

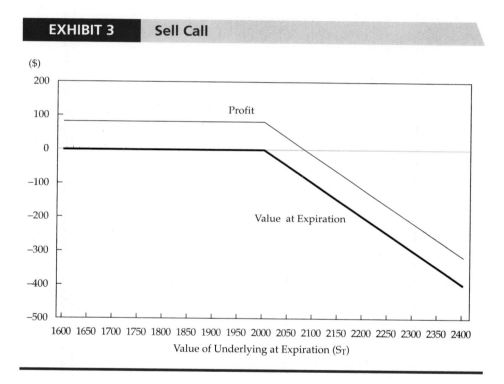

Value of Underlying at Expiration (S_T)

EXAMPLE 1

Consider a call option selling for $7 in which the exercise price is $100 and the price of the underlying is $98.

A. Determine the value at expiration and the profit for a buyer under the following outcomes:

   i. The price of the underlying at expiration is $102.

   ii. The price of the underlying at expiration is $94.

B. Determine the value at expiration and the profit for a seller under the following outcomes:

  i. The price of the underlying at expiration is $91.

  ii. The price of the underlying at expiration is $101.

C. Determine the following:

  i. The maximum profit to the buyer (maximum loss to the seller)

  ii. The maximum loss to the buyer (maximum profit to the seller)

D. Determine the breakeven price of the underlying at expiration.

Solutions:

A. Call buyer

  i. Value at expiration $= c_T = \max(0, S_T - X) = \max(0, 102 - 100) = 2$
     $\Pi = c_T - c_0 = 2 - 7 = -5$

  ii. Value at expiration $= c_T = \max(0, S_T - X) = \max(0, 94 - 100) = 0$
     $\Pi = c_T - c_0 = 0 - 7 = -7$

B. Call seller

  i. Value at expiration $= -c_T = -\max(0, S_T - X) = -\max(0, 91 - 100) = 0$
     $\Pi = -c_T + c_0 = -0 + 7 = 7$

  ii. Value at expiration $= -c_T = -\max(0, S_T - X) = -\max(0, 101 - 100) = -1$
     $\Pi = -c_T + c_0 = -1 + 7 = 6$

C. Maximum and minimum

  i. Maximum profit to buyer (loss to seller) $= \infty$

  ii. Maximum loss to buyer (profit to seller) $= c_0 = 7$

D. $S_T{}^* = X + c_0 = 100 + 7 = 107$

2.1.2 Puts

The value of a put at expiration is $p_T = \max(0, X - S_T)$. Broken down into parts,

$$p_T = X - S \qquad \text{if } S_T < X$$
$$p_T = 0 \qquad \text{if } S_T \geq X$$

The profit is obtained by subtracting the premium on the put from the value at expiration:

$$\Pi = p_T - p_0$$

Broken down into parts,

$$\Pi = X - S_T - p_0 \qquad \text{if } S_T < X$$
$$\Pi = -p_0 \qquad \text{if } S_T \geq X$$

For our example and outcomes of $S_T = 1900$ and 2100, the results are as follows:

$S_T = 1900$:

$$p_T = \max(0, 2000 - 1900) = 100$$
$$\Pi = 100 - 79.25 = 20.75$$

$S_T = 2100$:

$$p_T = \max(0, 2000 - 2100) = 0$$
$$\Pi = 0 - 79.25 = -79.25$$

These results are shown in Exhibit 4. We see that the put has a maximum value and profit and a limited loss, the latter of which is the premium. The maximum value is obtained when the underlying goes to zero.[5] In that case, $p_T = X$. So the maximum profit is $X - p_0$. Here that will be $2000 - 79.25 = 1920.75$.

The breakeven is found by breaking up the profit equation into its parts, $\Pi = X - S_T - p_0$ for $S_T < X$ and $\Pi = -p_0$ for $S_T \geq X$. In the latter case, there is no possibility of breaking even. It refers to the range over which the entire premium is lost. In the former case, we denote the breakeven index value as S_T^*, set the equation to zero, and solve for S_T^* to obtain $S_T^* = X - p_0$. In our example, the breakeven is $S_T^* = 2000 - 79.25 = 1920.75$.

EXHIBIT 4	Buy Put

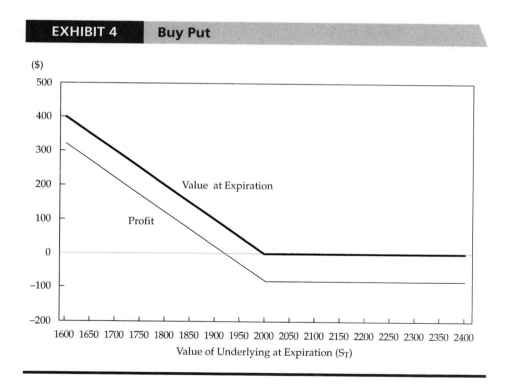

($)

Value at Expiration

Profit

Value of Underlying at Expiration (S_T)

---

[5] The maximum value and profit are not visible on the graph because we do not show S_T all the way down to zero.

In summary, for the strategy of buying a put we have

$p_T = \max(0, X - S_T)$
Value at expiration $= p_T$
Profit: $\Pi = p_T - p_0$
Maximum profit $= X - p_0$
Maximum loss $= p_0$
Breakeven: $S_T^* = X - p_0$

Now consider the *likely* outcomes for the holder of the put. In this case, the underlying must move down by almost 4 percent in one month to cover the premium. One would hardly ever expect the underlying to move down at an annual rate of almost 50 percent. Moreover, if the underlying does not move downward at all (a likely outcome given the positive expected return on most assets), the loss is 100 percent of the premium.

For the sale of a put, we simply change the sign on the value at expiration and profit. The maximum profit for the buyer becomes the maximum loss for the seller and the maximum loss for the buyer becomes the maximum profit for the seller. The breakeven for the seller is the same as for the buyer. So, for the seller,

$p_T = \max(0, X - S_T)$
Value at expiration $= -p_T$
Profit: $\Pi = -p_T + p_0$
Maximum profit $= p_0$
Maximum loss $= X - p_0$
Breakeven: $S_T^* = X - p_0$

Exhibit 5 graphs the value at expiration and the profit for this transaction.

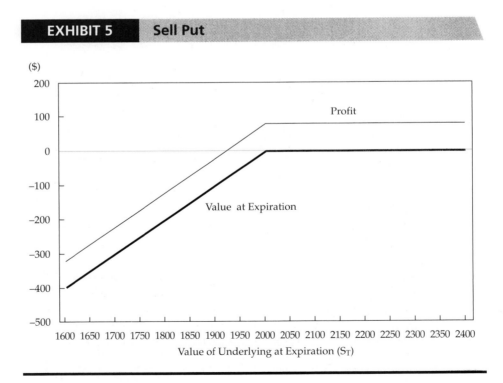

| **EXHIBIT 5** | **Sell Put** |

($)

Profit

Value at Expiration

Value of Underlying at Expiration (S_T)

EXAMPLE 2

Consider a put option selling for $4 in which the exercise price is $60 and the price of the underlying is $62.

A. Determine the value at expiration and the profit for a buyer under the following outcomes:

    i. The price of the underlying at expiration is $62.

    ii. The price of the underlying at expiration is $55.

B. Determine the value at expiration and the profit for a seller under the following outcomes:

    i. The price of the underlying at expiration is $51.

    ii. The price of the underlying at expiration is $68.

C. Determine the following:

    i. The maximum profit to the buyer (maximum loss to the seller)

    ii. The maximum loss to the buyer (maximum profit to the seller)

D. Determine the breakeven price of the underlying at expiration.

Solutions:

A. Put buyer

    i. Value at expiration = $p_T = \max(0, X - S_T) = \max(0, 60 - 62) = 0$
       $\Pi = p_T - p_0 = 0 - 4 = -4$

    ii. Value at expiration = $p_T = \max(0, X - S_T) = \max(0, 60 - 55) = 5$
       $\Pi = p_T - p_0 = 5 - 4 = 1$

B. Put seller

    i. Value at expiration = $-p_T = -\max(0, X - S_T) = -\max(0, 60 - 51) = -9$
       $\Pi = -p_T + p_0 = -9 + 4 = -5$

    ii. Value at expiration = $-p_T = -\max(0, X - S_T) = -\max(0, 60 - 68) = 0$
       $\Pi = -p_T + p_0 = 0 + 4 = 4$

C. Maximum and minimum

    i. Maximum profit to buyer (loss to seller) = $X - p_0 = 60 - 4 = 56$

    ii. Maximum loss to buyer (profit to seller) = $p_0 = 4$

D. $S_T^* = X - p_0 = 60 - 4 = 56$

It may be surprising to find that we have now covered all of the information we need to examine all of the other option strategies. We need to learn only a few basic facts. We must know the formula for the value at expiration of a call and a put. Then we need to know how to calculate the profit for the purchase of a call and a put, but that calculation is simple: the value at expiration minus the initial value. If we know these results, we can calculate the value at expiration of the option and the profit for any value of the underlying at expiration. If we can do that, we can graph the results for a range of possible values of the underlying at expiration. Because graphing can take a long time, however, it is probably helpful to learn the basic shapes of the value and profit graphs for calls and puts. Knowing

To summarize the covered call, we have the following:

Value at expiration: $V_T = S_T - \max(0, S_T - X)$
Profit: $\Pi = V_T - S_0 + c_0$
Maximum profit $= X - S_0 + c_0$
Maximum loss $= S_0 - c_0$
Breakeven: $S_T^* = S_0 - c_0$

Because of the importance and widespread use of covered calls, it is worthwhile to discuss this strategy briefly to dispel some misunderstandings. First of all, some investors who do not believe in using options fail to see that selling a call on a position in the underlying reduces the risk of that position. Options do not automatically increase risk. The option part of this strategy alone, viewed in isolation, seems an extremely risky strategy. We noted in Section 2.1.1 that selling a call without owning the stock exposes the investor to unlimited loss potential. But selling a covered call—adding a short call to a long position in a stock—reduces the overall risk. Thus, any investor who holds a stock cannot say he is too conservative to use options.

Following on that theme, however, one should also view selling a covered call as a strategy that reduces not only the risk but also the expected return compared with simply holding the underlying. Hence, one should not expect to make a lot of money writing calls on the underlying. It should be apparent that in fact the covered call writer could miss out on significant gains in a strong bull market. The compensation for this willingness to give up potential upside gains, however, is that in a bear market the losses on the underlying will be cushioned by the option premium.

It may be disconcerting to some investors to look at the profit profile of a covered call. The immediate response is to think that no one in their right mind would invest in a strategy that has significant downside risk but a limited upside. Just owning the underlying has significant downside risk, but at least there is an upside. But it is important to note that the visual depiction of the strategy, as in Exhibit 6, does not tell the whole story. It says nothing about the likelihood of certain outcomes occurring.

For example, consider the covered call example we looked at here. The underlying starts off at 2000. The maximum profit occurs when the option expires with the underlying at 2050 or above, an increase of 2.5 percent over the life of the option. We noted that this option has a one-month life. Thus, the underlying would have to increase at an approximate annual rate of at least $2.5\%(12) = 30\%$ for the covered call writer to forgo all of the upside gain. There are not many stocks, indices, or other assets in which an investor would expect the equivalent of an annual move of at least 30 percent. Such movements obviously do occur from time to time, but they are not common. Thus, covered call writers do not often give up large gains.

But suppose the underlying did move to 2050 or higher. As we previously showed, the value of the position would be 2050. Because the initial value of the position is $2000 - 59.98 = 1940.02$, the rate of return would be 5.7 percent for one month. Hence, the maximum return is still outstanding by almost anyone's standards.[7]

Many investors believe that the initial value of a covered call should not include the value of the underlying if the underlying had been previously pur-

---

[7] Of course, we are not saying that the performance reflects a positive alpha. We are saying only that the upside performance given up reflects improbably high returns, and therefore the limits on the upside potential are not too restrictive.

chased. Suppose, for example, that this asset, currently worth 2000, had been bought several months ago at 1900. It is tempting to ignore the current value of the underlying; there is no current outlay. This view, however, misses the notion of opportunity cost. If an investor currently holding an asset chooses to write a call on it, she has made a conscious decision not to sell the asset. Hence, the current value of the asset should be viewed as an opportunity cost that is just as real as the cost to an investor buying the underlying at this time.

Sellers of covered calls must make a decision about the chosen exercise price. For example, one could sell the call with an exercise price of 1950 for 108.43, or sell the call with an exercise price of 2000 for 81.75, or sell the call with an exercise price of 2050 for 59.98. The higher the exercise price, the less one receives for the call but the more room for gain on the upside. There is no clear-cut solution to deciding which call is best; the choice depends on the risk preferences of the investor.

Finally, we should note that anecdotal evidence suggests that writers of call options make small amounts of money, but make it often. The reason for this phenomenon is generally thought to be that buyers of calls tend to be overly optimistic, but that argument is fallacious. The real reason is that the expected profits come from rare but large payoffs. For example, consider the call with exercise price of 2000 and a premium of 81.75. As we learned in Section 2.1, the breakeven underlying price is 2081.75—a gain of about 4.1 percent in a one-month period, which would be an exceptional return for almost any asset. These prices were obtained using the Black–Scholes–Merton model, so they are fair prices. Yet the required underlying price movement to profit on the call is exceptional. Obviously someone buys calls, and naturally, someone must be on the other side of the transaction. Sellers of calls tend to be holders of the underlying or other calls, which reduces the enormous risk they would assume if they sold calls without any other position.[8] Hence, it is reasonable to expect that sellers of calls would make money often, because large underlying price movements occur only rarely. Following this line of reasoning, however, it would appear that sellers of calls can consistently take advantage of buyers of calls. That cannot possibly be the case. What happens is that buyers of calls make money less often than sellers, but when they do make money, the leverage inherent in call options amplifies their returns. Therefore, when call writers lose money, they tend to lose big, but most call writers own the underlying or are long other calls to offset the risk.

EXAMPLE 3

Consider a bond selling for $98 per $100 face value. A call option selling for $8 has an exercise price of $105. Answer the following questions about a covered call.

A. Determine the value of the position at expiration and the profit under the following outcomes:

   i. The price of the bond at expiration is $110.

   ii. The price of the bond at expiration is $88.

B. Determine the following:

   i. The maximum profit

   ii. The maximum loss

---

[8] Sellers of calls who hold other calls are engaged in transactions called spreads.

–500

1600 1650 1700 1750 1800 1850 1900 1950 2000 2050 2100 2150 2200 2250 2300 2350 2400
Value of Underlying at Expiration (S_T)

---

[9] Note that the graph for a protective put looks like the graph for a call. This result is due to put–call parity, as covered in Reading 73.

> **C.** Determine the breakeven bond price at expiration.
>
> **Solutions:**
> **A.** **i.** $V_T = S_T - \max(0, S_T - X) = 110 - \max(0, 110 - 105)$
> $= 110 - 110 + 105 = 105$
> $\Pi = V_T - V_0 = 105 - (S_0 - c_0) = 105 - (98 - 8) = 15$
> **ii.** $V_T = S_T - \max(0, S_T - X) = 88 - \max(0, 88 - 105) = 88 -$

To break even, the underlying must be at least as high as the amount expended up front to establish the position. In this problem, this amount is 2000 + 56.01 = 2056.01.

To summarize the protective put, we have the following:

Value at expiration: $V_T = S_T + \max(0, X - S_T)$
Profit: $\Pi = V_T - S_0 - p_0$
Maximum profit $= \infty$
Maximum loss $= S_0 + p_0 - X$
Breakeven: $S_T^* = S_0 + p_0$

A protective put can appear to be a great transaction with no drawbacks. It provides downside protection with upside potential, but let us take a closer look. First recall that this is a one-month transaction and keep in mind that the option has been priced by the Black–Scholes–Merton model and is, therefore, a fair price. The maximum loss of 106.01 is a loss of 106.01/2056.01 = 5.2%. The breakeven of 2056.01 requires an upward move of 2.8 percent, which is an annual rate of about 34 percent. From this angle, the protective put strategy does not look quite as good, but in fact, these figures simply confirm that protection against downside loss is expensive. When the protective put is fairly priced, the protection buyer must give up considerable upside potential that may not be particularly evident from just looking at a graph.

The purchase of a protective put also presents the buyer with some choices. In this example, the buyer bought the put with exercise price of 1950 for 56.01. Had he bought the put with exercise price of 2000, he would have paid 79.25. The put with exercise price of 2050 would have cost 107.39. The higher the price for which the investor wants to be able to sell the underlying, the more expensive the put will be.

The protective put is often viewed as a classic example of insurance. The investor holds a risky asset and wants protection against a loss in value. He then buys insurance in the form of the put, paying a premium to the seller of the insurance, the put writer. The exercise price of the put is like the insurance deductible because the magnitude of the exercise price reflects the risk assumed by the party holding the underlying. The higher the exercise price, the less risk assumed by the holder of the underlying and the more risk assumed by the put seller. The lower the exercise price, the more risk assumed by the holder of the underlying and the less risk assumed by the put seller. In insurance, the higher the deductible, the more risk assumed by the insured party and the less risk assumed by the insurer. Thus, a higher exercise price is analogous to a lower insurance deductible.

Like traditional insurance, this form of insurance provides coverage for a period of time. At the end of the period of time, the insurance expires and either pays off or not. The buyer of the insurance may or may not choose to renew the insurance by buying another put.

EXAMPLE 4

Consider a currency selling for $0.875. A put option selling for $0.075 has an exercise price of $0.90. Answer the following questions about a protective put.

A. Determine the value at expiration and the profit under the following outcomes:

    i. The price of the currency at expiration is $0.96.

    ii. The price of the currency at expiration is $0.75.

B. Determine the following:

    i. The maximum profit

    ii. The maximum loss

C. Determine the breakeven price of the currency at expiration.

Solutions:

A. **i.** $V_T = S_T + \max(0, X - S_T) = 0.96 + \max(0, 0.90 - 0.96) = 0.96$
$\Pi = V_T - V_0 = 0.96 - (S_0 + p_0) = 0.96 - (0.875 + 0.075) = 0.01$

    ii. $V_T = S_T + \max(0, X - S_T) = 0.75 + \max(0, 0.90 - 0.75) = 0.90$
$\Pi = V_T - V_0 = 0.90 - (S_0 + p_0) = 0.90 - (0.875 + 0.075) = -0.05$

B. **i.** Maximum profit $= \infty$

    ii. Maximum loss $= S_0 + p_0 - X = 0.875 + 0.075 - 0.90 = 0.05$

C. $S_T^* = S_0 + p_0 = 0.875 + 0.075 = 0.95$

Finally, we note that a protective put can be modified in a number of ways. One in particular is to sell a call to generate premium income to pay for the purchase of the put. This strategy is known as a collar.

SUMMARY

► The profit from buying a call is the value at expiration, $\max(0, S_T - X)$, minus c_0, the option premium. The maximum profit is infinite, and the maximum loss is the option premium. The breakeven underlying price at expiration is the exercise price plus the option premium. When one sells a call, these results are reversed.

► The profit from buying a put is the value at expiration, $\max(0, X - S_T)$, minus p_0, the option premium. The maximum profit is the exercise price minus the option premium, and the maximum loss is the option premium. The breakeven underlying price at expiration is the exercise price minus the option premium. When one sells a put, these results are reversed.

► The profit from a covered call—the purchase of the underlying and sale of a call—is the value at expiration, $S_T - \max(0, S_T - X)$, minus $S_0 - c_0$, the cost of the underlying minus the option premium. The maximum profit is the exercise price minus the original underlying price plus the option premium, and the maximum loss is the cost of the underlying less the option premium. The breakeven underlying price at expiration is the original price of the underlying minus the option premium.

► The profit from a protective put—the purchase of the underlying and a put—is the value at expiration, $S_T + \max(0, X - S_T)$, minus the cost of the underlying plus the option premium, $S_0 + p_0$. The maximum profit is infinite, and the maximum loss is the cost of the underlying plus the option premium minus the exercise price. The breakeven underlying price at expiration is the original price of the underlying plus the option premium.

PRACTICE PROBLEMS FOR READING 75

1. Consider a call option selling for $4 in which the exercise price is $50.

   A. Determine the value at expiration and the profit for a buyer under the following outcomes:

   i. The price of the underlying at expiration is $55.
   ii. The price of the underlying at expiration is $51.
   iii. The price of the underlying at expiration is $48.

   B. Determine the value at expiration and the profit for a seller under the following outcomes:

   i. The price of the underlying at expiration is $49.
   ii. The price of the underlying at expiration is $52.
   iii. The price of the underlying at expiration is $55.

   C. Determine the following:

   i. The maximum profit to the buyer (maximum loss to the seller)
   ii. The maximum loss to the buyer (maximum profit to the seller)

   D. Determine the breakeven price of the underlying at expiration.

2. Suppose you believe that the price of a particular underlying, currently selling at $99, is going to increase substantially in the next six months. You decide to purchase a call option expiring in six months on this underlying. The call option has an exercise price of $105 and sells for $7.

   A. Determine the profit under the following outcomes for the price of the underlying six months from now.

   i. $99
   ii. $104
   iii. $105
   iv. $109
   v. $112
   vi. $115

   B. Determine the breakeven price of the underlying at expiration. Check that your answer is consistent with the solution to Part A of this problem.

3. Consider a put option on the Nasdaq 100 selling for $106.25 in which the exercise price is 2100.

   A. Determine the value at expiration and the profit for a buyer under the following outcomes:

   i. The price of the underlying at expiration is 2125.
   ii. The price of the underlying at expiration is 2050.
   iii. The price of the underlying at expiration is 1950.

   B. Determine the value at expiration and the profit for a seller under the following outcomes:

   i. The price of the underlying at expiration is 1975.
   ii. The price of the underlying at expiration is 2150.

   C. Determine the following:

   i. The maximum profit to the buyer (maximum loss to the seller)
   ii. The maximum loss to the buyer (maximum profit to the seller)

   D. Determine the breakeven price of the underlying at expiration.

4. Suppose you believe that the price of a particular underlying, currently selling at $99, will decrease considerably in the next six months. You decide to purchase a put option expiring in six months on this underlying. The put option has an exercise price of $95 and sells for $5.

A. Determine the profit for you under the following outcomes for the price of the underlying six months from now:

   i. $100

   ii. $95

   iii. $93

   iv. $90

   v. $85

B. Determine the breakeven price of the underlying at expiration. Check that your answer is consistent with the solution to Part A of this problem.

C. **i.** What is the maximum profit that you can have?

   ii. At what expiration price of the underlying would this profit be realized?

5. You simultaneously purchase an underlying priced at $77 and write a call option on it with an exercise price of $80 and selling at $6.

A. What is the term commonly used for the position that you have taken?

B. Determine the value at expiration and the profit for your strategy under the following outcomes:

   i. The price of the underlying at expiration is $70.

   ii. The price of the underlying at expiration is $75.

   iii. The price of the underlying at expiration is $80.

   iv. The price of the underlying at expiration is $85.

C. Determine the following:

   i. The maximum profit

   ii. The maximum loss

   iii. The expiration price of the underlying at which you would realize the maximum profit

   iv. The expiration price of the underlying at which you would incur the maximum loss

D. Determine the breakeven price at expiration.

6. Suppose you simultaneously purchase an underlying priced at $77 and a put option on it, with an exercise price of $75 and selling at $3.

A. What is the term commonly used for the position that you have taken?

B. Determine the value at expiration and the profit for your strategy under the following outcomes:

   i. The price of the underlying at expiration is $70.

   ii. The price of the underlying at expiration is $75.

   iii. The price of the underlying at expiration is $80.

   iv. The price of the underlying at expiration is $85.

   v. The price of the underlying at expiration is $90.

C. Determine the following:

   i. The maximum profit

   ii. The maximum loss

   iii. The expiration price of the underlying at which you would incur the maximum loss

D. Determine the breakeven price at expiration.

7. The recent price per share of Dragon Vacations Inc. is $50 per share. Calls with exactly six months left to expiration are available on Dragon with strikes of $45, $50, and $55. The prices of the calls are $8.75, $6.00, and $4.00, respectively. Assume that each call contract is for 100 shares of stock and that at initiation of the strategy the investor purchases 100 shares of Dragon at the current market price. Further assume that the investor will close out the strategy in six months when the options expire, including the sale of any stock not delivered against exercise of a call, whether the stock price goes up or goes down. If the closing price of Dragon stock in six months is exactly $60, calculate the profit to a covered call using the $50 strike call.

  A. −$100

  B. $400

  C. $600

  D. $1,600

8. The recent price per share of Win Big Inc. is €50 per share. Verna Hillsborough buys 100 shares at €50. To protect against a fall in price, Verna Hillsborough buys one put, covering 100 shares of Win Big, at a strike price of €40. The put premium is €1 per share. If Win Big closes at €45 per share at the expiration of the put and Hillsborough sells her shares at €45, Hillsborough's profit from the stay/put is *closest* to

  A. −€1,100.

  B. −€600.

  C. €0.

  D. €900.

ANALYSIS OF ALTERNATIVE INVESTMENTS

TOPIC LEVEL LEARNING OUTCOME

The candidate should be able to demonstrate a working knowledge of the analysis of alternative investments, including mutual funds, exchange traded funds, real estate, private equity, venture capital, hedge funds, closely held companies, distressed securities, and commodities and commodity derivatives.

4⅝ 4⅜
5½   5½ —   ⅜
5½   21¾₁₆ —   ⅛
20⅝ 21¾₁₆ —   ⅛
17⅜ 18⅛ +   ⅞
16½ 6½   6½ —   ½
7¼   6½   6½ —
15⁄16   3¹⁄32 —   ⅛
9⁄16   9⁄16
⁷⁄32 7¹³⁄16 7¹⁵⁄16
7¹⁵⁄16 7¹³⁄16 7¹⁵⁄16
25⅝ 2¹¹⁄32 2½ +
546   2¾   2¼   2¼
327   2¾   2¼   2¼
5⅛   12¹⁄16 11⅜   11¾ +
87   33¾   33   33¹⁄16 —
502   25⅝   24⁹⁄16 25⅝ +
833   12   11⅝   11⅞ +
16   10½   10½   10½ —
78   15⅞   15¹³⁄16 15⅞ —
4608 9¹⁄16   8¼   8⅝ +
430   11¼   10⅛   10⅛
4⅞

STUDY SESSION 18
ALTERNATIVE INVESTMENTS

Due to diversification benefits and higher expectations of investment returns, investors are increasingly turning to alternative investments. This study session describes the common types of alternative investments, methods for their valuation, unique risks and opportunities associated with them, and the relation between alternative investments and traditional investments.

Although finding a single definition of an "alternative" investment is difficult, certain features (e.g., limited liquidity, infrequent valuations, and unique legal structures) are typically associated with alternative investments. This study session discusses these features and how to evaluate their impact on expected returns and investment decisions in more detail. The reading provides an overview of the major categories of alternative investments, including real estate, private equity, venture capital, hedge funds, closely held companies, distressed securities, and commodities.

Each one of these categories has several unique characteristics, and the readings discuss valuation methods for illiquid assets (such as direct real estate or closely held companies), performance measures for private equity and venture capital investments, differences between various hedge fund strategies, and implementation vehicles for investments in alternative assets.

READING ASSIGNMENT

Reading 76   Alternative Investments

LEARNING OUTCOMES

Reading 76: Alternative Investments
The candidate should be able to:

a. differentiate between an open-end and a closed-end fund, and explain how net asset value of a fund is calculated and the nature of fees charged by investment companies;

173

2.2 Fund Management Fees

Investment companies charge fees, some as one-time charges and some as annual charges. By setting an initial selling price above the NAV, the unmanaged company charges a fee for the effort of setting up the fund. For managed funds, loads are simply sales commissions charged at purchase (front-end) as a percentage of the investment. A redemption fee (back-end load) is a charge to exit the fund. Redemption fees discourage quick trading turnover and are often set up so that the fees decline the longer the shares are held (in this case, the fees are sometimes called contingent deferred sales charges). Loads and redemption fees provide sales incentives but not portfolio management performance incentives.

Annual charges are composed of operating expenses including management fees, administrative expenses, and continuing distribution fees (12b-1 fees in the U.S.). The ratio of operating expenses to average assets is often referred to as the fund's "expense ratio." Distribution fees are fees paid back to the party that arranged the initial sale of the shares and are thus another type of sales incentive fee. Only management fees can be considered a portfolio management incentive fee. Example 1 is an illustration of the effects of investment company fees on fund performance.

EXAMPLE 1

Investment Company Fees: Effects on Performance

An investor is considering the purchase of TriGroup International Equity Fund (TRIEF) for her portfolio. Like many U.S.-based mutual funds today, TRIEF has more than one class of shares. Although all classes hold the same portfolio of securities, each class has a different expense structure. This particular mutual fund has three classes of shares, A, B, and C. The expenses of these classes are summarized in the following table:

Expense Comparison for Three Classes of TRIEF

	Class A	Class B[a]	Class C
Sales charge (load) on purchases	3%	None	None
Deferred sales charge (load) on redemptions	None	5% in the first year, declining by 1 percentage point each year thereafter	1% for the initial two years

	Class A	Class B[a]	Class C
Annual expenses:			
Distribution fee	0.25%	0.50%	0.50%
Management fee	0.75%	0.75%	0.75%
Other expenses	0.25%	0.25%	0.25%
	1.25%	1.50%	1.50%

[a]Class B shares automatically convert to Class A shares 72 months (6 years) after purchase, reducing future annual expenses.

The time horizon associated with the investor's objective in purchasing TRIEF is six years. She expects equity investments with risk characteristics similar to TRIEF to earn 8 percent per year, and she decides to make her selection of fund share class based on an assumed 8 percent return each year, gross of any of the expenses given in the preceding table.

A. Based on only the information provided here, determine the class of shares that is most appropriate for this investor. Assume that expense percentages given will be constant at the given values. Assume that the deferred sales charges are computed on the basis of NAV.

B. Suppose that, as a result of an unforeseen liquidity need, the investor needs to liquidate her investment at the end of the first year. Assume an 8 percent rate of return has been earned. Determine the relative performance of the three fund classes, and interpret the results.

C. Based on your answers to A and B, discuss the appropriateness of these share classes as it relates to an investor's time horizon; for example, a one-, six- and ten-year horizon.

Solutions:

A. To address this question, we compute the terminal value of $1 invested at the end of year 6. The share class with the highest terminal value, net of all expenses, would be the most appropriate for this investor, as all classes are based on the same portfolio and thus have the same portfolio risk characteristics.

Class A. $1 \times (1 - 0.03) = \$0.97$ is the amount available for investment at $t = 0$, after paying the front-end sales charge. Because this amount grows at 8 percent for six years, reduced by annual expenses of 0.0125, the terminal value per $1 invested after six years is $\$0.97 \times 1.08^6 \times (1 - 0.0125)^6 = \$1.4274$.

Class B. After six years, $1 invested grows to $\$1 \times 1.08^6 \times (1 - 0.015)^6 = \$1.4493$. According to the table, the deferred sales charge disappears after year 5; therefore, the terminal value is $1.4493.

Class C. After six years, $1 invested grows to $\$1 \times 1.08^6 \times (1 - 0.015)^6 = \$1.4493$. There is no deferred sales charge in the sixth year, so $1.4493 is the terminal value.

In summary, the ranking by terminal value after six years is Class B and Class C ($1.4493), followed by Class A ($1.4274). Class B or Class C appears to be the most appropriate for this investor with a six-year horizon.

B. For Class A shares, the terminal value per $1 invested is $\$0.97 \times 1.08 \times (1 - 0.0125) = \$1.0345$. For Class B shares, it is $\$1 \times 1.08 \times (1 - 0.015) \times (1 - 0.05) = \$1.0106$, reflecting a 5 percent redemption charge; for Class C shares, it is $\$1 \times 1.08 \times (1 - 0.015) \times (1 - 0.01) = \$1.0532$, reflecting a 1 percent redemption charge. Thus, the ranking is Class C ($1.0532), Class A ($1.0345), and Class B ($1.0106).

C. Although Class B is appropriate given a six-year investment horizon, it is a costly choice if the fund shares need to be liquidated soon after investment. That eventuality would need to be assessed by the investor we are discussing. Class B, like Class A, is more attractive the longer the holding period, in general. Because Class C has higher annual expenses than Class A and Class B (after six years), it becomes less attractive the longer the holding period, in general. After 10 years Class B shares would return $1 \times 1.08^{10} \times (1 - 0.015)^6 \times (1 - 0.0125)^4 = \$1.8750$, reflecting conversion to Class A after six years. Class C would return $\$1 \times 1.08^{10} \times (1 - 0.0150)^{10} = \$1.8561$. Class A shares would return the smallest amount, $\$0.97 \times 1.08^{10} \times (1 - 0.0125)^{10} = \$1.8466$. Though Class A underperforms Class C for a ten-year investment horizon, one could verify that Class A outperforms Class C for an investment horizon of 13 years or more. Also, in practice, the sales charge for Class A shares may be lower for purchases over certain sizes, making them more attractive in such comparisons.

2.3 Investment Strategies

Investment companies primarily invest in equity. Investment strategies can be characterized as style, sector, index, global, or stable value strategies. Style strategies focus on the underlying characteristics common to certain investments. Growth is a different style than value, and large capitalization investing is a different style than small stock investing. A growth strategy may focus on high price-to-earnings stocks, and a value strategy on low price-to-earnings stocks. Clearly, there are many styles.[2] A sector investment fund focuses on a particular industry. An index fund tracks an index. In the simplest implementation, the fund owns the securities in the index in exactly the same proportion as the market value weights of those securities in the index. A global fund includes securities from around the world and might keep portfolio weights similar to world market capitalization weights. An international fund is one that does not include the home country's securities, whereas a global fund includes the securities from the home country. A stable value fund invests in securities such as short-term fixed income instruments and guaranteed investment contracts which are guaranteed by the issuing insurance company and pay principal and a set rate of interest.

2.4 Exchange Traded Funds

Exchange traded funds (ETFs) are index-based investment products that allow investors to buy or sell exposure to an index through a single financial instrument. ETFs are funds that trade on a stock market like shares of any individual companies. Gastineau (2001) gives a good introduction to ETFs. They can be traded at any time during market hours, can be sold short or margined. But they are shares of a portfolio, not of an individual company. They represent shares of ownership in either **open-end funds** or unit investment trusts that hold portfolios

---

[2] See, for example, Richard Bernstein, *Style Investing*, Wiley, 1995, and Richard Michaud, *Investment Styles, Market Anomalies, and Global Stock Selection*, The Research Foundation of AIMR, 1999.

of stocks or bonds in custody, which are designed to track the price and yield performance of their underlying indexes—broad market, sector/industry, single country/region (multiple countries), or fixed income. Although many investors regard ETFs simply as a form of diversified equity investment, their novelty and legal specificity suggested their inclusion in this reading.

2.4.1 Recent Developments of ETFs

ETFs first appeared as TIP 35 (Toronto Index Participation Fund) in Canada in 1989, and appeared in the United States in 1993 with the introduction of Standard & Poor's 500 (S&P 500) Depositary Receipts. The first Asian ETF, the Hong Kong Tracker Fund, was launched in 1999. The first ETF launched in Europe, Euro STOXX 50, did not appear until 2000. Japan did not trade ETFs until 2001, when eight were listed. Their popularity has grown so quickly that they have become one of the most successful financial products of the decade.

According to Merrill Lynch (2002), there were 102 ETFs listed in the United States as of June 2002, 14 in Canada, 106 in Europe, and approximately 24 in Asia, including Japan—a total of 246.[3] Total global assets under management approached $130 billion, 75 percent of which are invested in U.S.-listed products. Although ETFs had a slow trading start in the United States, the trading volume of ETFs has grown rapidly in the last few years. According to Goldman Sachs (2002), the total shares outstanding for U.S. ETFs amounts to 1.9 million shares, with total assets of $92 billion, while average daily trading volume reached $7.0 billion, or 146.6 million shares per day, in mid-2002. ETFs based on international indexes have shown a strong growth and now represent almost 10 percent of total U.S.-listed ETF assets. The latest additions to the universe of ETFs are fixed-income ETFs, which started trading in July 2002 on the American Stock Exchange.

In Europe, the first ETF was launched by Merrill Lynch in April 2000 to track the Euro STOXX 50, which is the most actively replicated index in Europe. Listings of multiple ETFs on the same underlying index are common in Europe. In general, ETFs traded in Europe fall into four categories: single-country ETFs, regional ETFs based mostly on some pan-European or Eurozone indexes, European-sector ETFs, and global ETFs. The most popular ETFs are based on Euro STOXX 50, CAC 40, and the DAX. Although assets under management ($8 billion in mid-2002) and average daily volumes are still small compared with U.S. figures, the growth in terms of volume and number of outstanding products has been impressive. The daily trading volume grew from $6 million in the third quarter of 2000 to over $250 million in the first quarter of 2002 (Mussavian and Hirsch, 2002).

In Asia, the growth in ETFs comes primarily from Japan. Merrill Lynch (2002) estimates that the total assets under management in Asian ETFs were in excess of $13.9 billion in mid-2002.

2.4.2 ETF Structure

The usual ETF structure adopted worldwide is that of open-end funds with special characteristics, such as the "in-kind" process for creation and redemption of shares described subsequently (see Gastineau, 2001). Details of the legal structure vary depending on the country where the ETF is incorporated. In the United States, ETFs have adopted three different legal structures:

---

[3] Complete listings of ETFs can be found at www.indexfunds.com.

▶ *Managed investment companies:* Managed investment companies are open-ended investment companies registered under the Investment Company Act of 1940. They offer the most flexible ETF structure. The index can be tracked using various techniques, such as holding only a sample of the underlying securities in the index, lending of securities, and trading in derivatives. Dividends paid on the securities can be immediately reinvested in the fund. Sector SPDRs, iShares, and WEBS use this legal structure.

▶ *Unit investment trusts:* Unit investment trusts (UITs) are also registered investment companies, but they operate under more constraints, because they do not have a manager per se (but trustees). UITs are required to be fully invested in all underlying securities forming the index and must hold dividends received on securities in cash until the ETF pays a dividend to shareholders. This could result in a slight cash drag on performance. UITs are not permitted to lend securities and do not generally use derivatives. S&P 500 SPDR, Midcap 400 SPDR and NASDAQ-100 QQQQ use this legal structure.

▶ *Grantor trusts:* Grantor trusts are not registered investment companies. Accordingly, owning a grantor trust is substantially similar to holding a basket of securities. A grantor trust often takes the form of an American Depositary Receipt (ADR) and trades as such. Because a grantor trust is fully invested in the basket of securities, no investment discretion is exercised by the trust. This is basically an unmanaged (and unregistered) investment company with a limited life. The trust passes all dividends on the underlying securities to shareholders as soon as practicable. Securities lending and use of derivatives are generally not practiced. HOLDRs use this legal structure. Grantor trusts are a structure that allows investors to indirectly own an unmanaged basket of stocks rather than tracking an index, and some do not classify them as ETFs.

We will now introduce the unique "in-kind" creation and redemption process used by open-end and UIT ETFs. This in-kind process is a major distinguishing feature of ETFs. Creation/redemption units are created in large multiples of individual ETF shares, for example, 50,000 shares. These units are available to exchange specialists (*authorized participants* or *creation agents*) that are authorized by the fund and who will generally act as market makers on the individual ETF shares. The fund publishes the index **tracking portfolio** that it is willing to accept for in-kind transactions. When there is excess demand for ETF shares, an authorized participant will create a *creation unit* (a large block of ETF shares) by depositing with the trustee of the fund the specified portfolio of stocks used to track the index. In return, the authorized participant will receive ETF shares that can be sold to investors on the stock market. The redemption process is the same but in reverse. If there is an excess number of ETF shares sold by investors, an authorized participant will decide to redeem ETF shares; it will do so by exchanging with the fund a *redemption unit* (a large block of ETF shares) for a portfolio of stocks held by the fund and used to track the index. Exhibit 1 depicts the ETF structure and the creation/redemption process.

As opposed to traditional open-end funds, the in-kind redemption means that no capital gain will be realized in the fund's portfolio on redemption. If the redemption were in cash, the fund would have to sell stocks held in the fund's portfolio. If their price had appreciated, the fund would realize a capital gain, and the tax burden would have to be passed to all existing fund shareholders. This is not the case with ETFs. This in-kind transfer for redemptions does not create a tax burden for the remaining ETF shareholders under current U.S. tax law, unlike the capital gains distributions on traditional mutual fund shareholders that could result from the sale of securities to meet redemption demand.[4] As in any **open-end fund**, individual ETF shareholders[5] can require in-cash redemption based on the NAV. Redemption in cash by individual ETF shareholders is discouraged in two ways:

▶ Redemption is based on the NAV computed a couple of days after the shareholder commits to redemption. So, the redemption value is unknown when the investor decides to redeem. This is a common feature of mutual funds.

▶ A large fee is assessed on in-cash redemptions.

It is more advantageous for individual shareholders to sell their shares on the market than to redeem them in cash. Arbitrage[6] by authorized participants ensures that the listed price is close to the fund's NAV, and the sale can take place immediately based on observed share prices and at a low transaction cost. Authorized participants maintain a market in the ETF share by posting bid-and-ask prices with a narrow spread, or by entering in an electronic order book buy-and-sell limit orders, which play the same role. The transaction cost of ETFs can be estimated as the sum of the commission charged by the broker plus half this bid–ask spread.

EXHIBIT 1	Creation/Redemption Process of Exchange Traded Funds

In comparing the ETF structure presented in Exhibit 1 with that of the traditional mutual fund structure, it is clear that market makers in the ETF structure play an instrumental role in the creation and redemption process. In the traditional mutual fund structure, an increase in demand for the shares of the mutual fund is met by the mutual fund, which simply issues new shares to the investor, and the fund manager will take the cash to the capital markets and buy securities appropriate to the fund's objective. When the customer wants to sell the mutual fund shares, the fund manager may need to raise cash by selling securities back to the capital markets. In contrast, when a customer wants to buy ETF shares, the order is not directed to the fund but to the market makers on the exchange. The market maker will exchange ETF shares for cash with the customer (via broker/dealer) and, when necessary, replenish the supply of ETFs through the creation process outlined earlier.

---

[4] As pointed out by Chamberlain and Jordan (2002), there are situations in which capital gains distributions are generated for the ETF, such as capital gains resulting from selling securities directly to the capital markets due to an index reconstitution. Thus, zero capital gains distributions are not guaranteed.

[5] But authorized participants commit to redeem only in kind.

[6] ETFs usually publish an indicative intraday NAV every 15 seconds that is available from major data providers.

2.4.3 Advantages/Disadvantages of ETFs

ETFs are used by a wide spectrum of investors, both individual and institutional, in a wide variety of investment strategies. This is because ETFs have the following advantages:

▶ Diversification can be obtained easily with a single ETF transaction. With equity-oriented ETFs, investors can gain instant exposure to different market capitalizations, style (value or growth), sector or industries, countries or geographic regions. With fixed income ETFs, they can gain exposure to different maturity segments and bond market sectors. Thus, ETFs provide a convenient way to diversify.

▶ Although ETFs represent interests in a portfolio of securities, they trade similarly to a stock on an organized exchange. For example, ETFs can be sold short and also bought on margin.

▶ ETFs trade throughout the whole trading day at market prices that are updated continuously, rather than only trading once a day at closing market prices, as do the traditional open-end mutual funds.

▶ For many ETFs, there exist futures and options contracts on the same index, which is convenient for risk management.

▶ Portfolio holdings of ETFs are transparent. The ETF sponsor publishes the constituents of the fund on a daily basis. This should closely resemble the constituents of the underlying index. This is in contrast to other funds, for which the manager publishes only the list of assets in the fund from time to time.

▶ ETFs are cost effective. There are no load fees. Moreover, because the ETFs are passively managed, the expense ratio (which includes management fee for open-end funds, trustee fee for UITs, and custody fee for HOLDRs) can be kept low relative to actively managed funds. The expense ratio is comparable to that of an index mutual fund. For example, management fee can be as low as 8 basis points for the most successful U.S. ETFs, and up to 90 basis points for sector and international products (Mussavian and Hirsch, 2002). ETFs have a cost advantage over traditional mutual funds because there is no shareholder accounting at the fund level.

▶ ETFs have an advantage over closed-end index funds because their structure can prevent a significant premium/discount. Although supply and demand determine the market price of an ETF just like any other security, arbitrage helps keep the traded price of an ETF much more in line with its underlying value. By simultaneously buying (or selling) the ETF basket of securities and selling (or buying) the ETF shares in the secondary market, and creating (or redeeming) ETF shares to be delivered against the sale, market makers can capture the price discrepancy and make an arbitrage profit. Thus, UIT and open-end ETFs have the capability to avoid trading at large premiums and discounts to the NAVs. This is in contrast to closed-end index funds, which offer a fixed supply of shares, and as demand changes, they frequently trade at appreciable discounts from—and sometimes premiums to—their NAVs.

▶ The exposure to capital gains distribution taxes is lower than for traditional funds, so the consequences of other shareholders' redemptions are limited. As mentioned, capital gains resulting from in-kind transfer for redemptions do not create a tax burden for the remaining ETF shareholders. For this reason, capital gains tax liability is expected to be lower for ETF shareholders than for mutual fund shareholders.

▶ Dividends are reinvested immediately for open-end ETFs (but not for UIT ETFs), whereas for index mutual funds, timing of dividend reinvestment varies.

However, ETFs are not necessarily the most efficient alternative for investing in a market segment.

▶ In many countries, actively traded ETFs track a narrow-based market index, including only stocks with large market capitalization. So, no ETF is available for mid or low market-cap stocks. This is not the case in the United States, where a variety of ETF products trade actively.

▶ Many investors do not require the intraday trading opportunity provided by ETFs, because they have a long investment horizon.

▶ Some ETFs do not have large trading volumes and the bid–ask spread can be quite large. For example, some U.S. ETFs based on some sector indexes or on some foreign indexes (e.g., emerging markets) do not trade actively, and directly investing in a managed fund can be a less costly alternative, especially for large investors. Sector and international ETFs have an expense ratio that can be substantial (close to 1 percent) compared with that of a managed portfolio.

▶ For large institutional investors, the alternative to international ETFs is to invest directly in an indexed, or actively managed, international portfolio; the costs could be less, and the tax situation equivalent or better.

2.4.4 Types of ETFs

ETFs can be grouped by investment category, based on their investment target (broad domestic market index, style, sector/industry, country or region). For a given investment target, ETFs can be created based on different indexes of the same market, as well as by different sponsors. The number of ETFs keeps growing, and the diversity of investment targets increases, although all ETFs launched are not successful. We only cite some notable examples under each of the following categories:

▶ *Broad domestic market index:* In many countries, the most active ETFs are those launched on the major local stock index. Hong Kong Tracker Fund was the first ETF listed in Asia and the largest ever IPO in Asia excluding Japan. In Japan, Nikkei 225 and TOPIX ETFs have amassed significant assets under management, and there are several competing sponsors offering ETFs on the same indexes. In Europe, ETFs based on the French CAC 40 index and the German DAX 30 index are, by far, the most actively traded. In the United States, there are many market indexes followed by investors, so there are many competing ETFs; the most notable examples in this category include S&P 500 Depositary Receipts (SPDRs or "spiders"), Nasdaq-100 Index Tracking Stock (QQQQ), and Diamonds Trust Series (DIAs or "diamonds"). There are also ETFs based on very broad U.S. market indexes, such as the Russell 1000, Russell 3000, or Wilshire 5000 indexes. It is fair to say that ETFs based on local market indexes now exist in most countries, including in many emerging countries.

▶ *Style:* Some ETFs track a specific investment style. This type of ETF is mostly found in the United States, because investors from other countries are less accustomed to style investing. ETFs exist on growth and value indexes developed by S&P/BARRA and Russell. Investors can also find ETFs specialized by market capitalization (large, mid, and small cap).

▶ *Sector or industry:* Some ETFs track a sector index or invest in baskets of stocks from specific industry sectors, including consumer, cyclicals, energy, financial, heath care, industrials, insurance, materials, media, staples, technology, telecommunications, transportation, and utilities. Sector and industry ETFs can be found in the United States, Europe, and Japan. Many European funds track pan-European or global-sector indexes. In the United States, industry HOLDRs offer a series of investment portfolios that are based not on an index, but on a basket of 20 to 50 companies in the same industry.

▶ *Country or region (multiple countries):* A fast-growing segment of the ETF market is funds tracking foreign-country indexes and regional indexes. In the United States, iShares are indexed to several developed and emerging equity markets, as well as to international indexes such as MSCI Europe and EAFE. Fresco introduced on the NYSE an ETF indexed on the Euro STOXX 50 index of the major 50 stocks of the Eurozone. Country and regional ETFs have also been launched in Europe and Japan. Again, several sponsors are competing for products on the same international indexes.

▶ *Fixed income:* This category is the latest addition to the universe of ETFs, and mostly in the United States. They have had limited success so far.

International ETFs have distinguishing features. An ETF indexed on some less-liquid emerging market is bound to have high bid–ask spreads. Managing an ETF on a broad international index means holding stocks from numerous countries with different custodial arrangement and time zones. Again, the bid–ask spreads are bound to be larger than for plain-vanilla ETFs. But the size (assets under management) of the ETF is an important factor influencing costs. The effect of non-overlapping time zones should be taken into account when comparing the ETF price and its NAV. Take the example of an ETF on a Japanese stock index, traded in New York. During Wall Street opening hours, the Tokyo stock market is closed. The NAV available in the morning in America is based on the closing prices in Tokyo several hours before New York opened. Except for currency fluctuations, the NAV will remain unchanged because Tokyo is closed throughout the New York trading session. However, the ETF price will be affected by expectations about future stock prices in Tokyo, so it could differ significantly from the official NAV. This is not an inefficiency and there are no arbitrage opportunities, because the NAV is stale and does not correspond to current market pricing.

2.4.5 Risks in ETFs

Listed next are the major risks faced by ETFs. They, however, do not affect all ETFs to the same extent. For example, market risk, trading risk, and tracking error risk affect all ETFs, while sector risk, currency risk, and country risk may affect sector and country ETFs. Likewise, derivatives risk affects only those funds that employ derivatives in their investment strategies. In addition, different ETFs may face risks that are unique to the fund (not discussed in this reading).

▶ *Market risk:* ETF shareholders are subject to risks similar to those of holders of other diversified portfolios. The NAV of the ETF will change with changes in the market index tracked by the fund.

▶ *Asset class/sector risk:* Some ETFs invest in some market segment. The returns from the type of securities in which an ETF invests may underperform returns from the general securities markets or different asset classes. For example, the performance of a sector ETF may be susceptible to any single economic, market, political, or regulatory occurrence. Thus, a sector ETF also may be adversely affected by the performance of that specific sector or group of industries on which it is based. This risk is directly implied by the investment strategy offered by the fund.

▶ *Trading risk:* Although an ETF is designed to make it likely that it will trade close to its NAV, impediments to the securities markets may result in trading prices that differ, sometimes significantly, from NAV. Moreover, there is no assurance that an active trading market will always exist for the ETF on the exchange, so the bid–ask spread can be large for some ETFs. The overall depth and liquidity of the secondary market also may fluctuate.

▶ *Tracking error risk:* Although ETFs are designed to provide investment results that generally correspond to the price and yield performance of their respective underlying indexes, the funds/trusts may not be able to exactly replicate the performance of the indexes because of fund/trust expenses and other factors. Tracking risk comes from trading risk (the ETF market price deviates from its NAV), but also from the fact that the ETF NAV differs from the index value.

▶ *Derivatives risk:* ETFs that invest in index futures contracts and other derivatives to track an index are subject to additional risks that accrue to derivatives, for example, counterparty credit risk and higher leverage.

▶ *Currency risk and country risk:* ETFs that are based on international indexes may involve risk of capital loss from unfavorable fluctuations in currency values or from economic and political instability in other nations. ETFs invested in emerging markets bear greater risk of market shutdown and of the imposition of capital controls than those typically found in a developed market. Country risk also includes the risk of expropriation. It could be that foreign investors are discriminated against, so that the return of an ETF will significantly underperform the local market index return achieved by a local investor.

2.4.6 Applications of ETFs

ETFs can be used in a wide variety of investment strategies. Following are some suggested popular applications:

▶ *Implementing asset allocation:* ETFs can be used to effect asset allocation among baskets of stocks and bonds at either the strategic or the tactical level.

▶ *Diversifying sector/industry exposure:* ETFs on broad market indexes can be used to diversify away the sector- or industry-specific event risks borne in an otherwise undiversified portfolio. Such ETF exposure is a natural complement to an investment strategy of holding only a few attractive stocks.

▶ *Gaining exposure to international markets:* Money managers can quickly and easily purchase ETFs for instant and extensive international exposure to a single country or multiple countries within a geographic region, compared with the expense and difficulty of assembling a portfolio of foreign securities.

▶ ***Equitizing cash****:* By investing in ETFs, money managers can put idle cash to work temporarily while determining where to invest for the longer term. For example, a fund manager using the Nikkei 225 as its benchmark could invest cash inflows into one of the ETFs tied to this benchmark before he decides which stocks to buy. This can minimize cash drag or benchmark risk. It is a convenient alternative to buying futures contract on the market index.

independent (right-hand side) variables are the ratings for each of the characteristics. The estimated slope coefficients are the valuation of each characteristic in the transaction price. The result is a benchmark monetary value associated with each characteristic's rating. It is then possible to estimate the selling price of a specific property by taking into account its rating on each feature. Although this has become a standard technique in residential property appraisal, it has also been applied to income producing property.[10]

EXAMPLE 2

Sales Comparison Approach: Hedonic Price Model

A real estate company has prepared a simple hedonic model to value houses in a specific area. A summary list of the house's characteristics that can affect pricing are:

- the number of main rooms,
- the surface area of the garden,
- the presence of a swimming pool, and
- the distance to a shopping center.

A statistical analysis of a large number of recent transactions in the area allowed the company to estimate the following slope coefficients:

Characteristics	Units	Slope Coefficient in Pounds per Unit
Number of rooms	Number	20,000
Surface area of the garden	Square feet	5
Swimming pool	0 or 1	20,000
Distance to shopping center	In miles	−10,000

A typical house in the area has five main rooms, a garden of 10,000 square feet, a swimming pool, and a distance of one mile to the nearest shopping center. The transaction price for a typical house was £160,000.

You wish to value a house that has seven rooms, a garden of 10,000 square feet, a swimming pool, and a distance of two miles to the nearest shopping center. What is the appraisal value based on this sales comparison approach of hedonic price estimation?

Solution: The appraised value is given by the equation

$$
\begin{aligned}
\text{Value} &= 20{,}000 \times (\text{\# Rooms}) + 5 \times (\text{Garden surface}) + 20{,}000 \times \\
&\quad (\text{Pool}) - 10{,}000 \times (\text{Distance to shopping center}) \\
&= 20{,}000 \times 7 + 5 \times 10{,}000 + 20{,}000 \times 1 - 10{,}000 \times 2 \\
&= £190{,}000
\end{aligned}
$$

---

[10] See Söderberg (2002), pp. 157–180.

This specific house has an appraised value of £190,000. Compared to the typical house in the area, it has two more rooms but is one mile farther from the nearest shopping center.

3.2.3 The Income Approach

The income approach to real estate valuation values property using a perpetuity discount type of model. The perpetuity is the annual net operating income (NOI). This perpetual stream is discounted at a market required rate of return (the market capitalization or cap rate). NOI is gross potential income minus expenses, which include estimated vacancy and collection losses, insurance, taxes, utilities, and repairs and maintenance. Technically, the market cap rate is the rate used by the market in recent transactions to capitalize future income into a present market value. For a constant and perpetual stream of annual NOI, we have

$$\text{Appraisal price} = \frac{\text{NOI}}{\text{Market cap rate}}$$

And the market cap rate is calculated on the benchmark transactions as

$$\text{Market cap rate} = \frac{\text{Benchmark NOI}}{\text{Benchmark transaction price}}$$

Benchmark may refer to a single comparable property or the median or mean of several comparable properties, with any appropriate adjustments.

It must be stressed that the income approach makes the simplifying assumption of a constant and perpetual amount of annual income. The income approach can also be adjusted for the special cases of a constant growth rate in rentals or a constant growth rate in rentals coupled with long-term leases. Valuation with a constant growth rate in rentals parallels the constant growth dividend discount model. Inflation could make NOI grow at the inflation rate over time. As long as inflation can be passed through, it will not affect valuation, because the market cap rate also incorporates the inflation rate. In the long-term lease case, the growth in rentals is not fully reflected in the NOI growth rate. The rent remains fixed over the term of the lease, while costs grow at the inflation rate. This is analogous to the inflation pass-through question raised in equity valuation (see Reading 58, Volume 5). If expected inflation will cause operating expenses to rise, how much of the inflation can the owner pass through to the tenants? Longer lease terms delay the pass-through. Another limitation of this approach is that all calculations are performed before tax.

EXAMPLE 3

The Income Approach

An investor wants to evaluate an apartment complex using the income approach. Recent sales in the area consist of an office building and an apartment complex. He gathers the following data on the apartment complex, as well as on recent sales in the area. All income items are on an annual basis. According to the income approach, what is the value of the apartment complex?

is sometimes called a fixed-income arbitrage fund. Other types of arbitrage make use of complex securities with option-like clauses, such as convertibles, warrants, or collateralized mortgage obligations (CMOs). Among the various techniques used by market-neutral funds are

► equity long/short,
► fixed-income hedging,
► pairs trading,
► warrant arbitrage,
► mortgage arbitrage,
► convertible bond arbitrage,
► closed-end fund arbitrage, and
► statistical arbitrage.

It must be stressed that despite their labels ("arbitrage," "neutral"), these funds are not riskless because hedges can never be perfect. Loss can be incurred if the model used is imperfect, and can be high because hedge funds tend to be highly leveraged.

EXAMPLE 7

Long/Short Market-Neutral Strategy

A hedge fund has a capital of $10 million and invests in a market-neutral long/short strategy on the British equity market. Shares can be borrowed from a primary broker with a cash margin deposit equal to 18 percent of the value of the shares. No additional costs are charged to borrow the shares. The hedge fund has drawn up a list of shares regarded as under-valued (list A) and a list of shares regarded as overvalued (list B). The hedge fund expects that shares in list A will outperform the British index by 5 percent over the year, while shares in list B will underperform the British index by 5 percent over the year. The hedge fund wishes to retain a cash cushion of $1 million for unforeseen events. What specific investment actions would you suggest?

Solution: The hedge fund would sell short shares from list B and use the proceeds to buy shares from list A for an equal amount such that the overall beta of the portfolio with respect to the market equals zero. Some capital needs to be invested in the margin deposit. The hedge funds could take long/short positions for $50 million:

► Keep $1 million in cash.
► Deposit $9 million in margin.
► Borrow $50 million of Shares B from a broker, and sell those shares short.
► Use the sale proceeds to buy $50 million worth of shares A.

The positions in shares A and B are established so that the portfolio's beta is zero. Also, note that the invested assets of $50 million equals $9 million divided by 0.18. The ratio of invested assets to equity capital is roughly 5:1.

If expectations materialize, the return for investors in the hedge fund will be high. The long/short portfolio of shares should have a gain over the year of 10 percent on $50 million, whatever the movement in the general market index. This $5 million gain will translate into an annual return before fees of 50 percent on the invested capital of $10 million. This calculation does not take into account the return on invested cash ($1 million) and assumes that the dividends on long positions will offset dividends on short positions.

▶ *Global macro funds* take bets on the direction of a market, a currency, an interest rate, a commodity, or any macroeconomic variable. These funds tend to be highly leveraged and make extensive use of derivatives. There are many subgroups in this category, including the following:

　▶ *Futures funds* (or *managed futures funds*) are commodity pools that include commodity trading advisor funds (CTAs). They take bets on directional moves in the positions they hold (long and short) in a single asset class, such as currency, fixed income, or commodities and tend to use many actively traded futures contracts.

　▶ *Emerging-market funds* primarily take bets on all types of securities in emerging markets. The securities markets in these economies are typically less efficient and less liquid than those in developed markets. There typically is not an organized lending market for securities, so it is difficult to sell short most issues. Emerging market investments tend to be fairly volatile and greatly influenced by economic and political factors.

▶ *Event-driven funds* take bets on some event specific to a company or a security. Typically the events are special situations or opportunities to capitalize on price fluctuations. These include the following, among others:

　▶ *Distressed securities funds:* The manager invests in the debt and/or equity of companies having financial difficulty. Such companies are generally in bankruptcy reorganization or are emerging from reorganization or appear likely to declare bankruptcy in the near future. Because of their distressed situations, the manager can buy such companies' securities at deeply discounted prices. The manager stands to make money should the company successfully reorganize and return to profitability. The manager may take short positions in companies whose situations he believes will worsen, rather than improve, in the short term.

　▶ *Risk arbitrage in mergers and acquisitions:* Before the effective date of a merger, the stock of the acquired company will typically sell at a discount to its acquisition value as officially announced. A hedge fund manager simultaneously buys stock in a company being acquired and sells stock in its acquirers. Even though a merger has been accepted by the board of directors of the two companies, there is always a chance that the merger will not go through, possibly because of objections by regulatory authorities. This is a reason for the existence of the discount. If the takeover falls through, fund managers can be left with large losses.

EXAMPLE 8

Merger Risk Arbitrage and Long/Short Market-Neutral Strategy

A merger has been announced between a French company A and a German company B. A will acquire B by offering one share of A for two shares of B. Shares of B were trading in a €15 to €20 range prior to the merger announcement. Shares of B currently trade at €24, while shares of A trade at €50. The merger has been approved by both boards of directors but is awaiting ratification by all shareholders (which is extremely likely) and approval by the EU commission (there is a slight risk of non-approval because the combined company has a large European market share in some products). How could a hedge fund take advantage of the situation? What are the risks?

Solution: The hedge fund should construct a hedged position whereby it buys two shares of B for every share of A that it sells short. Because the proceeds of the short sale of one share of A (€50) can be used to buy two shares of B (€48), the position can be highly leveraged. Of course, the cost of securities lending and margin deposit should also be taken into account. When the merger is completed, the hedge fund will make a profit of approximately two euros for each share of A.

The risk is that the merger will fall through. If it does, the stock price of B will drop sharply, because it was to be acquired at a price well above its premerger market value. If the stock price of A also falls, it should be by less than for B, resulting in an overall loss. The stock price of A might also rise, adding to the loss related to the position in B. That would mean a sizable loss for the hedge fund.

5.3 Funds of Funds

Funds of funds (FOF) have been created to allow easier access to small investors, but also to institutional investors. An FOF is open to investors and, in turn, invests in a selection of hedge funds. If an FOF has a large client base, it can invest large sums of money in each hedge fund. With their attractive benefits, FOF have grown rapidly and now compose more than a quarter of all hedge fund assets (McCrary [2002]). An FOF provides investors with several benefits:

▶ *Retailing:* Typically, a single hedge fund requires an investment of one to several hundred thousand dollars or euros. For the same amount, an investor can get exposure to a large number of hedge funds.

▶ *Access:* FOF managers may be able to offer investments in successful hedge funds that are closed to individual investors because the maximum number of investors has been reached. As long-time investors, they may have "old" money invested with funds that have been closed to new investment. They are also privileged clients that will have priority in buying shares of individual investors who cash out from the hedge fund for personal reasons.

▶ *Diversification:* An FOF allows investors to diversify the risk of a single hedge fund. The good performance of a single hedge fund could be due to specific market conditions prevailing in the past. An FOF can diversify across several types of hedge funds that may have good performance in different market conditions.

▶ *Expertise:* The manager of the FOF is supposed to have expertise in finding reliable and good-quality hedge funds in a world where information on the investment strategies of hedge funds is difficult to obtain. Selecting the right hedge fund and strategy requires a large database and intimate knowledge of strategies, and their advantages and potential pitfalls.

▶ *Due diligence process:* The due diligence (both at the outset and ongoing) that has to be performed by an institutional investor when selecting a hedge fund is highly specialized and time consuming, given the secretive nature of hedge funds and their complex investment strategies. An FOF may be better equipped to perform this due diligence than is a typical institutional investor.

However, there are drawbacks with an FOF:

▶ *Fee:* The fee charged by its manager is in addition to that charged by each hedge fund. The total fee can be quite hefty.

▶ *Performance:* Individual hedge funds are mostly selected by the FOF on the basis of past performance, which in practice often gives little indication of future performance. Biases of the existing databases on hedge funds used by FOFs in their selection process are described subsequently. There is little evidence of persistence in the performance delivered by FOFs.

▶ *Diversification is a two-edged sword:* Blending a high expected return hedge fund with many others for risk reduction purposes means that the overall FOF expected return will be lowered by this diversification. But the fees paid are still very high.

5.4 Leverage and Unique Risks of Hedge Funds

Prior to discussing the performance of hedge funds, we review the use of leverage by hedge funds and the unique risks for hedge funds. Some people regard the use of leverage as one of the main sources of risk for hedge funds, while others maintain that proper use of leverage with appropriate risk management benefits hedge fund investors. In addition, risks that are unique to hedge funds may make hedge funds look unduly risky. Thus, we can usefully discuss hedge funds' risks prior to presenting their historical track record.

5.4.1 Use of Leverage

One of the common characteristics of hedge funds is their use of leverage as part of their trading strategy, although some hedge funds do not use leverage at all.[18] For certain strategies (such as arbitrage strategies), leverage is essential because the arbitrage return is so small that leverage is needed for amplifying the profit. However, leverage is a double-edged sword that also magnifies losses on the downside. In this traditional sense, leveraged investments are more aggressive than those without leverage, and to some people, this may mean high risk.

Leverage in hedge funds often runs from 2:1 to 10:1 (depending on the type of assets held and strategies used) and can run higher than 100:1 (e.g., at one

---

[18] According to survey results, more than 70 percent of hedge funds use leverage to some degree (McCrary, 2002; Van Hedge Fund Advisors International, 2002).

5.5.2 *Talent*

The fee structure and flexibility of hedge funds attract talented fund managers. Someone having an outstanding investment idea can apply it in a hedge fund with few constraints. The investment idea can be leveraged to generate high returns for investors and for the manager. So, the search for an attractive hedge fund is based on its track record and also on the perceived talent of the manager to generate superior performance.

5.6 Caveats

Investors should exercise caution when using the historical track record of hedge funds in reaching asset allocation decisions. The hedge fund industry does not adhere to rigorous performance presentation standards. Biases in historical performance data can make it difficult to interpret hedge fund performance; past winners may also not repeat.

5.6.1 *Biases*

The performance data from hedge fund databases and indexes suffer from serious biases that are listed here. Both performance and risk measures are affected.

▶ *Self-selection bias:* Hedge fund managers decide themselves whether they want to be included in a database. Managers that have funds with an unimpressive track record will not wish to have that information exposed.

▶ *Instant history bias:* When a hedge fund enters a database, it brings with it its track record. Because only hedge funds with good track records enter the database, this creates a positive bias in past performance in the database, as stressed by Fung and Hsieh (2002).

▶ *Survivorship bias: Return:* In the investment industry, unsuccessful funds and managers tend to disappear over time. Only successful ones search for new clients and present their track records. This creates a survivor bias. This problem is acute with hedge funds because they often do not have to comply with performance presentation standards. It is not uncommon to see hedge fund managers present the track records of only their successful funds, omitting those that have been closed. If a fund begins to perform poorly, perhaps even starting to go out of business, it may stop reporting its performance entirely, thus inflating the reported average performance of hedge funds. Hedge fund indexes and databases may only include funds that have survived. Funds with bad performance disappear and are removed from the database that is used by investors to select among existing funds. Some data bases are now available that may be free from survivorship bias as defunct hedge funds are left in the data base; however, funds that simply stop reporting still pose a problem.

▶ *Survivorship bias: Risk:* Biases also affect risk measures. A similar survivorship bias applies to risk measures. Investors shy away from high risk, as well as from negative returns. Hedge funds that exhibited highly volatile returns in the past tend to disappear. Only strategies that have experienced low volatility in the past survive. So, reported volatility of existing funds will tend to be low. There is no guarantee that the same strategy will also be low risk in the future. Examples abound of hedge funds that were regarded as low risk but lost all of their capital.

▶ *Smoothed pricing: Infrequently traded assets:* Some assets trade infrequently. This is the case for many alternative assets that are not exchange-traded, such as real estate or private equity. This is also the case for illiquid exchange-traded securities or OTC instruments often used by hedge funds. Because prices used are often not up-to-date market prices, but estimates of fair value, their volatility is reduced (smoothing effect). The infrequent nature of price updates for alternative investments induces a significant downward bias to the measured risk of the assets. In addition, correlations of alternative investment returns with conventional equity and fixed income returns, and correlations among the alternative investments, are often artificially low simply because of the smoothing effect and the absence of market-observable returns. The bias can be very large,[20] so the true risk is much larger than the reported estimates.

EXAMPLE 9

Biases in Reported Performance

A manager without any expertise has decided to launch five long/short hedge funds with some seed money. The investment strategies of the five funds are quite different. Actually, the investment strategy of fund A is just the opposite of that of fund E. After a couple of years, some have performed well and some badly, as could be expected by pure chance. The annualized gross returns on the five funds are listed in the following table. All have an annualized standard deviation of 10 percent and the annual risk-free rate is 3 percent. The manager decides to close funds A, B, and C and to enter funds D and E in a well-known hedge fund database. The marketing pitch of the manager is that the funds have superior performance (Sharpe ratio of 1.7 and 2.7). What do you think?

Fund Name	Mean Annual Return	Standard Deviation	Sharpe Ratio
Fund A	−30%	10%	−3.3
Fund B	−20%	10%	−2.3
Fund C	0%	10%	−0.3
Fund D	+20%	10%	1.7
Fund E	+30%	10%	2.7

Solution: The performance on the funds is purely random. But only the good-performing funds are included in the hedge fund database. The performance reported for a selection of funds is misleading. There is obvious survivorship and self-selection bias. Similarly, the performance of the hedge fund index is biased upward and misleading.

---

[20] See, for example, Asness, Krail, and Liew (2001).

► *Option-like investment strategies:* Traditional risk measures used in performance appraisal assume that portfolio returns are drawn from normal or, at least symmetric, distributions. Many investment strategies followed by hedge funds have some option-like features that violate these distributional assumptions. For example, hedge funds following so-called arbitrage strategies will generally make a small profit when asset prices converge to their estimated fair value, but they run the risk of a huge loss if their arbitrage model fails. Standard deviation or traditional value at risk (VaR) measures understate the true risk of losses, and the Sharpe ratio can be an inappropriate performance measure.

► *Fee structure and gaming:* It is also important to remember the high fees charged by hedge funds: Typically a fixed fee of 1 percent plus an incentive fee of 20 percent of the total return, if positive. This compensation structure is option-like. Clearly, fund managers are paid to take risks. One can argue that they have strong incentives to take a huge amount of risk if their recent performance has been bad. However, one can also argue that because of the high water mark provision, hedge fund managers may not want to ruin their chance to stage a comeback by taking more risk as their performance diminishes. In either case, past risk measures may be misleading for forecasting future performance and risk for a fund that has performed badly in the recent past.

5.6.2 Persistence of Performance

Because of various biases, judging the average performance of the hedge fund industry by using the indexes discussed can be difficult. To appraise individual hedge funds, investors should look at their persistence of performance. Before a specific hedge fund is purchased, investors should judge whether their good track record will persist in the future. A similar attitude must be adopted when considering an FOF.[21]

Talented hedge fund managers can exploit market inefficiencies that cannot be exploited by conventional asset managers and/or design innovative investment strategies that may yield excellent returns. But, again, two caveats are in order. First, the size of the hedge fund industry is huge (some $600 billion by the end of 2001), and the leverage used means that the industry is a very large player in capital markets. But the existence of pricing inefficiencies, for which many managers search, is necessarily limited. Thus there is a very large pool of capital chasing after what is likely to be a limited supply of pricing inefficiencies. Second, any successful strategy will quickly be imitated by many other investors, thereby reducing its future profitability.

To summarize, investors need to exercise great caution in interpreting the reported performance of hedge funds; the risks in hedge fund investments are easily underestimated.

---

[21] In a study that may come as a surprise to proponents of hedge funds, Brown, Goetzmann, and Ibbotson (1999) found "no evidence of performance persistence in raw returns or risk-adjusted returns, even when we break funds down according to their returns-based style classification." They conclude that "the hedge fund arena provides no evidence that past performance forecasts future performance." It's important to note, however, that this study covers a relatively short time period and that determining accurate and comparable performance figures in the hedge fund arena is extremely complex.

CLOSELY HELD COMPANIES AND INACTIVELY TRADED SECURITIES

Investments in closely held companies and inactively traded securities require analysis of legal, financial, and ownership considerations with account taken of the effects of illiquidity. Closely held companies are those that are not publicly traded. Inactively traded securities are securities of companies that are infrequently traded; they generally do not trade on major exchanges. Illiquidity, limited information availability, and minority ownership issues are common to such companies.

6.1 Legal Environment

Closely held companies may be organized in various legal forms, such as special tax-advantaged corporations (subchapter S corporations in the United States), regular corporations, general partnerships, limited partnerships, and sole pro-prietorships. These forms have tax implications, as well as ownership differences, for the investor. Ownership is a bundle of rights, and these rights differ, depending on the business form. Because valuations can be required to provide evidence in litigation—for example, minority shareholder claims—much case law defines terms such as *intrinsic value, fundamental value,* and *fair value.* These definitions may vary in different jurisdictions. Even what is judged as evidence for a valuation can vary. There has long been a tension between the theory of value as based on projected cash flows and the acceptance of the *hard* evidence of recent cash flows. In a real sense, then, valuation of closely held and inactively traded securities requires extensive knowledge of the law and the purposes of the valuation.[22]

6.2 Valuation Alternatives

The basic types of valuation are the cost approach, the comparables approach, and the income approach.

6.2.1 The Cost Approach

This approach attempts to determine what it would cost to replace the company's assets in their present form.

6.2.2 The Comparables Approach

In the company comparison approach, market value is estimated relative to a benchmark value. The benchmark value may be the market price of a similar but actively traded company, or the average or median value of the market prices of similar companies, in transactions made near the time of the appraisal. The benchmark-based estimate needs to be adjusted for changing market conditions, the possibility that the benchmark itself is mispriced, and the unique features of the company relative to the benchmark. Companies with comparable characteristics might not have traded recently.

---

[22] See Pratt, Reilly, and Schweihs (1996) for an extensive treatment of the analysis and appraisal of closely held companies.

operate a separate airline that offers "a low-cost, no-frills" product in markets dominated by leisure customers and low-cost competition, Mr. Hacker said.

Lenders set conditions

UAL, the world's second-largest carrier, filed for protection from its creditors Monday in U.S. Bankruptcy Court in Chicago. As part of its filing, the company said it arranged $1.5 billion in interim financing to help it operate while under court protection. The lenders, who next week will extend an initial $800 million of that funding, insist that the airline meet strict financial benchmarks if it is to receive the balance.

Mr. Hacker, who served for several years as UAL's chief financial officer before leaving to head a United subsidiary, on Wednesday was named to the new post as strategy chief. Yesterday, he presented an overview of United's business plan to leaders of the carrier's union. In a telephone message to employees, he noted that the terms of the interim bankruptcy financing require lower labor costs "under very tight time frames."

In discussions with union leaders yesterday, it wasn't clear whether the company spelled out specific savings targets. A United spokesman last night declined to discuss details on the business plan or the savings targets.

Possible low-fare product

"We want to make the United brand relevant to as many customers as we can," Mr. Hacker told employees. "We'll do that through a family of products that meets customers' different needs."

Glenn Tilton, UAL's chairman and chief executive, has hinted in recent days that United would revive a product similar to its low-fare shuttle service that operated in the Western U.S. in the late 1990s to help the carrier fight off competition from Southwest Airlines. Mr. Tilton also hinted in employee meetings the past few days in the airline's hubs that UAL may seek government aid to facilitate its exit from Chapter 11.

The Air Transportation Stabilization Board, whose refusal to grant government-loan backing forced the airline into bankruptcy, has indicated it would consider a revised application from United for loan guarantees to back up financing to help the airline emerge from reorganization.

Source: Susan Carey, *The Wall Street Journal,* 13 December 2002, p. A2.

Investing in commodity futures is the most common strategy. Commodity trading advisers (CTAs) offer *managed futures funds* that take positions in exchange-traded derivatives on commodities and financials.[24]

8.1 Commodity Futures

Futures contracts are the easiest and cheapest way to invest in commodities. Commodities can be grouped into three major categories:

▶ *Agricultural products,* including fibers (wool, cotton), grains (wheat, corn, soybeans), food (coffee, cocoa, orange juice), and livestock (cattle, hogs, pork bellies). These are often called soft commodities by professionals.

▶ *Energy,* including crude oil, heating oil, and natural gas

▶ *Metals,* such as copper, aluminum, gold, silver, and platinum

Numerous commodity indexes have been developed. Some traditional indexes are broadly based, with a global economic perspective; they aim to track the evolution of input prices. Other indexes have been developed as

---

[24] See Jaeger (2002), p. 18.

investable indexes. They are based on the most liquid commodity futures contracts, so they can easily be replicated by taking positions in individual commodities. For example, the Goldman Sachs Commodity Index (GSCI) is a world-production weighted index of 26 commodities with liquid futures contracts. Futures contracts on the GSCI trade in Chicago. The composition and weights of the various commodity indexes differ widely, and so do their performances.

8.2 Motivation and Investment Vehicles

Commodities are sometimes treated as an asset class because they represent a direct participation in the real economy. The motivation for investing in commodities ranges from the diversification benefits achievable by a passive investor to the speculative profits sought by an *active* investor. The design of the investment vehicle used reflects these different motivations.

8.2.1 Passive Investment

A passive investor would buy commodities for their risk-diversification benefits. When inflation accelerates, commodity prices go up, whereas bond and stock prices tend to go down. A passive investor would typically invest through a collateralized position in a futures contract. Many banks and money managers offer collateralized futures funds based on one of the investable commodity indexes. A collateralized position in futures is a portfolio in which an investor takes a long position in futures for a given amount of underlying value and simultaneously invests the same amount in government securities, such as Treasury bills. The various investable indexes and collateralized futures indexes are published both in excess-return and in total-return form. The indexes reported assume that the *total return* on the index is continuously reinvested. The *excess return* is the return above the risk-free rate. The total return is the risk-free rate plus the excess return.

EXAMPLE 10

Collateralized Futures

Assume that the futures price is currently $100. If $100 million is added to the fund, the manager will take a long position in the futures contract for $100 million of underlying value and simultaneously buy $100 million worth of Treasury bills (part of this will be deposited as margin). If the futures price drops to $95 the next day, the futures position will be marked to market, and the manager will have to sell $5 million of the Treasury bills to cover the loss. Conversely, if the futures price rises to $105, the manager will receive a marked-to-market profit of $5 million, which will be invested in additional Treasury bills. Discuss the sources of total return from such an investment.

Solution: The total return on the collateralized futures position comes from the change in futures price and the interest income on the Treasury bills.

Generally, the volatility of commodity futures is higher than that of domestic or international equity, but commodities have a negative correlation with stock and bond returns and a desirable positive correlation with inflation. Nevertheless, the excellent long-term performance of some commodity indexes requires a word of caution. The commodities and weights selected to enter indexes reflect a selection bias when they include data from time periods prior to the initiation of the index, which biases any back-calculated performance.

8.3 Active Investment

Besides making inflation bets, another motivation for investing in commodities is that they provide good performance in periods of economic growth. In periods of rapid economic growth, commodities are in strong demand to satisfy production needs, and their prices go up. Because of productivity gains, the prices of finished goods are unlikely to rise as fast as those of raw materials. This suggests an active management strategy in which specific commodities are bought and sold at various times. Managed futures are proposed by a large number of institutions.

As with any investments, the return–risk characteristics of managed futures must be analyzed carefully. Schneeweis (2002) discusses the proposed attraction of managed futures: the possibility of positive returns in months when the market does well and in the months when it does poorly. Jaeger (2002) proposes several principles for the risk management of managed futures portfolios:

▶ Diversification

▶ Liquidity monitoring, because diversification into a larger universe of contracts can include illiquid contracts

▶ Volatility dependent allocation where the weight of the different contracts in the portfolio is determined by their historical or implied volatility

▶ Quantitative risk management techniques such as value at risk (VaR) and stress tests

▶ **Risk budgeting** on various aggregation levels to detect undesired risk concentrations

▶ Limits on leverage

▶ Use of derivatives to hedge any unwanted currency risk

▶ Care in model selection with respect to data mining, in and out of sample performance, and adequate performance adjustments for risk

8.4 The Example of Gold

Gold has always played a special role in investments. It is a commodity traded worldwide, but more important, it has been regarded by many Europeans and Asians as the ultimate store of value. It is considered an international monetary asset that offers protection in case of a major disruption. Furthermore, central banks and most non-U.S. investors regard gold as a monetary asset because it has been the core of domestic and international monetary systems for many centuries. This section focuses on gold investment because of the historical importance of gold in investment strategies, and as an example of a real asset investment. Of course, precious stones, stamps, or paintings could also be profitable long-term investments, but they usually require high transaction costs; moreover, each stone or painting is in a sense unique, which reduces its marketability. Gold is offered in a wide variety of investment vehicles that can be used in passive or active strategies. Gold-linked investments include gold bullion, coins, bonds, mining equity, futures, and options on gold and on mining equity or bonds.

8.4.1 The Motivation for Investing in Gold

The traditional role of gold as the ultimate hedge and store of value is well known. For centuries, Europeans and Asians alike have regarded gold as the best possible protection against inflation and social, political, or economic crises because it can easily be traded worldwide at any time, and its real value increases during crises. Europeans and others who have suffered revolutions, invasions, and periods of hyperinflation need no correlation coefficients to be convinced of this attractive portfolio hedge characteristic. For example, gold kept its real value during the U.S. stock market crash from 1929 to 1932 and the London Stock Exchange collapse in equity and bonds from 1973 to 1975. Furthermore, the central role gold has played in domestic and international monetary systems for thousands of years makes it, in part, a monetary asset with exceptional liquidity. Other real assets, such as diamonds or stamps, do not have this characteristic.

In general, gold often allows investors to diversify against the kinds of risks that affect all stock markets simultaneously. For example, in 1973 and 1974, the price of bullion tripled when stock markets worldwide dropped dramatically during the oil crisis; the NYSE dropped approximately 50 percent.

A theoretical comment is in order here. In modern portfolio theory, a small or negative beta implies that the expected return on gold should be small. For example, a negative beta caused by a negative correlation between gold and the market portfolio implies that in the capital asset pricing model (CAPM) framework, the expected return on gold should be less than the risk-free interest rate. Indeed, it can be claimed that we should expect a modest long-term performance in gold and a greater return on the other assets in the portfolio; however, gold assets will reduce the risk of the portfolio in the event of adverse economic conditions. The question for a prudent portfolio manager, then, is whether these hedge benefits are worth the implicit cost she must pay in the form of a smaller expected long-term return for a small part of the portfolio.

8.4.2 Gold Price Determinants

The following material is intended to indicate the kind of information and methods that analysts and investment managers use to analyze real asset investments. Commodities other than gold could also serve as examples.

Gold is a tangible international asset in limited supply. Gold can be extracted at a cost but cannot be produced artificially. Although gold is immune to the effects of weather, water, and oxygen, it suffers from human habits. The tradition of hiding gold treasures in the ground is consistent with the observation that gold is the ultimate physical store of value during major disruptions such as civil unrest, coup d'état, and war. During World War II, most Europeans dug a hole in their gardens or cellars to hide their gold holdings. Part of this hidden gold is never recovered if the owner dies. Most of the gold used in dentistry also disappears with the owner. Despite these losses, the stock of gold keeps slowly increasing with the amount extracted.

In a sense, the price of gold should be easy to forecast: The product is well defined. The supply sources are well identified, and reserves can be reasonably estimated. The major demands are clearly identified: carat jewelry, industrial needs, coins, and investment.

Supply and demand clearly determine the price of gold. It is therefore necessary to study the various components of supply and demand to forecast the price of gold. A different model may be required for each component. For example, Western mine production is affected by technological considerations, South African extraction policy, and political situations in sensitive countries. Russia's gold sales depend on their need for hard currencies. Official sales may also be induced by monetary and **balance of payments** problems. Industrial demand depends on technological innovation and the discovery of cheaper substitutes. Jewelry demand is sensitive to short-term gold price movements, as well as fashion; the investment motivation is often present in jewelry purchases. Investment demand for bullion and coins is a component of the total demand affecting gold price but is also determined by expectations of future price movements.

So, although gold is a single, well-identified, extensively researched product, its analysis and valuation is not a simple exercise. This difficulty may add another dimension to gold's mystical attraction.

8.5 Commodity-Linked Securities

Holding commodities provides no income, so the sole return to the owner is through price increase. Investors can also select securities that are linked to some commodity prices and also provide some income. This can be an attractive alternative for investors who wish to, or must, hold financial investments rather than real assets. The two major types of commodity-linked securities are bonds and equity. The indexation clause is explicit for commodity-linked bonds but implicit for equity. Again, we focus on the example of gold.

8.5.1 Commodity-Linked Bonds

There are many examples of commodity-linked bonds in the world capital markets.[25] In periods of high inflation, governments have often been forced to offer loans with coupons or principal indexed to either the price of a specific good or a global inflation index. Inflation-indexed gilts became popular in the United Kingdom during the 1980s. The capital and coupons of these bonds are indexed to British retail prices.

In 1997, the U.S. Treasury started to offer Inflation-Indexed Securities, also known as Treasury Inflation Protected Securities (TIPS).[26] The first such security was a 10-year bond, issued with a real yield of 3.45 percent. The principal value is adjusted for changes in the consumer price index (CPI) on each semiannual coupon payment date. So, the nominal coupon, equal to the real yield times the CPI-adjusted principal, increases with inflation. At maturity, the CPI-adjusted principal is reimbursed. In the United States, some government agencies, municipalities, and corporations have also issued inflation-indexed bonds. Often, the inflation adjustment to the principal is paid out immediately rather than at final maturity. This structure has been adopted because seeing their nominal credit exposure on nongovernment issues accumulate automatically over time worried investors.

---

[25] Jacquillat and Roll (1979) provide an empirical analysis of the benefits of commodity-linked bonds. Schwartz (1982) provides a theoretical model for an index-linked bond with an option to repay the bond at face value or at an index-linked price. Such a model was tested on a silver-linked bond issued by Sunshine Mining in Brauer and Ravichandran (1986). An interesting analysis of oil-linked securities is provided by Gibson and Schwartz (1990).

[26] McFall Lamm (1998) and Anderson and Moore (1998) provide an analysis of TIPS.

Several countries have issued inflation-indexed bonds, and corporations and governments have issued bonds indexed to a variety of specific prices, such as oil prices. Gold bonds, and bonds with warrants on gold, have been an attractive alternative to holding gold ingots.

8.5.2 Commodity-Linked Equity

The value of some companies is directly affected by commodity prices. This is clearly the case with the so-called *energy companies*. For example, companies in the oil and gas industries are affected by the evolution of oil prices. The link between commodity prices and stock prices is more evident for small, undiversified companies that specialize in one type of activity, for example, oil and gas exploration and production. However, large oil companies tend to be quite diversified across activities and the link between commodity prices and stock prices is weaker. An integrated exploration, production, and refining company will be less affected by oil price increases than a company operating in only one of the industry segments.

Gold mining companies are another example of commodity-linked equity. Gold mining shares differ from commodity-linked bonds in that the indexation clause is not fixed by contract but depends on mining economics. In fact, the mining industry is probably the simplest activity to describe in a valuation model. The economics of mining can be described by a simple discounted cash flow model. The principal relationship in the model is the cost structure of the mine as measured by the ratio of costs to revenues. The cost to remove an ounce or a gram of gold from so-called storage and refine it depends on several factors: technology, wage rates, power rates, and the grade and depth of the mine. Revenues depend on the world price of gold. Any movement in the market price of gold will directly affect the cash flows of a mine and therefore its market value; the higher the ratio of costs to revenues, the more sensitive will be the cash flows to gold price movements. However, note that the correlation between gold mine share prices and the price of gold is far from perfect. Gold mine values are influenced by factors other than gold prices; for example, social and political factors have strongly affected South African share prices over time.

SUMMARY

▶ Alternative investments usually involve illiquidity, difficulty in the determination of current market values, limited historical risk and return data, the requirement for extensive investment analysis, a liquidity risk premium, and a segmentation risk premium. Alternative assets are assets not traded on exchanges. Alternative strategies are strategies that mostly use traded assets for the purpose of isolating bets and generating alpha.

▶ An open-end fund stands ready to redeem investor shares at market value, but a closed-end fund does not. A load fund has sales commission charges, and a no-load fund does not. Sales fees may also appear in annual distribution fees.

▶ The net asset value of a fund is calculated as the per-share value of the investment company's assets minus liabilities.

▶ Mutual funds may charge several different fees: Loads and redemption fees provide sales incentives; distribution and operating fees are annual fees; the part of the operating fee that is allocated to the fund manager can be considered an investment performance incentive.

▶ An exchange traded fund (ETF) is a special type of fund that tracks some market index but that is traded on a stock market as any common share.

▶ A mutual fund's purchases and sales of stocks held in the fund lead to taxable gains at the level of the fund, but this is not the case for an ETF because of its in-kind creation and redemption process.

▶ The advantages of ETFs are diversification; trading similarly to a stock; management of their risk augmented by futures and options contracts on them; transparency; cost effectiveness; avoidance of significant premiums or discounts to NAV; tax savings from payment of in-kind redemption; and immediate dividend reinvestment for open-end ETFs. The disadvantages are only a narrow-based market index tracked in some countries; intraday trading opportunity is not important for long-horizon investors; large bid–ask spreads on some ETFs; and possibly better cost structures and tax advantages to direct index investing for large institutions.

▶ Some characteristics of real estate as an investable asset class are that each property is immovable, basically indivisible, and unique; not directly comparable to other properties; illiquid; and bought and sold intermittently in a generally local marketplace, with high transaction costs and market inefficiencies.

▶ The main approaches to real estate valuation are the cost approach, the sales comparison approach, the income approach, and the discounted after-tax cash flow approach.

▶ The net operating income from a real estate investment is gross potential income minus expenses, which include estimated vacancy and collection costs, insurance, taxes, utilities, and repairs and maintenance.

▶ The value of a property can be calculated as the cost to replace the building in its present form in the cost approach; an adjusted value from a benchmark of comparable sales in the sales comparison approach; or a hedonic price estimate from a regression model in the sales comparison approach; and capitalized net operating income in the income approach.

▶ The net present value of a property to an equity investor is obtained as the present value of the after tax cash flows, discounted at the investor's required rate of return on equity, minus the amount of equity required to make the investment.

► Venture capital investing is done in many stages from seed through mezzanine.

► Venture capital investment characteristics include illiquidity; long-term commitment required; difficulty in determining current market values; limited historical risk and return data; limited information; entrepreneurial/management mismatches; fund manager incentive mismatches; lack of knowledge of how many competitors exist; vintage cycles; and the requirement for extensive operations analysis and advice. The challenges to venture capital performance measurement are the difficulty in determining precise valuations, the lack of meaningful benchmarks, and the long-term nature of any performance feedback.

► The expected net present value of a venture capital project with a single, terminal payoff and a single, initial investment can be calculated, given its possible payoff and its conditional failure probabilities, as the present value of the expected payoff minus the required initial investment.

► The term *hedge fund* is not fully descriptive, because the hedged position is generally designed to isolate a bet rather than to reduce risk. Hedge funds can be defined as funds that seek absolute returns; have a legal structure avoiding some government regulations; and have option-like fees, including a base management fee and an incentive fee proportional to realized profits.

► The net performance of a hedge fund can be calculated by subtracting its fees from its gross performance.

► Hedge funds can be classified in a variety of ways. One classification of hedge funds comprises the categories: long/short, market neutral, global macro, and event driven.

► The advantages of fund of funds investing are availability to the small investor, access to funds closed to new investors, diversification, managerial expertise, and a due diligence process. The disadvantages to fund of funds investing are high fees, little evidence of persistent performance, and the absolute return loss through diversification.

► High leverage is often present in hedge funds as part of the trading strategy and is an essential part of some strategies in which the arbitrage return is so small that leverage is needed to amplify the profit. The unique risks of hedge funds are liquidity risk, pricing risk, counterparty credit risk, settlement risk, short squeeze risk, and financing squeeze risk.

► In terms of performance, hedge funds are generally viewed as having a net return higher than available for equity or bond investments, lower standard deviation of return than equity investments, a Sharpe ratio that is comparable to bonds and higher than that of equity investments, and a low correlation with conventional investments. The biases present in hedge fund performance reporting include self-selection bias, instant history bias, survivorship bias on return, survivorship bias on risk, smoothed pricing on infrequently traded assets, option-like investment strategies, and fee structure–induced gaming.

► For closely held companies and inactively traded securities, a discount is used for lack of liquidity, lack of marketability, and for a minority interest, but a control premium is added for controlling ownership. The base for the marketability discount is the market value of equity for a comparable publicly traded company.

► Distressed-securities investing usually means investing in distressed company bonds with a view to equity ownership in the eventually reconstituted company. Such investments are similar to venture capital investments because they are illiquid; they require a long investment horizon; they require intense investor participation/consulting; and they offer the possibility of alpha because of mispricing.

► As a vehicle for investing in production and consumption, commodities complement the investment opportunities offered by shares of corporations that extensively use these as raw materials in their production processes. Investing directly in agricultural products and other commodities gives the investor exposure to the commodity components of the country's production and consumption.

► Commodity trading advisors (CTAs) offer managed futures funds that take positions in exchange traded derivatives on commodities and financials.

► The return on a collateralized futures position comes from the change in the futures price plus the interest income on risk-free government securities.

► The motivation for investing in commodities, commodity derivatives, and commodity-linked securities is that they may have negative correlation with stock and bond returns and a desirable positive correlation with inflation. In the case of commodity-linked securities, the investor can receive some income rather than depending solely on commodity price changes.

► The risk of managed futures can be managed through diversification, liquidity monitoring, volatility dependent allocation, quantitative techniques such as VaR, risk budgeting on various aggregation levels, limits on leverage, use of derivatives, and care in model selection.

PRACTICE PROBLEMS FOR READING 76

Use the following information for Questions 1–2.

Global Leveraged Equity Fund (GLEF) has three classes of shares, each holding the same portfolio of securities but having a different expense structure. The following table summarizes the expenses of these classes of shares.

Expense Comparison for Four Classes of GLEF

	Class A	Class B[a]	Class C
Sales charge (load) on purchases	5%	None	None
Deferred sales charge (load) on redemptions	None	4% in the first year, declining by 1% each year thereafter	1% for the initial 2 years only
Annual expenses:			
Distribution fee	0.25%	0.50%	0.50%
Management fee	0.50%	0.50%	0.50%
Other expenses	0.50%	0.50%	0.50%
	1.25%	1.50%	1.50%

[a]Class B shares automatically convert to Class A shares 72 months (6 years) after purchase.

Assume that expense percentages given will be constant at the given values. Assume that the deferred sales charges are computed on the basis of NAV.

An investor is considering the purchase of GLEF shares. The investor expects equity investments with risk characteristics similar to GLEF to earn 9 percent per year. He decides to make his selection of fund share class based on an assumed 9 percent return each year, gross of any of the expenses given in the preceding table.

1. Decide which class of shares of GLEF is best for the investor if he plans to liquidate his investment toward the end of
   A. Year 1.
   B. Year 3.
   C. Year 5.
   D. Year 15.

2. You have analyzed the relative performance of different classes of GLEF shares for liquidation in several years. Specifically, you have looked at liquidation in years 1, 3, 5, and 15. Your results are as follows. (The > symbol implies that the class preceding the sign performs better than the class following and the = symbol implies equal performance of the two classes.)

   ► Liquidation in year 1: Class C > Class B > Class A
   ► Liquidation in year 3: Class C > Class B > Class A
   ► Liquidation in year 5: Class B = Class C > Class A
   ► Liquidation in year 15: Class B > Class C > Class A

   Provide an intuitive explanation for the pattern of relative performance that you observe.

3. Using the price data for several houses recently sold in a particular area, a real estate firm has identified the main characteristics that affect the prices of houses in that area. The characteristics identified include the living area, the number of bathrooms, whether the house has a fireplace, and how old the house is. The estimated slope coefficient for each of these characteristics and the constant term are as follows:

Characteristic	Units	Coefficient in Euros per Unit
Intercept	—	140,000
Living area	Square meters	210
Number of bathrooms	Number	10,000
Fireplace	0 or 1	15,000
Age of the house	Years	−6,000

   Use these above estimates to value a five-year-old house with a living area of 500 square meters, three bathrooms, and a fireplace.

4. A real estate firm is evaluating an office building, using the income approach. The real estate firm has compiled the following information for the office building. All information is on an annual basis.

Gross potential rental income	$350,000
Estimated vacancy and collection losses[a]	4%
Insurance and taxes	$26,000
Utilities	$18,000
Repairs and maintenance	$23,000
Depreciation	$40,000
Interest on proposed financing	$18,000

[a]As a percentage of gross potential rental income.

There have been two recent sales of office buildings in the area. The first building had a net operating income of $500,000 and was sold at $4 million. The second building had a net operating income of $225,000 and was sold at $1.6 million.

A. Compute the net operating income for the office building to be valued.

B. Use the income approach to compute the appraisal price of the office building.

5. An analyst is evaluating a real estate investment project using the discounted cash flow approach. The purchase price is $3 million, which is financed 15 percent by equity and 85 percent by a mortgage loan. It is expected that the property will be sold in five years. The analyst has estimated the following after-tax cash flows during the first four years of the five-year life of the real estate investment project.

Year	1	2	3	4
Cash flow	$60,000	$75,000	$91,000	$108,000

For the fifth year, that is, the year when the property would be sold by the investor, the after-tax cash flow without the property sale is estimated to be $126,000 and the after-tax cash flow from the property sale is estimated to be $710,000.

Compute the NPV of this project. State whether the investor should undertake the project. The investor's cost of equity for projects with level of risk comparable to this real estate investment project is 18 percent.

6. An investment firm is evaluating a real estate investment project, using the discounted cash flow approach. The purchase price is $1.5 million, which is financed 20 percent by equity and 80 percent by a mortgage loan at a 9 percent pre-tax interest rate. The mortgage loan has a long maturity and constant annual payments of $120,000. This includes interest payments on the remaining principal at a 9 percent interest rate and a variable principal repayment that steps up with time. The net operating income (NOI) in the first year is estimated to be $170,000. NOI is expected to grow at a rate of 4 percent every year. The interest on real estate financing for the project is tax deductible. The marginal income tax rate for the investment firm is 30 percent. Using straight-line depreciation, the annual depreciation of the property is $37,500.

   A. Compute the after-tax cash flows in years 1, 2, and 3 of the project.

   B. It is expected that the property will be sold at the end of three years. The projected sale price is $1.72 million. The property's sales expenses are 6.5 percent of the sale price. The capital gains tax rate is 20 percent. Compute the after-tax cash flow from the property sale in year 3.

   C. The investor's cost of equity for projects with level of risk comparable to this real estate investment project is 19 percent. Recommend whether to invest in the project or not, based on the NPV of the project.

7. Would you suggest using real estate appraisal-based indexes in a global portfolio optimization?

8. Suppose the estimated correlation matrix of the Wilshire 5000 U.S. stock index and two real estate indexes, the Federal Russell Company index (FRC) and the National Association of Real Estate Investment Trusts (NAREIT) is as follows:

	Wilshire 5000	NAREIT	FRC
Wilshire 5000	1.00	0.79	0.18
NAREIT	0.79	1.00	0.02
FRC	0.18	0.02	1.00

   Based on this above matrix, compare the expected price behavior of the two real estate indexes.

9. An investor is evaluating a venture capital project that will require an investment of $1.4 million. The investor estimates that she will be able to exit the venture successfully in eight years. She also estimates that there is an 80 percent chance that the venture will not survive until the end of the eighth year. If the venture does survive until then, she expects to exit the project then, and it is equally likely that the payoff at the time of exit will be either $25 million or $35 million. The investor is considering an equity investment in the project, and her cost of equity for a project with similar risk is 20 percent.

   A. Compute the net present value of the venture capital project.

   B. Recommend whether to accept or reject the project.

10. VenCap, Inc. is a venture capital financier. It estimates that investing €4.5 million in a particular venture capital project can return €60 million at the end of six years if it succeeds; however, it realizes that the project may fail at any time between now and the end of six years. The following table has VenCap's estimates of probabilities of failure for the project. First, 0.28 is the probability of failure in year 1. The probability that the project fails in the second year, given that it has survived through year 1, is 0.25. The probability that the project fails in the third year, given that it has survived through year 2, is 0.22; and so forth. VenCap is considering an equity investment in the project, and its cost of equity for a project with this level of risk is 22 percent.

Year	1	2	3	4	5	6
Failure probability	0.28	0.25	0.22	0.18	0.18	0.10

Compute the expected net present value of the venture capital project and recommend whether VenCap should accept or reject the project.

11. Consider a hedge fund that has an annual fee structure of 1.5 percent base management fee plus a 15 percent incentive fee applied to profits above the risk-free rate. If the risk-free rate is 5.5 percent, compute the net percentage return for an investor if the gross return during the year is

A. 35%

B. 5%

C. −6%

12. A hedge fund currently has assets of $2 billion. The annual fee structure of this fund consists of a fixed fee of 1 percent of portfolio assets plus a 20 percent incentive fee. The fund applies the incentive fee to the gross return each year in excess of the portfolio's previous high watermark, which is the maximum portfolio value since the inception of the fund. The maximum value the fund has achieved so far since its inception was a little more than a year ago when its value was $2.1 billion. Compute the fee that the manager would earn in dollars if the return on the fund this year turns out to be

A. 29%

B. 4.5%

C. −1.8%

13. Consider a hedge fund whose annual fee structure has a fixed fee and an incentive fee with a high watermark provision. The fund manager earns an incentive fee only if the fund is above the high watermark of the maximum portfolio value since the inception of the fund. Discuss the positive and negative implications of the high watermark provision for the investors of the hedge fund.

14. The shares of an Italian firm have been trading earlier around €6. Recently, a Spanish firm entered into talks with the Italian firm to acquire it. The Spanish firm offered two of its shares for every three shares of the Italian firm. The boards of directors of both firms have approved the merger, and ratification by shareholders is expected soon. The shares of the Spanish firm are currently trading at €12.50, and the shares of the Italian firm are trading at €8.

   A. Should the shares of the Italian firm trade at a discount? Explain.

   B. What position do you think a hedge fund that specializes in risk arbitrage in mergers and acquisitions will take in the two firms? Assume that the hedge fund's position will involve 250,000 shares of the Italian firm.

   C. It turns out that the European Union commission does not approve the merger because it fears that the merged firm will have a monopolistic position in its industry. After this announcement, the shares of the Italian firm fell to €6.10 each. The shares of the Spanish firm are still trading at €12.50 each. Discuss the consequences for the hedge fund. Ignore the cost of securities lending and margins deposit.

15. Global group manages hedge funds, and has three hedge funds invested in the stock market of a particular emerging country. These three hedge funds have very different investment strategies. As expected, the 2000 returns on the three funds were quite different. Over the year 2000, an index based on the overall stock market of the emerging country went up by 20 percent. Here are the performances of the three funds before management fees set at 15 percent of gross profits:

Fund	Gross Return
A	50%
B	20%
C	−10%

At year end, most clients had left fund C, and Global group closed this fund. At the start of 2001, Global group launched an aggressive publicity campaign among portfolio managers, stressing the remarkable return on fund A. If potential clients asked whether the firm had other hedge funds invested in the particular emerging market, it mentioned the only other fund, fund B, and claimed that the group's average gross performance during 2000 was 35 percent.

   A. Compare the average gross return and the average net return on the three hedge funds with the percentage increase in the stock market index.

   B. Comment on the publicity campaign launched by Global group.

16. An analyst is examining the performance of hedge funds. He looks at the 90 hedge funds that are in existence today, and notes that the average annual return on these funds during the last 10 years is 25.17 percent. The standard deviation of these returns is 17.43 percent and the Sharpe ratio is 1.15. The analyst also observes that the average of the annual returns on a stock market index during the last 10 years is 14.83 percent. The standard deviation of these returns is 11.87 percent and the Sharpe ratio is 0.81. The analyst concludes that the hedge funds have substantially outperformed the stock market index. Discuss why the comparison by the analyst could be misleading.

17. Consider the four major commodities traded on a commodity futures exchange today (year 10). The following table lists the average annualized price movements from year 1 to year 10, as well as the production volumes, expressed in the local currency unit, today (year 10) and ten years ago (year 1).

Commodity	Average Return	Annual Production Year 1	Year 10
A	20%	10	50
B	20%	5	20
C	−10%	50	10
D	0%	35	20

The futures exchange has now decided to create a commodity index based on the four commodities, with weights equal to their current relative importance in economic production. These indexes are back-calculated till year 1 using today's weights.

A. Would such an index give unbiased indications over the past 10 years?

B. What suggestions do you have regarding weights that can be used to back-calculate the indexes?

18. The beta of gold relative to the market portfolio is −0.3. The risk-free rate is 7 percent, and the market risk premium is 4 percent.

A. What is the expected return on gold based on the capital asset pricing model (CAPM)?

B. Give an intuitive explanation for the magnitude of the expected return on gold.

19. An analyst compared the performance of a hedge fund index with the performance of a major stock index over the past eight years. She noted that the hedge fund index (created from a database) had a higher average return, lower standard deviation, and higher Sharpe ratio than the stock index. All the successful funds that have been in the hedge fund database continued to accept new money over the eight-year period. Are the average return and the Sharpe ratio, respectively, for the hedge fund index *most likely* overstated or understated?

CFA
2005 exam

	Average Return for the Hedge Fund Index	Sharpe Ratio for the Hedge Fund Index
A.	Overstated	Overstated
B.	Overstated	Understated
C.	Understated	Overstated
D.	Understated	Understated

20. In-kind redemption is a process available to investors participating in:

   A. traditional mutual funds but not exchange traded funds.

   B. exchange traded funds but not traditional mutual funds.

   C. both traditional mutual funds and exchange traded funds.

   D. neither traditional mutual funds nor exchange traded funds.

21. Does trading take place only once a day at closing market prices in the case of:

	exchange traded funds?	traditional mutual funds?
A.	No	No
B.	No	Yes
C.	Yes	No
D.	Yes	Yes

22. Do funds that are likely to trade at substantial discounts from their net asset values include:

	exchange traded funds?	closed-end funds?
A.	No	No
B.	No	Yes
C.	Yes	No
D.	Yes	Yes

23. Forms of real estate investment that typically involve issuing shares that are traded on the stock market include:

   A. real estate investment trusts but not commingled funds.

   B. commingled funds but not real estate investment trusts.

   C. both real estate investment trusts and commingled funds.

   D. neither real estate investment trusts nor commingled funds.

24. An investor gathered the following information about a real estate investment:

Cost of the property	$800,000
Amount financed by mortgage loan	80%
Interest rate on mortgage loan	13%
Present value of after-tax cash flows from the investment	$226,000
Investor's required rate of return for an equity investment	16%

The investment's net present value (NPV) and yield to an equity investor, respectively, are best described as being:

	Investment's NPV	Investment's yield to an equity investor
A.	Positive	Greater than 16%
B.	Positive	Between 13% and 16%
C.	Negative	Less than 13%
D.	Negative	Between 13% and 16%

25. An investor is considering the purchase of an apartment building. The investor expects that net operating income will remain constant over the life of the investment. The investor plans to depreciate the property using straight-line depreciation and expects that his 35 percent tax rate will not change over the life of the investment. The investor will finance 80 percent of the purchase price with a long-term mortgage loan that will require a level annual payment of $62,600, and he intends to hold the property for at least ten years. During the years prior to the sale of the property, the investor's annual after-tax cash flow from the investment will *most likely:*

A. be lower in the third year than in the second year.

B. be higher in the third year than in the second year.

C. remain constant, because net operating income is expected to remain constant.

D. remain constant, because the cash inflows and outflows are expected to remain constant.

2005 exam

26. An investor gathered the following information about a real estate investment:

Amount financed by mortgage loan	$640,000
Interest rate on mortgage loan	10%
Term of mortgage loan	30 years
Year 1 gross potential rental income	$160,000
Year 1 estimated vacancy and collection losses	5%
Year 1 estimated insurance, taxes, and electricity	$35,000
Year 1 estimated repairs and maintenance	$20,000
Annual straight-line depreciation	$25,000
Investor's tax rate	30%

The mortgage loan requires level end-of-year annual payments of $67,891 and interest on the loan is tax-deductible. The investment's expected after-tax cash flow in year 1 is *closest* to:

A. $1,709.

B. $5,600.

C. $26,709.

D. $30,600.

2005 exam

27. A long time horizon is typically required for investments in:

A. distressed securities but not for investments in venture capital.

B. venture capital but not for investments in distressed securities.

C. both distressed securities and investments in venture capital.

D. neither distressed securities nor investments in venture capital.

2005 exam

28. An investor gathered the following information about a venture capital project

Initial investment in project	$400,000
Estimated payoff if project is successful	$12 million
Time to payoff for project	8 years
Probability of project's survival until end of year 8	15%
Investor's required rate of return	17%

The net present value of the venture capital project is *closest* to:

A. $52,608.

B. $112,608.

C. $172,608.

D. $452,608.

APPENDIX

Appendix A Solutions to End-of-Reading Problems

SOLUTIONS FOR READING 70

1. **B is correct.** A call option is not binding on both parties in the same sense that the other financial instruments are. The call option gives the holder a right but does not impose an obligation.

2. **B is correct.** If the market falls, the buyer of a forward contract could pay more for the index, as determined by the price that was contracted for at the inception of the contract, than the index is worth when the contract matures. Although it is possible that a rise in interest rates could cause the market to fall, this might not always happen and thus is a secondary consideration.

3. **D is correct.** Forward contracts are usually private transactions that do not have an intermediary such as a clearinghouse to guarantee performance by both parties. This type of transaction requires a high degree of credit-worthiness for both parties.

4. **B is correct.** Forward contracts are usually less liquid than futures contracts because they are typically private transactions tailored to suit both parties, unlike futures contracts, which are usually for standardized amounts and are exchange traded.

5. **A is correct.** A swap is most like a series of forward contracts. An example is a swap in which one party makes a set of fixed-rate payments over time in exchange for a set of floating-rate payments based on some notional amount.

6. **C is correct.** Unlike a contingent claim, a forward commitment typically requires no premium to be paid up front. An intuitive way to look at this is to realize that a forward commitment is binding on both parties, so any up-front fees would cancel, while a contingent claim is binding only on the party in the short position. For this, the party in the short position demands (and receives) compensation.

7. **C is correct.** Because the holder of a contingent claim (the party in the long position) has a right but not an obligation, she will only exercise when it is in her best interest to do so and not otherwise. This will happen only when she stands to gain and never when she stands to lose.

8. **A is correct.** The notional principal is the amount of the underlying asset covered by the derivative contract.

9. **A is correct.** The most widely used derivative contracts are written on underlying assets that are financial, such as Treasury instruments and stock indices.

10. **A is correct.** Arbitrage, or the absence of it, is the basis for pricing most derivative contracts. Consequently, it is relatively unusual, although certainly not impossible, for derivative markets to be used to generate arbitrage profits.

11. **B is correct.** One reason derivative markets have flourished is that they have relatively low transaction costs. For example, buying a risk-free Treasury security and a futures contract on the S&P 500 Index to replicate payoffs to the index is cheaper than buying the 500 stocks in the index in their proper proportions to get the same payoff.

12. B is correct. The clues that guide the response are (1) the transaction is private which eliminates both the futures contract answer and the exchange-traded answer, and (2) the transaction is a commitment ("agrees to make") thus eliminating the contingent claims answers. A swap with a single payment is equivalent to a forward contract.

13. B is correct. The transaction is a commitment which eliminates the contingent claims answers, the transaction is standardized which is a characteristic of futures contracts, and the transaction is for single delivery at a future date which is, in general, not a characteristic of a newly-initiated swap contract.

14. A is correct. In bankruptcy, the price of the bankrupt company's stock falls. In the limit it falls to zero. At a price of zero, the price cannot go any lower, and it would be advantageous to exercise the American put at that point in time rather than be forced to wait until the expiration date. Therefore, the American-style put is likely to have a higher price than an equivalent European-style put.

SOLUTIONS FOR READING 71

1. A. Taking a short position will hedge the interest rate risk for Company A. The gain on the contract will offset the reduced interest rate that can be earned when rates fall.

B. This is a 3×6 FRA.

C. $\$15,000,000 \left[\dfrac{(0.045 - 0.05)(90/360)}{1 + 0.045(90/360)} \right] = -\$18,541.41$

The negative sign indicates a gain to the short position, which Company A holds.

2. A. These instruments are called off-the-run FRAs.

B. $\$20,000,000 \left[\dfrac{(0.04 - 0.0475)(137/360)}{1 + 0.04(137/360)} \right] = -\$56,227.43$

Because the party is long, this amount represents a loss.

3. The contract is settled in cash, so the settlement would be €20,000,000(0.875 − 0.90) = −\$500,000. This amount would be paid by Sun Microsystems to the dealer. Sun would convert euros to dollars at the spot rate of \$0.90, receiving €20,000,000 × (0.90) = \$18,000,000. The net cash receipt is \$17,500,000, which results in an effective rate of \$0.875.

SOLUTIONS FOR READING 72

1. A. Parsons would close out his position in April by offsetting his long position with a short position. To do so, he would re-enter the market and offer for sale a June futures contract on the Nasdaq 100 index. When he has a buyer, he has both a long and a short position in the June futures contract on the Nasdaq 100 index. From the point of view of the clearinghouse, he no longer has a position in the contract.

B. Smith would close out her position in August by offsetting her short position with a long position. To do so, she would re-enter the market and purchase a September futures contract on the S&P 500. She then has both a short and a long position in the September futures contract on the S&P 500. From the point of view of the clearinghouse, she no longer has a position in the contract.

2. The difference between initial and maintenance margin requirements for one gold futures contract is $2,000 - $1,500 = $500. Because one gold futures contract is for 100 troy ounces, the difference between initial and maintenance margin requirements per troy ounce is $500/100, or $5.

A. Because Evans has a long position, he would receive a maintenance margin call if the price were to *fall* below $320 - $5, or $315 per troy ounce.

B. Because Tosca has a short position, he would receive a maintenance margin call if the price were to *rise* above $323 + $5, or $328 per troy ounce.

3. *Trader with a long position:* This trader loses if the price falls. The maximum loss would be incurred if the futures price falls to zero, and this loss would be $0.75/lb × 25,000 lbs, or $18,750. Of course, this scenario is only theoretical, not realistic.

Trader with a short position: This trader loses if the price increases. Because there is no limit on the price increase, there is no theoretical upper limit on the loss that the trader with a short position could incur.

4. A. The difference between the initial margin requirement and the maintenance margin requirement is $2. Because the initial futures price was $212, a margin call would be triggered if the price falls below $210.

B.

Day	Beginning Balance	Funds Deposited	Futures Price	Price Change	Gain/Loss	Ending Balance
0	0	200	212			200
1	200	0	211	−1	−20	180
2	180	0	214	3	60	240
3	240	0	209	−5	−100	140
4	140	60	210	1	20	220
5	220	0	204	−6	−120	100
6	100	100	202	−2	−40	160

Solutions to 1–6 taken from *Analysis of Derivatives for the CFA® Program*, by Don M. Chance. Copyright © 2003 by AIMR. Reprinted with permission. All other solutions copyright © 2007 by CFA Institute.

On day 0, you deposit $200 because the initial margin requirement is $10 per contract and you go long 20 contracts ($10 per contract times 20 contracts equals $200). At the end of day 3, the balance is down to $140, $20 below the $160 maintenance margin requirement ($8 per contract times 20 contracts). You must deposit enough money to bring the balance up to the initial margin requirement of $200. So, the next day (day 4), you deposit $60. The price change on day 5 causes a gain/loss of −$120, leaving you with a balance of $100 at the end of day 5. Again, this amount is less than the $160 maintenance margin requirement. You must deposit enough money to bring the balance up to the initial margin requirement of $200. So on day 6, you deposit $100.

C. By the end of day 6, the price is $202, a decrease of $10 from your purchase price of $212. Your loss so far is $10 per contract times 20 contracts, or $200.

You could also look at your loss so far as follows. You initially deposited $200, followed by margin calls of $60 and $100. Thus, you have deposited a total of $360 so far and have not withdrawn any excess margin. The ending balance, however, is only $160. Thus, the total loss incurred by you so far is $360 − $160, or $200.

5. A.

Day	Beginning Balance	Funds Deposited	Futures Price	Price Change	Gain/Loss	Ending Balance
0	0	2,700.00	96-06			2,700.00
1	2,700.00	0	96-31	25/32	−781.25	1,918.75
2	1,918.75	781.25	97-22	23/32	−718.75	1,981.25
3	1,981.25	718.75	97-18	−4/32	125.00	2,825.00
4	2,825.00	0	97-24	6/32	−187.50	2,637.50
5	2,637.50	0	98-04	12/32	−375.00	2,262.50
6	2,262.50	0	97-31	−5/32	156.25	2,418.75

On day 0, Moore deposits $2,700 because the initial margin requirement is $2,700 per contract and she has gone short one contract. At the end of day 1, the price has increased from 96-06 to 96-31—that is, the price has increased from $96,187.50 to $96,968.75. Because Moore has taken a short position, this increase of $781.25 is an adverse price movement for her, and the balance is down by $781.25 to $1,918.75. Because this amount is less than the $2,000 maintenance margin requirement, she must deposit additional funds to bring her account back to the initial margin requirement of $2,700. So, the next day (day 2), she deposits $781.25. Another adverse price movement takes place on day 2 as the price further increases by $718.75 to $97,687.50. Her ending balance is again below the maintenance margin requirement of $2,000, and she must deposit enough money to bring her account back to the initial margin requirement of $2,700. So, the next day (day 3), she deposits $718.75. Subsequently, even though her balance falls below the initial margin requirement, it does not go below the maintenance margin requirement, and she does not need to deposit any more funds.

B. Moore bought the contract at a futures price of 96-06. By the end of day 6, the price is 97-31, an increase of 1 25/32. Therefore, her loss so far is 1.78125 percent of $100,000, which is $1,781.25.

You could also look at her loss so far as follows: She initially deposited $2,700, followed by margin calls of $781.25 and $718.75. Thus, she has deposited a total of $4,200 so far, and has not withdrawn any excess margin. Her ending balance is $2,418.75. Thus, the total loss so far is $4,200 − $2,418.75, or $1,781.25.

6. A. Because the IMM index price is 95.23, the annualized LIBOR rate priced into the contract is 100 − 95.23 = 4.77 percent. With each contract based on $1 million notional principal of 90-day Eurodollars, the actual futures price is $1,000,000[1 − 0.0477(90/360)] = $988,075.

B. Because the IMM index price is 95.25, the annualized LIBOR rate priced into the contract is 100 − 95.25 = 4.75 percent. The actual futures price is $1,000,000[1 − 0.0475(90/360)] = $988,125. So, the change in actual futures price is $988,125 − $988,075 = $50.

You could also compute the change in price directly by noting that the IMM index price increased by 2 basis points. Because each basis point move in the rate moves the actual futures price by $25, the increase in the actual futures price is 2 × $25, or $50.

7. D is correct. Both statements describe functions of a clearinghouse.

8. B is correct. Initial margin is 20 contracts × $7.50 margin per contract = $150. At the end of day one, the short position has lost $20 [(85 − 86) × 20 contracts]. To meet the required maintenance margin of $140, the short deposits $10 variation margin. On day 2, the short position has a daily gain of $35 [(86 − 84.25) × 20], bringing the margin account to a balance of $175. The short position loses $25 on day 3 [(84.25 − 85.50) × 20], leaving a margin balance of $150.

9. B is correct. The short initiates the delivery process, and actual delivery typically can occur on any business day of the delivery month.

SOLUTIONS FOR READING 73

1. A. $S_T = 579.32$
   i. Call payoff, X = 450: $\text{Max}(0,579.32 - 450) \times 100 = \$12,932$
   ii. Call payoff, X = 650: $\text{Max}(0,579.32 - 650) \times 100 = 0$
   B. $S_T = 579.32$
   i. Put payoff, X = 450: $\text{Max}(0,450 - 579.32) \times 100 = 0$
   ii. Put payoff, X = 650: $\text{Max}(0,650 - 579.32) \times 100 = \$7,068$

2. A. $S_T = \$0.95$
   i. Call payoff, X = 0.85: $\text{Max}(0,0.95 - 0.85) \times 100,000 = \$10,000$
   ii. Call payoff, X = 1.15: $\text{Max}(0,0.95 - 1.15) \times 100,000 = \$0$
   B. $S_T = \$0.95$
   i. Put payoff, X = 0.85: $\text{Max}(0,0.85 - 0.95) \times 100,000 = \$0$
   ii. Put payoff, X = 1.15: $\text{Max}(0,1.15 - 0.95) \times 100,000 = \$20,000$

3. A. $S_T = 0.0653$
   i. Call payoff, X = 0.05: $\text{Max}(0,0.0653 - 0.05) \times (180/360) \times 10,000,000 = \$76,500$
   ii. Call payoff, X = 0.08: $\text{Max}(0,0.0653 - 0.08) \times (180/360) \times 10,000,000 = 0$
   B. $S_T = 0.0653$
   i. Put payoff, X = 0.05: $\text{Max}(0,0.05 - 0.0653) \times (180/360) \times 10,000,000 = 0$
   ii. Put payoff, X = 0.08: $\text{Max}(0,0.08 - 0.0653) \times (180/360) \times 10,000,000 = \$73,500$

4. A. $S_T = \$1.438$
   i. Call payoff, X = 1.35: $\text{Max}(0,1.438 - 1.35) \times 125,000 = \$11,000$
   ii. Call payoff, X = 1.55: $\text{Max}(0,1.438 - 1.55) \times 125,000 = \$0$
   B. $S_T = \$1.438$
   i. Put payoff, X = 1.35: $\text{Max}(0,1.35 - 1.438) \times 125,000 = \$0$
   ii. Put payoff, X = 1.55: $\text{Max}(0,1.55 - 1.438) \times 125,000 = \$14,000$

5. A. $S_T = 1136.76$
   i. Call payoff, X = 1130: $\text{Max}(0,1136.76 - 1130) \times 1,000 = \$6,760$
   ii. Call payoff, X = 1140: $\text{Max}(0,1136.76 - 1140) \times 1,000 = 0$
   B. $S_T = 1136.76$
   i. Put payoff, X = 1130: $\text{Max}(0,1130 - 1136.76) \times 1,000 = 0$
   ii. Put payoff, X = 1140: $\text{Max}(0,1140 - 1136.76) \times 1,000 = \$3,240$

6. A. $S_0 = 1240.89$, $T = 75/365 = 0.2055$, X = 1225 or 1255, call options
   i. X = 1225
      Maximum value for the call: $c_0 = S_0 = 1240.89$
      Lower bound for the call: $c_0 = \text{Max}[0,1240.89 - 1225/(1.03)^{0.2055}] = 23.31$
   ii. X = 1255
      Maximum value for the call: $c_0 = S_0 = 1240.89$
      Lower bound for the call: $c_0 = \text{Max}[0,1240.89 - 1255/(1.03)^{0.2055}] = 0$
   B. $S_0 = 1240.89$, $T = 75/365 = 0.2055$, X = 1225 or 1255, put options
   i. X = 1225
      Maximum value for the put: $p_0 = 1225/(1.03)^{0.2055} = 1217.58$
      Lower bound for the put: $p_0 = \text{Max}[0,1225/(1.03)^{0.2055} - 1240.89] = 0$

ii. X = 1255

Maximum value for the put: $p_0 = 1255/(1.03)^{0.2055} = 1247.40$

Lower bound for the put: $p_0 = Max[0,1255/(1.03)^{0.2055} - 1240.89]$
$= 6.51$

7. A. $S_0 = 1.05$, T = 60/365 = 0.1644, X = 0.95 or 1.10, American-style options

   i. X = $0.95

      Maximum value for the call: $C_0 = S_0 = \$1.05$

      Lower bound for the call: $C_0 = Max[0,1.05 - 0.95/(1.055)^{0.1644}]$
      $= \$0.11$

      Maximum value for the put: $P_0 = X = \$0.95$

      Lower bound for the put: $P_0 = Max(0,0.95 - 1.05) = \$0$

   ii. X = $1.10

      Maximum value for the call: $C_0 = S_0 = \$1.05$

      Lower bound for the call: $C_0 = Max[0,1.05 - 1.10/(1.055)^{0.1644}] = \$0$

      Maximum value for the put: $P_0 = X = \$1.10$

      Lower bound for the put: $P_0 = Max(0,1.10 - 1.05) = \$0.05$

B. $S_0 = 1.05$, T = 60/365 = 0.1644, X = 0.95 or 1.10, European-style options

   i. X = $0.95

      Maximum value for the call: $c_0 = S_0 = \$1.05$

      Lower bound for the call: $c_0 = Max[0,1.05 - 0.95/(1.055)^{0.1644}]$
      $= \$0.11$

      Maximum value for the put: $p_0 = 0.95/(1.055)^{0.1644} = \$0.94$

      Lower bound for the put: $p_0 = Max[0,0.95/(1.055)^{0.1644} - 1.05] = \$0$

   ii. X = $1.10

      Maximum value for the call: $c_0 = S_0 = \$1.05$

      Lower bound for the call: $c_0 = Max[0,1.05 - 1.10/(1.055)^{0.1644}] = \$0$

      Maximum value for the put: $p_0 = 1.10/(1.055)^{0.1644} = \$1.09$

      Lower bound for the put: $p_0 = Max[0,1.10/(1.055)^{0.1644} - 1.05]$
      $= \$0.04$

8. We can illustrate put–call parity by showing that for the fiduciary call and the protective put, the current values and values at expiration are the same.

Call price, $c_0 = \$6.64$

Put price, $p_0 = \$2.75$

Exercise price, X = $30

Risk-free rate, r = 4 percent

Time to expiration = 219/365 = 0.6

Current stock price, $S_0 = \$33.19$

Bond price, $X/(1 + r)^T = 30/(1 + 0.04)^{0.6} = \$29.30$

Transaction	Current Value	Value at Expiration	
		$S_T = 20$	$S_T = 40$
Fiduciary call			
Buy call	6.64	0	40 − 30 = 10
Buy bond	29.30	30	30
Total	35.94	30	40
Protective put			
Buy put	2.75	30 − 20 = 10	0
Buy stock	33.19	20	40
Total	35.94	30	40

The asset manager owes this amount to the dealer.
The overall payment made by the dealer to the asset manager is
$2,006,092 − $1,182,092 = $824,000.

6. A. The small-cap equity payment is $\left(\dfrac{238.41}{234.10} - 1\right)(50,000,000) =$
$920,547.

The asset manager owes the dealer this amount.
The fixed interest payment is $(50,000,000)(0.055)(180/365)$
= $1,356,164.
The dealer owes this amount to the asset manager.
So the dealer pays to the asset manager $1,356,164 − $920,547
= $435,617.

B. The small-cap equity payment is $\left(\dfrac{241.27}{234.10} - 1\right)(50,000,000)$
= $1,531,397.
The asset manager owes the dealer this amount.
The fixed interest payment is $(50,000,000)(0.055)(180/365)$
= $1,356,164.
The dealer owes this amount to the asset manager.
So the asset manager pays to the dealer $1,531,397 − $1,356,164
= $175,233.

7. A. The large-cap equity payment is $\left(\dfrac{622.54}{578.50} - 1\right)(25,000,000)$
= $1,903,198.
The dealer owes this amount to the asset manager.
The fixed interest payment is $(25,000,000)(0.045)(180/365)$
= $554,795.
The asset manager owes this amount to the dealer.
So the dealer pays to the asset manager $1,903,198 − $554,795
= $1,348,403.

B. The large-cap equity payment is $\left(\dfrac{581.35}{578.50} - 1\right)(25,000,000) =$
$123,163.
The dealer owes this amount to the asset manager.
The fixed interest payment is $(25,000,000)(0.045)(180/365)$
= $554,795.
The asset manager owes this amount to the dealer.
So the asset manager pays to the dealer $554,795 − $123,163
= $431,632.

8. A is correct. If the equity referenced in the equity swap shows a negative
return for a settlement date, the receive equity, pay fixed party would pay
both a variable payment based on the negative equity return and the fixed
rate payment. Given that interest rates will not go negative, an analogous
situation cannot occur in interest rate swaps.

9. B is correct. A 3 × 9 FRA uses the 180-day LIBOR contract as the underlying rate. Solve $(0.048 − 0.52) × (180/360)/[1 + 0.048 × (180/360)]$ =
−0.001953125. Multiply by 10,000,000. The answer is approximately
−$19,531.

10. A is correct. Agrawal would owe floating rate interest on the LIBOR loans.
The receive floating part of the swap would offset those payments, while the
pay fixed side of the swap resembles the fixed coupon payments on the
6.75% coupon bonds.

11. C is correct. The calculation is $5,000,000 × 0.08 × (180/365) −
$5,000,000 × 0.0725 × (180/360) = $16,010.

SOLUTIONS FOR READING 75

1. A. Call buyer

i. $c_T = \max(0, S_T - X) = \max(0, 55 - 50) = 5$

$\Pi = c_T - c_0 = 5 - 4 = 1$

ii. $c_T = \max(0, S_T - X) = \max(0, 51 - 50) = 1$

$\Pi = c_T - c_0 = 1 - 4 = -3$

iii. $c_T = \max(0, S_T - X) = \max(0, 48 - 50) = 0$

$\Pi = c_T - c_0 = 0 - 4 = -4$

B. Call seller

i. Value $= -c_T = -\max(0, S_T - X) = -\max(0, 49 - 50) = 0$

$\Pi = -c_T + c_0 = -0 + 4 = 4$

ii. Value $= -c_T = -\max(0, S_T - X) = -\max(0, 52 - 50) = -2$

$\Pi = -c_T + c_0 = -2 + 4 = 2$

iii. Value $= -c_T = -\max(0, S_T - X) = -\max(0, 55 - 50) = -5$

$\Pi = -c_T + c_0 = -5 + 4 = -1$

C. Maximum and minimum

i. Maximum profit to buyer (loss to seller) $= \infty$

ii. Maximum loss to buyer (profit to seller) $= c_0 = 4$

D. $S_T^* = X + c_0 = 50 + 4 = 54$

2. A.   **i.** $c_T = \max(0, S_T - X) = \max(0, 99 - 105) = 0$

$\Pi = c_T - c_0 = 0 - 7 = -7$

ii. $c_T = \max(0, S_T - X) = \max(0, 104 - 105) = 0$

$\Pi = c_T - c_0 = 0 - 7 = -7$

iii. $c_T = \max(0, S_T - X) = \max(0, 105 - 105) = 0$

$\Pi = c_T - c_0 = 0 - 7 = -7$

iv. $c_T = \max(0, S_T - X) = \max(0, 109 - 105) = 4$

$\Pi = c_T - c_0 = 4 - 7 = -3$

v. $c_T = \max(0, S_T - X) = \max(0, 112 - 105) = 7$

$\Pi = c_T - c_0 = 7 - 7 = 0$

vi. $c_T = \max(0, S_T - X) = \max(0, 115 - 105) = 10$

$\Pi = c_T - c_0 = 10 - 7 = 3$

B. $S_T^* = X + c_0 = 105 + 7 = 112$

Clearly, this result is consistent with our solution above, where the profit is exactly zero in Part A(v), in which the price at expiration is 112.

3. A. Put buyer

i. $p_T = \max(0, X - S_T) = \max(0, 2100 - 2125) = 0$

$\Pi = p_T - p_0 = 0 - 106.25 = -106.25$

ii. $p_T = \max(0, X - S_T) = \max(0, 2100 - 2050) = 50$

$\Pi = p_T - p_0 = 50 - 106.25 = -56.25$

Solutions to 1–6 taken from *Analysis of Derivatives for the CFA® Program*, by Don M. Chance. Copyright © 2003 by AIMR. Reprinted with permission. All other solutions copyright © 2007 by CFA Institute.

iii. $p_T = \max(0, X - S_T) = \max(0, 2100 - 1950) = 150$

A priori probability A probability based on logical analysis rather than on observation or personal judgment.

Abandonment option The ability to terminate a project at some future time if the financial results are disappointing.

Abnormal rate of return The amount by which a security's actual return differs from its expected rate of return which is based on the market's rate of return and the security's relationship with the market.

Above full-employment equilibrium A macroeconomic equilibrium in which real GDP exceeds potential GDP.

Absolute dispersion The amount of variability present without comparison to any reference point or benchmark.

Absolute frequency The number of observations in a given interval (for grouped data).

Accelerated method A method of depreciation that allocates relatively large amounts of the depreciable cost of an asset to earlier years and reduced amounts to later years.

Accelerated methods of depreciation Depreciation methods that allocate a relatively large proportion of the cost of an asset to the early years of the asset's useful life.

Account With the accounting systems, a formal record of increases and decreases in a specific asset, liability, component of owners' equity, revenue, or expense.

Account format A method of presentation of accounting transactions in which effects on assets appear at the left and effects on liabilities and equity appear at the right of a central dividing line; also known as T-account format.

Accounting risk The risk associated with accounting standards that vary from country to country or with any uncertainty about how certain transactions should be recorded.

Accounts payable Amounts that a business owes to its vendors for goods and services that were purchased from them but which have not yet been paid.

Accounts receivable turnover Ratio of sales on credit to the average balance in accounts receivable.

Accrual accounting The system of recording financial transactions as they come into existence as a legally enforceable claim, rather than when they settle.

Accrued expenses (accrued liabilities) Liabilities related to expenses that have been incurred but not yet paid as of the end of an accounting period—an example of an accrued expense is rent that has been incurred but not yet paid, resulting in a liability "rent payable."

Accrued interest Interest earned but not yet paid.

Accumulated depreciation An offset to property, plant, and equipment (PPE) reflecting the amount of the cost of PPE that has been allocated to current and previous accounting periods.

Active factor risk The contribution to active risk squared resulting from the portfolio's different-than-benchmark exposures relative to factors specified in the risk model.

Active return The return on a portfolio minus the return on the portfolio's benchmark.

Active risk The standard deviation of active returns.

Active risk squared The variance of active returns; active risk raised to the second power.

Active specific risk or asset selection risk The contribution to active risk squared resulting from the portfolio's active weights on individual assets as those weights interact with assets' residual risk.

Active strategy In reference to short-term cash management, an investment strategy characterized by monitoring and attempting to capitalize on market conditions to optimize the risk and return relationship of short-term investments.

Activity ratios (asset utilization or operating efficiency ratios) Ratios that measure how efficiently a company performs day-to-day tasks, such as the collection of receivables and management of inventory.

Addition rule for probabilities A principle stating that the probability that A or B occurs (both occur) equals the probability that A occurs, plus the probability that B occurs, minus the probability that both A and B occur.

Additional information Information that is required or recommended under the GIPS standards and is not considered as "supplemental information" for the purposes of compliance.

Additions Enlargements to the physical layout of a plant asset.

Add-on interest A procedure for determining the interest on a bond or loan in which the interest is added onto the face value of a contract.

Adjusted beta Historical beta adjusted to reflect the tendency of beta to be mean reverting.

G-1

Business cycle The periodic but irregular up-and-down movement in production.

Business risk (or sales risk) Risk that is related to the uncertainty of revenues

Butterfly spread An option strategy that combines two bull or bear spreads and has three exercise prices.

Buy-and-hold strategy A passive portfolio management strategy in which securities (bonds or stocks) are bought and held to maturity.

Call An option that gives the holder the right to buy an underlying asset from another party at a fixed price over a specific period of time.

Call market A market in which trading for individual stocks only takes place at specified times. All the bids and asks available at the time are combined and the market administrators specify a single price that will possibly clear the market at that time.

Call option Option to buy an asset within a certain period at a specified price called the *exercise price*.

Call premium Amount above par that an issuer must pay to a bondholder for retiring the bond before its stated maturity.

Call provisions Specifies when and how a firm can issue a call for bonds outstanding prior to their maturity.

Cannibalization Cannibalization occurs when an investment takes customers and sales away from another part of the company.

Cap (1) A contract on an interest rate, whereby at periodic payment dates, the writer of the cap pays the difference between the market interest rate and a specified cap rate if, and only if, this difference is positive. This is equivalent to a stream of call options on the interest rate. (2) A combination of interest rate call options designed to hedge a borrower against rate increases on a floating-rate loan.

Capital The tools, equipment, buildings, and other constructions that businesses now use to produce goods and services.

Capital account (1) The record of transactions with foreigners that involve either (a) the exchange of ownership rights to real or financial assets or (b) the extension of loans. (2) A component of the balance of payments that reflects unrequited (or unilateral) transfers corresponding to capital flows entailing no compensation (in the form of goods, services, or assets). Examples include investment capital given (without future repayment) in favor of poor countries, debt forgiveness, and expropriation losses.

Capital accumulation The growth of capital resources.

Capital allocation line (CAL) A graph line that describes the combinations of expected return and standard deviation of return available to an investor from combining the optimal portfolio of risky assets with the risk-free asset.

Capital appreciation A return objective in which the investor seeks to increase the portfolio value, primarily through capital gains, over time to meet a future need rather than dividend yield.

Capital asset pricing model (CAPM) An equation describing the expected return on any asset (or portfolio) as a linear function of its beta relative to the market portfolio.

Capital budgeting The allocation of funds to relatively long-range projects or investments.

Capital Employed (Real Estate) The denominator of the return expressions, defined as the "weighted-average equity" (weighted-average capital) during the measurement period. Capital employed should not include any income or capital return accrued during the measurement period. Beginning capital is adjusted by weighting the cash flows (contributions and distributions) that occurred during the period. Cash flows are typically weighted based on the actual days the flows are in or out of the portfolio. Other weighting methods are acceptable; however, once a methodology is chosen, it should be consistently applied.

Capital expenditure An expenditure for the purchase or expansion of a long-term asset, recorded in an asset account.

Capital market line (CML) The line with an intercept point equal to the risk-free rate that is tangent to the efficient frontier of risky assets; represents the efficient frontier when a risk-free asset is available for investment.

Capital preservation A return objective in which the investor seeks to minimize the risk of loss; generally a goal of the risk-averse investor.

Capital rationing A capital rationing environment assumes that the company has a fixed amount of funds to invest.

Capital return (real estate) The change in the market value of the real estate investments and cash/cash equivalent assets held throughout the measurement period (ending market value less beginning market value) adjusted for all capital expenditures (subtracted) and the net proceeds from sales (added). The return is computed as a percentage of the capital employed through the measurement period. Synonyms: capital appreciation return, appreciation return.

Capital stock   The total quantity of plant, equipment, buildings, and inventories.

Capital structure   A company's specific mixture of long-term financing.

Caplet   Each component call option in a cap.

Capped swap   A swap in which the floating payments have an upper limit.

Captive finance subsidiary   A wholly-owned subsidiary of a company that is established to provide financing of the sales of the parent company.

Carried interest (private equity)   The profits that general partners earn from the profits of the investments made by the fund (generally 20-25%). Also known as "carry."

Carrying value   The unexpired part of an asset's cost. Also called *book value*.

Cartel   A group of firms that has entered into a collusive agreement to limit output and increase prices and profits.

Carve-Out   A single or multiple asset class segment of a multiple asset class portfolio.

Cash   In accounting contexts, cash on hand (e.g., petty cash and cash not yet deposited to the bank) and demand deposits held in banks and similar accounts that can be used in payment of obligations.

Cash conversion cycle (net operating cycle)   A financial metric that measures the length of time required for a company to convert cash invested in its operations to cash received as a result of its operations; equal to days of inventory on hand + days of sales outstanding − number of days of payables.

Cash equivalents   Very liquid short-term investments, usually maturing in 90 days or less.

Cash flow additivity principle   The principle that dollar amounts indexed at the same point in time are additive.

Cash flow at risk (CFAR)   A variation of VAR that reflects the risk of a company's cash flow instead of its market value.

Cash flow coverage ratio   Ratio of cash flow from operations + interest payments + tax payments to interest payments; a comparison of the cash flows available to meet interest obligations with existing interest obligations.

Cash flow from operations (cash flow from operating activities or operating cash flow)   The net amount of cash provided from operating activities.

Cash flow statement (statement of cash flows)   A financial statement that reconciles beginning-of-period and end-of-period balance sheet values of cash; consists of three parts: cash flows from operating activities, cash flows from investing activities, and cash flows from financing activities.

Cash-flow-to-debt ratio   Ratio of cash flow from operations to total debt; a measure of debt coverage that estimates the length of time it would take for the company to repay its debt if it were to apply all of its cash flow from operations toward debt repayment.

Cash-generating efficiency   A company's ability to generate cash from its current or continuing operations.

Cash price or spot price   The price for immediate purchase of the underlying asset.

Cash ratio   The ratio of cash + short-term marketable investments to current liabilities; provides an indication of a company's ability to satisfy current liabilities with just the cash and cash equivalents on hand.

Cash settlement   A procedure used in certain derivative transactions that specifies that the long and short parties engage in the equivalent cash value of a delivery transaction.

CD equivalent yield   *See* Money market yield.

Central bank   A bank's bank and a public authority that regulates a nation's depository institutions and controls the quantity of money.

Central limit theorem   A result in statistics that states that the sample mean computed from large samples of size n from a population with finite variance will follow an approximate normal distribution with a mean equal to the population mean and a variance equal to the population variance divided by n.

Centralized risk management or companywide risk management   When a company has a single risk management group that monitors and controls all of the risk-taking activities of the organization. Centralization permits economies of scale and allows a company to use some of its risks to offset other risks. See also *enterprise risk management*.

Certificates of deposit (CDs)   Instruments issued by banks and S&Ls that require minimum deposits for specified terms and that pay higher rates of interest than deposit accounts.

Ceteris paribus   Other things being equal—all other relevant things remaining the same.

Chain rule of forecasting   A forecasting process in which the next period's value as predicted by the forecasting equation is substituted into the right-hand side of the equation to give a predicted value two periods ahead.

Conditional expected value (1) Expected value of a variable conditional on some available information set. The expected value changes over time with changes in the information set. (2) The expected value of a stated event given that another event has occurred.

Conditional heteroskedasticity Heteroskedasticity in the error variance that is correlated with the values of the independent variable(s) in the regression.

Conditional probability The probability of an event given (conditioned on) another event.

Conditional variance (1) Variance of a variable conditional on some available information set. (2) The variance of one variable, given the outcome of another.

Conditional variances The variance of one variable, given the outcome of another.

Confidence interval A range that has a given probability that it will contain the population parameter it is intended to estimate.

Consistency A desirable property of estimators; a consistent estimator is one for which the probability of estimates close to the value of the population parameter increases as sample size increases.

Consistent With reference to estimators, describes an estimator for which the probability of estimates close to the value of the population parameter increases as sample size increases.

Consolidated Quotation System (CQS) An electronic quotation service for issues listed on the NYSE, the AMEX, or regional exchanges and traded on the Nasdaq InterMarket.

Constant maturity swap or CMT swap A swap in which the floating rate is the rate on a security known as a constant maturity treasury or CMT security.

Constant maturity treasury or CMT A hypothetical U.S. Treasury note with a constant maturity. A CMT exists for various years in the range of 2 to 10.

Constant returns to scale Features of a firm's technology that leads to constant long-run average cost as output increases. When constant returns to scale are present, the *LRAC* curve is horizontal.

Consumer Price Index (CPI) An index that measures the average of the prices paid by urban consumers for a fixed "basket" of the consumer goods and services.

Consumer surplus The value of a good minus the price paid for it, summed over the quantity bought.

Consumption expenditure The total payment for consumer goods and services.

Contango A situation in a futures market where the current futures price is greater than the current spot price for the underlying asset.

Contestable market A market in which firms can enter and leave so easily that firms in the market face competition from potential entrants.

Contingent claims Derivatives in which the payoffs occur if a specific event occurs; generally referred to as options.

Continuous market A market where stocks are priced and traded continuously by an auction process or by dealers when the market is open.

Continuous random variable A random variable for which the range of possible outcomes is the real line (all real numbers between $-\infty$ and ∞) or some subset of the real line.

Continuous time Time thought of as advancing in extremely small increments.

Continuously compounded return The natural logarithm of 1 plus the holding period return, or equivalently, the natural logarithm of the ending price over the beginning price.

Contra account An account that offsets another account.

Contract price The transaction price specified in a forward or futures contract.

Convenience yield The nonmonetary return offered by an asset when the asset is in short supply, often associated with assets with seasonal production processes.

Conventional cash flow A conventional cash flow pattern is one with an initial outflow followed by a series of inflows.

Conversion factor An adjustment used to facilitate delivery on bond futures contracts in which any of a number of bonds with different characteristics are eligible for delivery.

Conversion value The value of the convertible security if converted into common stock at the stock's current market price.

Convertible bonds A bond with the added feature that the bondholder has the option to turn the bond back to the firm in exchange for a specified number of common shares of the firm.

Convexity (1) A measure of the change in duration with respect to changes in interest rates. (2) A measure of the degree to which a bond's price-yield curve departs from a straight line. This characteristic affects estimates of a bond's price volatility for a given change in yields.

Cooperative equilibrium The outcome of a game in which the players make and share the monopoly profit.

Copyright A government-sanctioned exclusive right granted to the inventor of a good, service, or productive process to produce, use, and sell the invention for a given number of years.

Correlation A number between −1 and 1 that measures the co-movement (linear association) between two random variables.

Correlation analysis The analysis of the strength of the linear relationship between two data series.

Correlation coefficient A standardized measure of the relationship between two variables that ranges from 2 1.00 to 1 1.00.

Cost averaging The periodic investment of a fixed amount of money.

Cost of capital The rate of return that the suppliers of capital-bondholders and owners-require as compensation for their contribution of capital.

Cost of carry The cost associated with holding some asset, including financing, storage, and insurance costs. Any yield received on the asset is treated as a negative carrying cost.

Cost of carry model A model for pricing futures contracts in which the futures price is determined by adding the cost of carry to the spot price.

Cost of debt The cost of debt financing to a company, such as when it issues a bond or takes out a bank loan.

Cost of goods sold For a given period, equal to beginning inventory minus ending inventory plus the cost of goods acquired or produced during the period.

Cost of preferred stock The cost to a company of issuing preferred stock; the dividend yield that a company must commit to pay preferred stock holders.

Cost recovery method A method of revenue recognition in which is the seller does not report any profit until the cash amounts paid by the buyer—including principal and interest on any financing from the seller——are greater than all the seller's costs for the merchandise sold.

Cost-push inflation An inflation that results from an initial increase in costs.

Council of Economic Advisers In the executive branch of the U.S. government, a council whose main work is to monitor the economy and keep the President and the public well informed about the current state of the economy and the best available forecasts of where it is heading.

Counterparty A participant to a derivative transaction.

Country risk Uncertainty due to the possibility of major political or economic change in the country where an investment is located. Also called *political risk*.

Coupon Indicates the interest payment on a debt security. It is the coupon rate times the par value that indicates the interest payments on a debt security.

Covariance A measure of the co-movement (linear association) between two random variables.

Covariance matrix A matrix or square array whose entries are covariances; also known as a variance-covariance matrix.

Covariance stationary Describes a time series when its expected value and variance are constant and finite in all periods and when its covariance with itself for a fixed number of periods in the past or future is constant and finite in all periods.

Covered call An option strategy involving the holding of an asset and sale of a call on the asset.

Covered interest arbitrage A transaction executed in the foreign exchange market in which a currency is purchased (sold) and a forward contract is sold (purchased) to lock in the exchange rate for future delivery of the currency. This transaction should earn the risk-free rate of the investor's home country.

Credit With respect to double-entry accounting, a credit records increases in liability, owners' equity, and revenue accounts or decreases in asset accounts; with respect to borrowing, the willingness and ability of the borrower to make promised payments on the borrowing.

Credit analysis The evaluation of credit risk; the evaluation of the creditworthiness of a borrower or counterparty.

Credit derivatives A contract in which one party has the right to claim a payment from another party in the event that a specific credit event occurs over the life of the contract.

Credit-linked notes Fixed-income securities in which the holder of the security has the right to withhold payment of the full amount due at maturity if a credit event occurs.

Credit risk (or default risk) The risk of loss caused by a counterparty's or debtor's failure to make a promised payment.

Credit scoring model A statistical model used to classify the creditworthiness of borrowers.

Credit spread option An option on the yield spread on a bond.

Credit swap A type of swap transaction used as a credit derivative in which one party makes periodic payments to the other and receives the promise of a payoff if a third party defaults.

changes through time, and the position must be revised to maintain the hedge.

Delta-normal method A measure of VAR equivalent to the analytical method but that refers to the use of delta to estimate the option's price sensitivity.

Demand The relationship between the quantity of a good that consumers plan to buy and the price of the good when all other influences on buyers' plans remain the same. It is described by a demand schedule and illustrated by a demand curve.

Demand curve A curve that shows the relationship between the quantity demanded of a good and its price when all other influences on consumers' planned purchases remain the same.

Demand for labor The relationship between the quantity of labor demanded and the real wage rate when all other influences on firm's hiring plans remain the same.

Demand-pull inflation An inflation that results from an initial increase in aggregate demand.

Dependent With reference to events, the property that the probability of one event occurring depends on (is related to) the occurrence of another event.

Dependent variable The variable whose variation about its mean is to be explained by the regression; the left-hand-side variable in a regression equation.

Depletion The exhaustion of a natural resource through mining, cutting, pumping, or other extraction, and the way in which the cost is allocated.

Depository institution A firm that takes deposits from households and firms and makes loans to other households and firms.

Depreciable cost The cost of an asset less its residual value.

Depreciation The process of systematically allocating the cost of long-lived (tangible) assets to the periods during which the assets are expected to provide economic benefits.

Derivative A financial instrument that offers a return based on the return of some other underlying asset or factor (e.g., a stock price, an interest rate, or exchange rate).

Derivative security An instrument whose market value ultimately depends upon, or derives from, the value of a more fundamental investment vehicle called the underlying asset or security.

Derivatives (1) Securities bearing a contractual relation to some underlying asset or rate. Options, futures, forward, and swap contracts, as well as many forms of bonds, are derivative securities. (2) A financial instrument that offers a return based on the return of some other underlying asset.

Derivatives dealers Commercial and investment banks that make markets in derivatives. .

Derived demand The demand for a productive resource, which is derived from the demand for the goods and services produced by the resource.

Descriptive statistics The study of how data can be summarized effectively.

Diff swaps A swap in which the payments are based on the difference between interest rates in two countries but payments are made in only a single currency.

Diffuse prior The assumption of equal prior probabilities.

Diluted earnings per share Net income, minus preferred dividends, divided by the number of common shares outstanding considering all dilutive securities (e.g., convertible debt and options); the EPS that would result if all dilutive securities were converted into common shares.

Diluted shares The number of shares that would be outstanding if all potentially dilutive claims on common shares (e.g., convertible debt, convertible preferred stock, and employee stock options) were exercised.

Diminishing balance method An accelerated depreciation method, i.e., one that allocates a relatively large proportion of the cost of an asset to the early years of the asset's useful life.

Diminishing marginal returns The tendency for the marginal product of an additional unit of a factor of production to be less than the marginal product of the previous unit of the factor.

Diminishing marginal utility The decrease in marginal utility as the quantity consumed increases.

Direct debit program An arrangement whereby a customer authorizes a debit to a demand account; typically used by companies to collect routine payments for services.

Direct format (direct method) With reference to the cash flow statement, a format for the presentation of the statement in which cash flow from operating activities is shown as operating cash receipts less operating cash disbursements.

Direct method The procedure for converting the income statement from an accrual basis to a cash basis by adjusting each item on the income statement.

Direct write-off method An approach to recognizing credit losses on customer receivables in which the company waits until such time as a customer has defaulted and only then recognizes the loss.

Disbursement float The amount of time between check issuance and a check's clearing back against the company's account.

Discount To reduce the value of a future payment in allowance for how far away it is in time; to calculate the present value of some future amount. Also, the amount by which an instrument is priced below its face value.

Discount interest A procedure for determining the interest on a loan or bond in which the interest is deducted from the face value in advance.

Discounting The conversion of a future amount of money to its present value.

Discouraged workers People who are available and willing to work but have not made specific efforts to find a job within the previous four weeks.

Discrete random variable A random variable that can take on at most a countable number of possible values.

Discrete time Time thought of as advancing in distinct finite increments.

Discretionary fiscal policy A policy action that is initiated by an act of Congress.

Discretionary policy A policy that responds to the state of the economy in a possibly unique way that uses all the information available, including perceived lessons from past "mistakes."

Discriminant analysis A multivariate classification technique used to discriminate between groups, such as companies that either will or will not become bankrupt during some time frame.

Diseconomies of scale Features of a firm's technology that leads to rising long-run average cost as output increases.

Dispersion The variability around the central tendency.

Disposable income Aggregate income minus taxes plus transfer payments.

Distinct business entity A unit, division, department, or office that is organizationally and functionally segregated from other units, divisions, departments, or offices and retains discretion over the assets it manages and autonomy over the investment decision-making process. Possible criteria that can be used to determine this include: (a) being a legal entity; (b) having a distinct market or client type (e.g., institutional, retail, private client, etc.); (c) using a separate and distinct investment process.

Dividend discount model (DDM) A technique for estimating the value of a stock issue as the present value of all future dividends.

Dividend discount model based approach or implied risk premium approach An approach for estimating a country's equity risk premium. The market rate of return is estimated as the sum of the dividend yield and the growth rate in dividends for a market index. Subtracting the risk-free rate of return from the estimated market return produces an estimate for the equity risk premium.

Dividend payout ratio The ratio of dividends paid to earnings for a period; more specifically, the ratio of dividends paid to common shareholders to net income attributable to common shares.

Dividends per share The dollar amount of cash dividends paid during a period per share of common stock.

Dominant strategy equilibrium A Nash equilibrium in which the best strategy of each player is to cheat (deny) regardless of the strategy of the other player.

Double declining balance depreciation An accelerated depreciation method that involves depreciating the asset at double the straight-line rate.

Double-declining-balance method An accelerated method of depreciation in which a fixed rate equal to twice the straight-line percentage is applied to the carrying value (the declining balance) of a tangible long-lived asset.

Double-entry accounting The accounting system of recording transactions in which every recorded transaction affects at least two accounts so as to keep the basic accounting equation (assets = liabilities + owners' equity) in balance.

Down transition probability The probability that an asset's value moves down in a model of asset price dynamics.

Drag on liquidity When receipts lag, creating pressure from the decreased available funds.

Dummy variable A type of qualitative variable that takes on a value of 1 if a particular condition is true and 0 if that condition is false.

Dumping The sale by a foreign firm of exports at a lower price that the cost of production.

Duopoly A market structure in which two producers of a good or service compete.

DuPont analysis An approach to decomposing return on investment, e.g., return on equity, as the product of other financial ratios.

DuPont system A method of examining ROE by breaking it down into three component parts: (1) profit margin, (2) total asset turnover, and (3) financial leverage.

Duration A measure of an option-free bond's average maturity. Specifically, the weighted average maturity of all future cash flows paid by a security, in which the weights are the present value of these cash flows as a fraction of the bond's price. A measure of a bond's price sensitivity to interest rate movements.

Dutch Book Theorem   A result in probability theory stating that inconsistent probabilities create profit opportunities.

Dynamic comparative advantage   A comparative advantage that a person or country possesses as a result of having specialized in a particular activity and then, as a result of learning-by-doing, having become the producer with the lowest opportunity cost.

Dynamic hedging   A strategy in which a position is hedged by making frequent adjustments to the quantity of the instrument used for hedging in relation to the instrument being hedged.

Earnings at risk (EAR)   A variation of VAR that reflects the risk of a company's earnings instead of its market value.

Earnings momentum   A strategy in which portfolios are constructed of stocks of firms with rising earnings.

Earnings multiplier model   A technique for estimating the value of a stock issue as a multiple of its earnings per share.

Earnings per share (EPS)   The amount of income earned during a period per share of common stock; (net income − preferred dividends) divided by the weighted average number of common shares outstanding.

Earnings surprise   A company announcement of earnings that differ from analysts' prevailing expectations.

Earnings yield   Earnings per share divided by price; the reciprocal of the P/E ratio.

EBITDA   Earnings before interest, taxes, depreciation, and amortization.

Economic depreciation   The change in the market value of capital over a given period.

Economic efficiency   A situation that occurs when the firm produces a given output at the least cost.

Economic exposure   The risk associated with changes in the relative attractiveness of products and services offered for sale, arising out of the competitive effects of changes in exchange rates.

Economic growth   The expansion of production possibilities that results from capital accumulation and technological change.

Economic information   Data on prices, quantities, and qualities of goods and services and factors of production.

Economic model   A description of some aspect of the economic world that includes only those features of the world that are needed for the purpose at hand.

Economic order quantity-reorder point   An approach to managing inventory based on expected demand and the predictability of demand; the ordering point for new inventory is determined based on the costs of ordering and carrying inventory, such that the total cost associated with inventory is minimized.

Economic profit   A firm's total revenue minus its opportunity cost.

Economic rent   The income received by the owner of a factor of production over and above the amount required to induce that owner to offer the factor for use.

Economic theory   A generalization that summarizes what we think we understand about the economic choices that people make and the performance of industries and entire economies.

Economic value added (EVA)   Internal management performance measure that compares net operating profit to total cost of capital. Indicates how profitable company projects are as a sign of management performance.

Economics   The social science that studies the *choices* that individuals, businesses, governments, and entire societies make and how they cope with *scarcity* and the *incentives* that influence and reconcile those choices.

Economies of scale   Features of a firm's technology that leads to a falling long-run average cost as output increases.

Economies of scope   Decreases in average total cost that occur when a firm uses specialized resources to produce a range of goods and services.

Effective annual rate   The amount by which a unit of currency will grow in a year with interest on interest included.

Effective annual yield (EAY)   An annualized return that accounts for the effect of interest on interest; EAY is computed by compounding 1 plus the holding period yield forward to one year, then subtracting 1.

Effective duration   Direct measure of the interest rate sensitivity of a bond (or any financial instrument) based upon price changes derived from a pricing model.

Efficiency   In statistics, a desirable property of estimators; an efficient estimator is the unbiased estimator with the smallest variance among unbiased estimators of the same parameter.

Efficient capital market   A market in which security prices rapidly reflect all information about securities.

Efficient frontier   The portion of the minimum-variance frontier beginning with the global minimum-variance portfolio and continuing above it; the graph of the set of portfolios offering the maximum expected return for their level of variance of return.

Efficient market A market in which the actual price embodies all currently available relevant information. Resources are sent to their highest valued use.

Efficient portfolio A portfolio offering the highest expected return for a given level of risk as measured by variance or standard deviation of return.

Elastic demand Demand with a price elasticity greater than 1; other things remaining the same, the percentage change in the quantity demanded exceeds the percentage change in price.

Elasticity of demand The responsiveness of the quantity demanded of a good to a change in its price, other things remaining the same.

Elasticity of supply The responsiveness of the quantity supplied of a good to a change in its price, other things remaining the same.

Electronic funds transfer The use of computer networks to conduct financial transactions electronically.

Empirical probability The probability of an event estimated as a relative frequency of occurrence.

Employment Act of 1946 A landmark Congressional act that recognized a role for government actions to keep unemployment, keep the economy expanding, and keep inflation in check.

Employment-to-population ratio The percentage of people of working age who have jobs.

Ending market value (private equity) The remaining equity that a limited partner has in a fund. Also referred to as net asset value or residual value.

Enhanced derivatives products companies (EDPC or special purpose vehicles SPVs) A type of subsidiary engaged in derivatives transactions that is separated from the parent company in order to have a higher credit rating than the parent company.

Enterprise risk management A form of *centralized risk management* that typically encompasses the management of a broad variety of risks, including insurance risk.

Entrepreneurship The human resource that organizes labor, land, and capital. Entrepreneurs come up with new ideas about what and how to produce, make business decisions, and bear the risks that arise from their decisions.

Equation of exchange An equation that states that the quantity of money multiplied by the velocity of circulation equals GDP.

Equilibrium price The price at which the quantity demanded equals the quantity supplied.

Equilibrium quantity The quantity bought and sold at the equilibrium price.

Equitizing cash A strategy used to replicate an index. It is also used to take a given amount of cash and turn it into an equity position while maintaining the liquidity provided by the cash.

Equity Assets less liabilities; the residual interest in the assets after subtracting the liabilities.

Equity forward A contract calling for the purchase of an individual stock, a stock portfolio, or a stock index at a later date at an agreed-upon price.

Equity options Options on individual stocks; also known as stock options.

Equity risk premium The expected return on equities minus the risk-free rate; the premium that investors demand for investing in equities.

Equity swap A swap transaction in which at least one cash flow is tied to the return to an equity portfolio position, often an equity index.

Error autocorrelation The autocorrelation of the error term.

Error term The portion of the dependent variable that is not explained by the independent variable(s) in the regression.

Estimate The particular value calculated from sample observations using an estimator.

Estimated (or fitted) parameters With reference to regression analysis, the estimated values of the population intercept and population slope coefficient(s) in a regression.

Estimated rate of return The rate of return an investor anticipates earning from a specific investment over a particular future holding period.

Estimated useful life The total number of service units expected from a long-term asset.

Estimation With reference to statistical inference, the subdivision dealing with estimating the value of a population parameter.

Estimator An estimation formula; the formula used to compute the sample mean and other sample statistics are examples of estimators.

Eurobonds Bonds denominated in a currency not native to the country in which they are issued.

Eurodollar A dollar deposited outside the United States.

European option An option contract that can only be exercised on its expiration date.

European terms With reference to U.S. dollar exchange rate quotations, the price of a U.S. dollar in terms of another currency.

European-style option or European option An option exercisable only at maturity.

European Union (EU)   A formal association of European countries founded by the Treaty of Rome in 1957. Formerly known as the EEC.

Event   Any outcome or specified set of outcomes of a random variable.

Event study   Research that examines the reaction of a security's price to a specific company, world event, or news announcement.

Ex-ante   Before the fact.

Excess kurtosis   Degree of peakedness (fatness of tails) in excess of the peakedness of the normal distribution.

Excess reserves   A bank's actual reserves minus its required reserves.

Exchange for physicals (EFP)   A permissible delivery procedure used by futures market participants, in which the long and short arrange a delivery procedure other than the normal procedures stipulated by the futures exchange.

Exchange rate risk   Uncertainty due to the denomination of an investment in a currency other than that of the investor's own country.

Exchange-traded fund (ETF)   A tradable depository receipt that gives investors a pro rata claim to the returns associated with a portfolio of securities (often designed to mimic an index, such as the Standard & Poor's 500) held in trust by a financial institution.

Exercise (or exercising the option)   The process of using an option to buy or sell the underlying.

Exercise price (or strike price or striking price, or strike)   The fixed price at which an option holder can buy or sell the underlying.

Exercise rate or strike rate   The fixed rate at which the holder of an interest rate option can buy or sell the underlying.

Exhaustive   Covering or containing all possible outcomes.

Expansion   A business cycle phase between a trough and a peak-phase in which real GDP increases.

Expected rate of return   The return that analysts' calculations suggest a security should provide, based on the market's rate of return during the period and the security's relationship to the market.

Expected return   The rate of return that an investor expects to get on an investment.

Expected utility   The average utility arising from all possible outcomes.

Expected value   The probability-weighted average of the possible outcomes of a random variable.

Expenditure   A payment or obligation to make future payment for an asset or a service.

Expensed   Taken as a deduction in arriving at net income.

Expenses   Outflows of economic resources or increases in liabilities that result in decreases in equity (other than decreases because of distributions to owners).

Expiration date   The date on which a derivative contract expires.

Expiry   The expiration date of a derivative security.

Exports   The goods and services that we sell to people in other countries.

Extended DuPont System   A method of examining *ROE* by breaking it down into five component parts.

External benefits   Benefits that accrue to people other than the buyer of the good.

External cash flow   Cash, securities, or assets that enter or exit a portfolio.

External costs   Costs that are not borne by the producer of the good but borne by someone else.

External diseconomies   Factors outside the control of a firm that raise the firm's costs as the industry produces a larger output.

External economies   Factors beyond the control of a firm that lower the firm's costs as the industry produces a larger output.

External valuation (real estate)   An external valuation is an assessment of market value performed by a third party who is a qualified, professionally designated, certified, or licensed commercial property valuer/appraiser. External valuations must be completed following the valuation standards of the local governing appraisal body.

Externality   A cost or a benefit that arises from production that falls on someone other than the producer or a cost or a benefit that arises from consumption that falls on someone other than the consumer.

Extraordinary repairs   Repairs that affect the estimated residual value or estimated useful life of an asset thereby increasing its carrying value.

Face value   The promised payment at maturity separate from any coupon payment.

Factor   A common or underlying element with which several variables are correlated.

Factor risk premium (or factor price)   The expected return in excess of the risk-free rate for a portfolio with a sensitivity of 1 to one factor and a sensitivity of 0 to all other factors.

Factor sensitivity (also factor betas or factor loadings)   A measure of the response of return to each unit of increase in a factor, holding all other factors constant.

Factors of production   The productive resources that businesses use to produce goods and services.

Fair market value   The market price of an asset or liability that trades regularly.

Fair value   The amount at which an asset could be exchanged or a liability settled, between knowledgeable, willing parties in an arm's-length transaction.

Federal budget   The annual statement of the expenditures and tax revenues of the government of the United States together with the laws and regulations that approve and support those expenditures and taxes.

Federal funds rate   The interest rate that banks charge each other on overnight loans of reserves.

Federal Open Market Committee   The main policy-making organ of the Federal Reserve System.

Federal Reserve System   The central bank of the United States.

Fee Schedule   The firm's current investment management fees or bundled fees for a particular presentation. This schedule is typically listed by asset level ranges and should be appropriate to the particular prospective client.

Feedback-rule policy   A rule that specifies how policy actions respond to changes in the state of the economy.

Fiduciary   A person who supervises or oversees the investment portfolio of a third party, such as in a trust account, and makes investment decisions in accordance with the owner's wishes.

Fiduciary call   A combination of a European call and a risk-free bond that matures on the option expiration day and has a face value equal to the exercise price of the call.

FIFO method   The first in, first out, method of accounting for inventory, which matches sales against the costs of items of inventory in the order in which they were placed in inventory.

Financial account   A component of the balance of payments covering investments by residents abroad and investments by nonresidents in the home country. Examples include direct investment made by companies, portfolio investments in equity and bonds, and other investments and liabilities.

Financial analysis   The process of selecting, evaluating, and interpreting financial data, along with other pertinent information, in order to formulate an assessment of the company's present and future financial condition and performance.

Financial flexibility   The ability to react and adapt to financial adversities and opportunities.

Financial futures   Futures contracts in which the underlying is a stock, bond, or currency.

Financial innovation   The development of new financial products—new ways of borrowing and lending.

Financial leverage   The extent to which a company can effect, through the use of debt, a proportional change in the return on common equity that is greater than a given proportional change in operating income; also, short for the financial leverage ratio.

Financial leverage ratio (or equity multiplier)   A measure of financial leverage calculated as average total assets divided by average total equity; indicates the extent to which assets are financed with debt relative to equity.

Financial risk   Uncertainty of net income and net cash flows attributed to the use of financing that has a fixed cost, such as debt and leases.

Financing activities   Activities related to obtaining or repaying capital to be used in the business (e.g., equity and long-term debt).

Firm   (1) For purposes of the GIPS standards, the term "firm" refers to the entity defined for compliance with the GIPS standards. See the term "distinct business entity." (2) An economic unit that hires factors of production and organizes those factors to produce and sell goods and services.

First-differencing   A transformation that subtracts the value of the time series in period $t-1$ from its value in period t.

First-order serial correlation   Correlation between adjacent observations in a time series.

Fiscal imbalance   The present value of the government's commitments to pay benefits minus the present value of its tax revenues.

Fiscal policy   The government's attempt to achieve macroeconomic objectives such as full employment, sustained economic growth, and price level stability by setting and changing taxes, making transfer payments, and purchasing goods and services.

Fixed asset turnover   An activity ratio calculated as total revenue divided by average net fixed assets.

Fixed charge coverage   A solvency ratio measuring the number of times interest and lease payments are covered by operating income, calculated as (EBIT + lease payments) divided by (interest payments + lease payments).

Fixed costs   Costs that stay the same within some range of activity.

Fixed exchange rate   An exchange rate that is set at a determined amount by government policy.

Fixed exchange rate regime   A system in which the exchange rate between two currencies remains fixed at a preset level, known as official parity.

Fixed rate perpetual preferred stock Nonconvertible, noncallable preferred stock that has a fixed dividend rate and no maturity date.

Fixed-income forward A forward contract in which the underlying is a bond.

Fixed-income investments Loans with contractually mandated payment schedules from firms or governments to investors.

Fixed-rule policy A rule that specifies an action to be pursued independently of the state of the economy.

Flat trend channel The range defined by security prices as they maintain a relatively steady level.

Flexible exchange rate system A system in which exchange rates are determined by supply and demand.

Flexible exchange rates Exchange rates that are determined by the market forces of supply and demand. They are sometimes called floating exchange rates.

Float In the context of customer receipts, the amount of money that is in transit between payments made by customers and the funds that are usable by the company.

Float factor An estimate of the average number of days it takes deposited checks to clear; average daily float divided by average daily deposit.

Floating-rate loan A loan in which the interest rate is reset at least once after the starting date.

Floor A combination of interest rate put options designed to hedge a lender against lower rates on a floating-rate loan.

Floor brokers Independent members of an exchange who act as brokers for other members.

Floor traders or locals Market makers that buy and sell by quoting a bid and an ask price. They are the primary providers of liquidity to the market.

Floored swap A swap in which the floating payments have a lower limit.

Floorlet Each component put option in a floor.

Flotation cost Fees charged to companies by investment bankers and other costs associated with raising new capital.

Flow A quantity per unit of time.

Foreign bond A bond issued by a foreign company on the local market and in the local currency (e.g., Yankee bonds in the United States, Bulldog bonds in the United Kingdom, or Samurai bonds in Japan).

Foreign exchange expectation A relation that states that the forward exchange rate, quoted at time 0 for delivery at time 1, is equal to the expected value of the spot exchange rate at time 1. When stated relative to the current spot exchange rate, the relation states that the forward discount (premium) is equal to the expected exchange rate movement.

Foreign exchange market The market in which the currency of one country is exchanged for the currency of another.

Foreign exchange rate The price at which one currency exchanges for another.

Forward contract An agreement between two parties in which one party, the buyer, agrees to buy from the other party, the seller, an underlying asset at a later date for a price established at the start of the contract.

Forward discount A situation where, from the perspective of the domestic country, the spot exchange rate is smaller than the forward exchange rate with a foreign country.

Forward P/E *See* Leading P/E.

Forward premium A situation where, from the perspective of the domestic country, the spot exchange rate is larger than the forward exchange rate with a foreign country.

Forward price or forward rate The fixed price or rate at which the transaction scheduled to occur at the expiration of a forward contract will take place. This price is agreed on at the initiation date of the contract.

Forward rate A short-term yield for a future holding period implied by the spot rates of two securities with different maturities.

Forward rate agreement (FRA) A forward contract calling for one party to make a fixed interest payment and the other to make an interest payment at a rate to be determined at the contract expiration.

Forward swap A forward contract to enter into a swap.

Four-firm concentration ratio A measure of market power that is calculated as the percentage of the value of sales accounted for by the four largest firms in an industry.

Franchise The right or license to an exclusive territory or market.

Franchise factor A firm's unique competitive advantage that makes it possible for a firm to earn excess returns (rates of return above a firm's cost of capital) on its capital projects. In turn, these excess returns and the franchise factor cause the firm's stock price to have a *P/E* ratio above its base *P/E* ratio that is equal to $1/k$.

Free cash flow The excess of operating cash flow over capital expenditures.

Free cash flow to equity The cash flow available to holders of the company's common equity after all operating expenses, interest, and principal payments have been paid and necessary investments in working capital and fixed capital have been made.

Free cash flow to the firm The cash flow available to the company's suppliers of capital after all operating expenses (including taxes) have been paid and necessary investments in working capital (e.g., inventory) and fixed capital (e.g., plant and equipment) have been made.

Free-rider problem The absence of an incentive for people to pay for what they consume.

Frequency distribution A tabular display of data summarized into a relatively small number of intervals.

Frequency polygon A graph of a frequency distribution obtained by drawing straight lines joining successive points representing the class frequencies.

Frictional unemployment The unemployment that arises from normal labor turnover-from people entering and leaving the labor force and from the ongoing creation and destruction of jobs.

Full employment A situation in which the quantity of labor demanded equal the quantity supplied. At full employment, there is no cyclical unemployment—all unemployment is frictional and structural.

Full price The price of a security including accrued interest.

Full-costing A method of accounting for the costs of exploring and developing oil and gas resources in which all costs are recorded as assets and depleted over the estimated life of the producing resources.

Full-costing method A method of accounting for the costs of exploring and developing oil and gas resources in which all costs are recorded as assets and depleted over the estimated life of the producing resources.

Fundamental beta A beta that is based at least in part on fundamental data for a company.

Fundamental factor models A multifactor model in which the factors are attributes of stocks or companies that are important in explaining cross-sectional differences in stock prices.

Future value (FV) The amount to which a payment or series of payments will grow by a stated future date.

Futures commission merchants (FCMs) Individuals or companies that execute futures transactions for other parties off the exchange.

Futures contract A variation of a forward contract that has essentially the same basic definition but with some additional features, such as a clearinghouse guarantee against credit losses, a daily settlement of gains and losses, and an organized electronic or floor trading facility.

Futures exchange A legal corporate entity whose shareholders are its members. The members of the exchange have the privilege of executing transactions directly on the exchange.

Gains Asset inflows not directly related to the ordinary activities of the business.

Game theory A tool that economists use to analyze strategic behavior—behavior that takes into account the expected behavior of others and the mutual recognition of independence.

Gamma A numerical measure of how sensitive an option's delta is to a change in the underlying.

GDP deflator One measure of the price level, which is the average of current-year prices as a percentage of base-year prices.

General Agreement on Tariffs and Trade An international agreement signed in 1947 to reduce tariffs on international trade.

Generalized least squares A regression estimation technique that addresses heteroskedasticity of the error term.

Generally accepted accounting principles (GAAP) Accounting principles formulated by the Financial Accounting Standards Board and used to construct financial statements.

Generational accounting An accounting system that measures the lifetime tax burden and benefits of each generation.

Generational imbalance The division of the fiscal imbalance between the current and future generations, assuming that the current generation will enjoy the existing levels of taxes and benefits

Generic *See* Plain-vanilla.

Geometric mean A measure of central tendency computed by taking the nth root of the product of n non-negative values.

Giro system An electronic payment system used widely in Europe and Japan.

Goods and services The objects that people value and produce to satisfy their wants.

Goodwill An intangible asset that represents the excess of the purchase price of an acquired company over the fair value of the net assets acquired.

Government budget deficit The deficit that arises when federal government spends more than it collects in taxes.

Government budget surplus   The surplus that arises when the federal government collects more in taxes than it spends.

Government debt   The total amount of borrowing that the government has borrowed. It equals the sum of past budget deficits minus budget surpluses.

Government purchases   Goods and services bought by the government.

Government purchases multiplier   The magnification effect of a change in government purchases of goods and services on aggregate demand.

Government sector surplus or deficit   An amount equal to net taxes minus government purchases of goods and services.

Great Depression   A decade (1929-1939) of high unemployment and stagnant production throughout the world economy.

Gross domestic product (GDP)   The market value of all the final goods and services produced within a country during a given time period—usually a year.

Gross investment   The total amount spent on purchases of new capital and on replacing depreciated capital.

Gross-Of-Fees Return   The return on assets reduced by any trading expenses incurred during the period.

Gross profit (gross margin)   Sales minus the cost of sales (i.e., the cost of goods sold for a manufacturing company).

Gross profit margin   A profitability ratio calculated as gross profit divided by revenue; indicates how much of every dollar of revenues is left after the cost of goods sold.

Group depreciation   The grouping of similar items to calculate depreciation.

Grouping by function   With reference to the presentation of expenses in an income statement, the grouping together of expenses serving the same function, e.g. all items that are costs of good sold.

Grouping by nature   With reference to the presentation of expenses in an income statement, the grouping together of expenses by similar nature, e.g., all depreciation expenses.

Growth company   A company that consistently has the opportunities and ability to invest in projects that provide rates of return that exceed the firm's cost of capital. Because of these investment opportunities, it retains a high proportion of earnings, and its earnings grow faster than those of average firms.

Growth investors   With reference to equity investors, investors who seek to invest in high-earnings-growth companies.

Growth option or expansion option   The ability to make additional investments in a project at some future time if the financial results are strong.

Growth stock   A stock issue that generates a higher rate of return than other stocks in the market with similar risk characteristics.

Harmonic mean   A type of weighted mean computed by averaging the reciprocals of the observations, then taking the reciprocal of that average.

Hedge   A trading strategy in which derivative securities are used to reduce or completely offset a counter-party's risk exposure to an underlying asset.

Hedge fund   An investment vehicle designed to manage a private, unregistered portfolio of assets according to any of several strategies. The investment strategy often employs arbitrage trading and significant financial leverage (e.g., short selling, borrowing, derivatives) while the compensation arrangement for the manager typically specifies considerable profit participation.

Hedge ratio   The relationship of the quantity of an asset being hedged to the quantity of the derivative used for hedging.

Hedging   A general strategy usually thought of as reducing, if not eliminating, risk.

Held-for-trading securities (trading securities)   Securities that a company intends to trade.

Held-to-maturity securities (Fixed-income)   Securities that a company intends to hold to maturity; these are presented at their original cost, updated for any amortization of discounts or premiums.

Herfindahl-Hirschman Index   A measure of market power that is calculated as the square of the market share of each firm (as a percentage) summed over the largest 50 firms (or over all firms if there are fewer than 50) in a market.

Heteroskedastic   With reference to the error term of a regression, having a variance that differs across observations.

Heteroskedasticity   The property of having a nonconstant variance; refers to an error term with the property that its variance differs across observations.

Heteroskedasticity-consistent standard errors   Standard errors of the estimated parameters of a regression that correct for the presence of heteroskedasticity in the regression's error term.

High-yield bond   A bond rated below investment grade. Also referred to as *speculative-grade bonds* or *junk bonds*.

Histogram   A bar chart of data that have been grouped into a frequency distribution.

Historical cost In reference to assets, the amount paid to purchase an asset, including any costs of acquisition and/or preparation; with reference to liabilities, the amount of proceeds received in exchange in issuing the liability.

Historical equity risk premium approach An estimate of a country's equity risk premium that is based upon the historical averages of the risk-free rate and the rate of return on the market portfolio.

Historical method A method of estimating VAR that uses data from the returns of the portfolio over a recent past period and compiles this data in the form of a histogram.

Historical simulation (or back simulation) method Another term for the historical method of estimating VAR. This method involves not a *simulation* of the past but rather what *actually happened* in the past, sometimes adjusted to reflect the fact that a different portfolio may have existed in the past than is planned for the future.

Holding period return (HPR) The return that an investor earns during a specified holding period; a synonym for total return.

Holding period yield (HPY) The return that an investor earns during a specified holding period; holding period return with reference to a fixed-income instrument.

Homogenization Creating a contract with standard and generally accepted terms, which makes it more acceptable to a broader group of participants.

Homoskedasticity The property of having a constant variance; refers to an error term that is constant across observations.

Horizontal analysis Common-size analysis that involves comparing a specific financial statement with that statement in prior or future time periods; also, cross-sectional analysis of one company with another.

Horizontal common-size analysis An analysis in which financial statement accounts are compared to a benchmark in a different reporting period. Accounts in subsequent periods are restated as a percentage of the base period's value for the same account.

Human capital The value of skills and knowledge possessed by the workforce.

Hurdle rate The rate of return that must be met for a project to be accepted.

Hypothesis With reference to statistical inference, a statement about one or more populations.

Hypothesis testing With reference to statistical inference, the subdivision dealing with the testing of hypotheses about one or more populations.

Identifiable intangible An intangible that can be acquired singly and is typically linked to specific rights or privileges having finite benefit periods (e.g., a patent or trademark).

If-converted method A method for accounting for the effect of convertible securities on earnings per share (EPS) that specifies what EPS would have been if the convertible securities had been converted at the beginning of the period, taking account of the effects of conversion on net income and the weighted average number of shares outstanding.

Impairment Diminishment in value.

Implicit rental rate The firm's opportunity cost of using its own capital.

Implied repo rate The rate of return from a cash-and-carry transaction implied by the futures price relative to the spot price.

Implied volatility The volatility that option traders use to price an option, implied by the price of the option and a particular option-pricing model.

Implied yield A measure of the yield on the underlying bond of a futures contract implied by pricing it as though the underlying will be delivered at the futures expiration.

Imports The goods and services that we buy from people in other countries.

In the money An option that has positive intrinsic value.

Incentive A reward that encourages or a penalty that discourages an action.

Incentive system A method of organizing production that uses a market-like mechanism inside the firm.

Income Increases in economic benefits in the form of inflows or enhancements of assets, or decreases of liabilities that result in an increase in equity (other than increases resulting from contributions by owners).

Income effect The effect of a change in income on consumption, other things remaining the same.

Income elasticity of demand The responsiveness of demand to a change in income, other things remaining the same. It is calculated as the percentage change in the quantity demanded divided by the percentage change in income.

Income statement (statement of operations or profit and loss statement) A financial statement that provides information about a company's profitability over a stated period of time.

Income statement A financial statement that shows the flow of the firm's sales, expenses, and earnings over a period of time.

Incremental cash flows The changes or increments to cash flows resulting from a decision or action;

the cash flow with a decision minus the cash flow without that decision.

Indenture   The legal agreement that lists the obligations of the issuer of a bond to the bondholder, including payment schedules, call provisions, and sinking funds.

Independent   With reference to events, the property that the occurrence of one event does not affect the probability of another event occurring.

Independent and identically distributed (IID)   With respect to random variables, the property of random variables that are independent of each other but follow the identical probability distribution.

Independent projects   Independent projects are projects whose cash flows are independent of each other.

Independent variable   A variable used to explain the dependent variable in a regression; a right-hand-side variable in a regression equation.

Index amortizing swap   An interest rate swap in which the notional principal is indexed to the level of interest rates and declines with the level of interest rates according to a predefined scheduled. This type of swap is frequently used to hedge securities that are prepaid as interest rates decline, such as mortgage-backed securities.

Index option   An option in which the underlying is a stock index.

Indexing   An investment strategy in which an investor constructs a portfolio to mirror the performance of a specified index.

Indirect format (indirect method)   With reference to cash flow statements, a format for the presentation of the statement which, in the operating cash flow section, begins with net income then shows additions and subtractions to arrive at operating cash flow.

Indirect method   The procedure for converting the income statement from an accrual basis to a cash basis by adjusting net income for items that do not affect cash flows, including depreciation, amortization, depletion, gains, losses, and changes in current assets and current liabilities.

Individual transferable quota (ITQ)   A production limit that is assigned to an individual who is free to transfer the quota to someone else.

Induced taxes   Taxes that vary with real GDP.

Industry life cycle analysis   An analysis that focuses on the industry's stage of development.

Inelastic demand   A demand with a price elasticity between 0 and 1; the percentage change in the quantity demanded is less than the percentage change in price.

Infant-industry argument   The argument that it is necessary to protect a new industry to enable it to grow into a mature industry that can compete in world markets.

Inferior good   A good for which demand decreases as income increases.

Inflation   A process in which the price level is rising and money is losing value.

Inflation premium   An extra return that compensates investors for expected inflation.

Inflation rate   The percentage change in the price level from one year to the next.

Inflationary gap   The amount by which real GDP exceeds potential GDP.

Information   An attribute of a good market that includes providing buyers and sellers with timely, accurate information on the volume and prices of past transactions and on all currently outstanding bids and offers.

Information ratio (IR)   Mean active return divided by active risk.

Information ratio   Statistic used to measure a portfolio's average return in excess of a comparison, benchmark portfolio divided by the standard deviation of this excess return.

Informationally efficient market   A more technical term for an efficient capital market that emphasizes the role of information in setting the market price.

Initial margin requirement   The margin requirement on the first day of a transaction as well as on any day in which additional margin funds must be deposited.

Initial public offering (IPO)   A new issue by a firm that has no existing public market.

In-sample forecast errors   The residuals from a fitted time-series model within the sample period used to fit the model.

Instability in the minimum-variance frontier   The characteristic of minimum-variance frontiers that they are sensitive to small changes in inputs.

Installment   Said of a sale in which proceeds are to be paid in installments over an extended period of time.

Installment method (installment-sales method)   With respect to revenue recognition, a method that specifies that the portion of the total profit of the sale that is recognized in each period is determined by the percentage of the total sales price for which the seller has received cash.

Intangible asset   An asset without physical substance.

Intellectual property rights   Property rights for discoveries owned by the creators of knowledge.

Interest coverage   A solvency ratio calculated as EBIT divided by interest payments.

Interest coverage ratio (or times-interest-earned ratio)   Ratio of EBIT to interest payments; a comparison of the earnings available to meet interest obligations with existing interest obligations.

Interest rate   A rate of return that reflects the relationship between differently dated cash flows; a discount rate.

Interest rate call   An option in which the holder has the right to make a known interest payment and receive an unknown interest payment.

Interest rate cap or cap   A series of call options on an interest rate, with each option expiring at the date on which the floating loan rate will be reset, and with each option having the same exercise rate. A cap in general can have an underlying other than an interest rate.

Interest rate collar   A combination of a long cap and a short floor, or a short cap and a long floor. A collar in general can have an underlying other than an interest rate.

Interest rate floor or floor   A series of put options on an interest rate, with each option expiring at the date on which the floating loan rate will be reset, and with each option having the same exercise rate. A floor in general can have an underlying other than the interest rate.

Interest rate forward   (See *forward rate agreement*)

Interest rate option   An option in which the underlying is an interest rate.

Interest rate parity   A formula that expresses the equivalence or parity of spot and forward rates, after adjusting for differences in the interest rates.

Interest rate put   An option in which the holder has the right to make an unknown interest payment and receive a known interest payment.

Interest rate risk   The uncertainty of returns on an investment due to possible changes in interest rates over time.

Interest rate swap   A swap in which the underlying is an interest rate. Can be viewed as a currency swap in which both currencies are the same and can be created as a combination of currency swaps.

Interest   The income that capital earns.

Interest-on-interest   Bond income from reinvestment of coupon payments.

Intergenerational data mining   A form of data mining that applies information developed by previous researchers using a dataset to guide current research using the same or a related dataset.

Intermarket Trading System (ITS)   A computerized system that connects competing exchanges and dealers who trade stocks listed on a U.S. exchange. Its purpose is to help customers find the best market for these stocks at a point in time.

Internal liquidity (solvency) ratios   Financial ratios that measure the ability of the firm to meet future short-term financial obligations.

Internal rate of return (IRR)   The discount rate that makes net present value equal 0; the discount rate that makes the present value of an investment's costs (outflows) equal to the present value of the investment's benefits (inflows).

Internal Rate of Return (Private Equity) (IRR)   IRR is the annualized implied discount rate (effective compounded rate) that equates the present value of all the appropriate cash inflows (paid-in capital, such as drawdowns for net investments) associated with an investment with the sum of the present value of all the appropriate cash outflows (such as distributions) accruing from it and the present value of the unrealized residual portfolio (unliquidated holdings). For an interim cumulative return measurement, any IRR depends on the valuation of the residual assets.

Internal Valuation (Real Estate)   An internal valuation is an advisor's or underlying third-party manager's best estimate of market value based on the most current and accurate information available under the circumstances. An internal valuation could include industry practice techniques, such as discounted cash flow, sales comparison, replacement cost, or a review of all significant events (both general market and asset specific) that could have a material impact on the investment. Prudent assumptions and estimates must be used, and the process must be applied consistently from period to period, except where a change would result in better estimates of market value.

International Fisher relation   The assertion that the interest rate differential between two countries should equal the expected inflation rate differential over the term of the interest rates.

Interquartile range   The difference between the third and first quartiles of a dataset.

Interval   With reference to grouped data, a set of values within which an observation falls.

Interval scale   A measurement scale that not only ranks data but also gives assurance that the differences between scale values are equal.

In-the-money option   An option that, if exercised, would result in the value received being worth more than the payment required to exercise (apart from transaction costs).

Intrinsic value   The portion of a call option's total value equal to the greater of either zero or the difference between the current value of the underlying asset and the exercise price; for a put option, intrinsic value is the greater of either zero or the exercise price less the underlying asset price. For a stock, it is the value derived from fundamental analysis of the stock's expected returns or cash flows.

Intrinsic value or exercise value   The value obtained if an option is exercised based on current conditions.

Inventory   The unsold units of product on hand.

Inventory blanket lien   The use of inventory as collateral for a loan. Though the lender has claim to some or all of the company's inventory, the company may still sell or use the inventory in the ordinary course of business.

Inventory turnover   An activity ratio calculated as cost of goods sold divided by average inventory; an indication of the resources tied up in inventory relative to the speed at which inventory is sold during the period.

Inverse floater   A floating-rate note or bond in which the coupon is adjusted to move opposite to a benchmark interest rate.

Inverse relationship   A relationship between variables that move in opposite directions.

Invested Capital (Private Equity)   The amount of paid-in capital that has been invested in portfolio companies.

Investing activities   Activities which are associated with the acquisition and disposal of property, plant, and equipment; intangible assets; other long-term assets; and both long-term and short-term investments in the equity and debt (bonds and loans) issued by other companies.

Investment   The purchase of new plant, equipment, and buildings and additions to inventories.

Investment Advisor (Private Equity)   Any individual or institution that supplies investment advice to clients on a per fee basis. The investment advisor inherently has no role in the management of the underlying portfolio companies of a partnership/fund.

Investment company   A firm that sells shares of the company and uses the proceeds to buy portfolios of stock, bonds, or other financial instruments.

Investment decision process   Estimation of intrinsic value for comparison with market price to determine whether or not to invest.

Investment demand   The relationship between investment and real interest rate, other things remaining the same.

Investment horizon   The time period used for planning and forecasting purposes or the future time at which the investor requires the invested funds.

Investment management company   A company separate from the investment company that manages the portfolio and performs administrative functions.

Investment Management Fee   The fee payable to the investment management firm for the on-going management of a portfolio. Investment management fees are typically asset based (percentage of assets), performance based (based on performance relative to a benchmark), or a combination of the two but may take different forms as well.

Investment Multiple (TVPI Multiple) (Private Equity)   The ratio of total value to paid-in-capital. It represents the total return of the investment to the original investment not taking into consideration the time invested. Total value can be found by adding the residual value and distributed capital together.

Investment opportunity schedule   A graphical depiction of a company's investment opportunities ordered from highest to lowest expected return. A company's optimal capital budget is found where the investment opportunity schedule intersects with the company's marginal cost of capital.

Investment strategy   A decision by a portfolio manager regarding how he or she will manage the portfolio to meet the goals and objectives of the client. This will include either active or passive management and, if active, what style in terms of top-down or buttom-up or fundamental versus technical.

IRR   The discount rate which forces the PV of a project's inflows to equal the PV of its costs.

IRR rule   An investment decision rule that accepts projects or investments for which the IRR is greater than the opportunity cost of capital.

January effect   A frequent empirical anomaly where risk-adjusted stock returns in the month of January are significantly larger than those occurring in any other month of the year.

Job search   The activity of looking for acceptable vacant jobs.

Joint probability   The probability of the joint occurrence of stated events.

Joint probability function   A function giving the probability of joint occurrences of values of stated random variables.

Just-in-time method (JIT)   Method of managing inventory that minimizes in-process inventory stocks.

Keynesian An economist who believes that left alone, the economy would rarely operate at full employment and that to achieve full employment, active help from fiscal policy and monetary policy is required.

***k*th Order autocorrelation** The correlation between observations in a time series separated by *k* periods.

Kurtosis The statistical measure that indicates the peakedness of a distribution.

Labor The work time and work effort that people devote to producing goods and services.

Labor force The sum of the people who are employed and who are unemployed.

Labor force participation rate The percentage of the working-age population who are members of the labor force.

Labor productivity Real GDP per hour of work.

Labor union An organized group of workers whose purpose is to increase wages and to influence other job conditions.

Laddering strategy A form of active strategy which entails scheduling maturities on a systematic basis within the investment portfolio such that investments are spread out equally over the term of the ladder.

Laffer curve The relationship between the tax rate and the amount of tax revenue collected.

Land The gifts of nature that we use to produce goods and services.

Law of demand Other things remaining the same, the higher the price of a good, the smaller is the quantity demanded of it.

Law of diminishing returns As a firm uses more of a variable input, with a given quantity of other inputs (fixed inputs), the marginal product of the variable input eventually diminishes.

Law of one price The condition in a financial market in which two financial instruments or combinations of financial instruments can sell for only one price. Equivalent to the principle that no arbitrage opportunities are possible.

Law of supply Other things remaining the same, the higher the price of a good, the greater is the quantity supplied of it.

Leading indicators A set of economic variables whose values reach peaks and troughs in advance of the aggregate economy.

Leading P/E (or forward P/E or prospective P/E) A stock's current price divided by the next year's expected earnings.

Learning-by-doing People become more productive in an activity (learn) just by repeatedly producing a particular good or service (doing).

Leasehold A right to occupy land or buildings under a long-term rental contract.

Leasehold improvements Improvements to leased property that become the property of the lessor at the end of the lease.

Legal monopoly A market structure in which there is one firm and entry is restricted by the granting of a public franchise, government license, patent, or copyright.

Legal risk The risk that the legal system will not enforce a contract in case of dispute or fraud.

Leptokurtic Describes a distribution that is more peaked than a normal distribution.

Level of significance The probability of a Type I error in testing a hypothesis.

Leveraged floating-rate note or leveraged floater A floating-rate note or bond in which the coupon is adjusted at a multiple of a benchmark interest rate.

Liabilities Present obligations of an enterprise arising from past events, the settlement of which is expected to result in an outflow of resources embodying economic benefits; creditors' claims on the resources of a company.

License The right to use a formula, technique, process, or design.

LIFO layer liquidation With respect to the application of the LIFO inventory method, the liquidation of old, relatively low-priced inventory; happens when the volume of sales rises above the volume of recent purchases so that some sales are made from relatively old, low-priced inventory.

LIFO method The last in, first out, method of accounting for inventory, which matches sales against the costs of items of inventory in the reverse order the items were placed in inventory (i.e., inventory produced or acquired last are assumed to be sold first).

Likelihood The probability of an observation, given a particular set of conditions.

Limit down A limit move in the futures market in which the price at which a transaction would be made is at or below the lower limit.

Limit move A condition in the futures markets in which the price at which a transaction would be made is at or beyond the price limits.

Limit order An order that lasts for a specified time to buy or sell a security when and if it trades at a specified price.

Limit pricing The practice of setting the price at the highest level that inflicts a loss on an entrant.

Limit up A limit move in the futures market in which the price at which a transaction would be made is at or above the upper limit.

Limited Partnership (Private Equity) The legal structure used by most venture and private equity funds. Usually fixed life investment vehicles. The general partner or management firm manages the partnership using the policy laid down in a partnership agreement. The agreement also covers terms, fees, structures, and other items agreed between the limited partners and the general partner.

Linear association A straight-line relationship, as opposed to a relationship that cannot be graphed as a straight line.

Linear interpolation The estimation of an unknown value on the basis of two known values that bracket it, using a straight line between the two known values.

Linear regression Regression that models the straight-line relationship between the dependent and independent variable(s).

Linear relationship A relationship between two variables that is illustrated by a straight line.

Linear trend A trend in which the dependent variable changes at a constant rate with time.

Liquid Term used to describe an asset that can be quickly converted to cash at a price close to fair market value.

Liquid assets Those company assets that are most readily converted to cash.

Liquidity In the context of financial analysis, a company's ability to satisfy its short-term obligations using assets that are most readily converted into cash.

Liquidity premium An extra return that compensates investors for the risk of loss relative to an investment's fair value if the investment needs to be converted to cash quickly.

Liquidity ratios Financial ratios measuring a company's ability to meet its short-term obligations.

Liquidity risk The risk that a financial instrument cannot be purchased or sold without a significant concession in price due to the size of the market.

Living wage An hourly wage rate that enables a person who works a 40-hour week to rent adequate housing for not more than 30 percent of the amount earned.

Lockbox system A payment system in which customer payments are mailed to a post office box and the banking institution retrieves and deposits these payments several times a day, enabling the company to have use of the fund sooner than in a centralized system in which customer payments are sent to the company.

Locked limit A condition in the futures markets in which a transaction cannot take place because the price would be beyond the limits.

Logit model A qualitative-dependent-variable multiple regression model based on the logistic probability distribution.

Log-linear model With reference to time-series models, a model in which the growth rate of the time series as a function of time is constant.

Log-log regression model A regression that expresses the dependent and independent variables as natural logarithms.

London Interbank Offer Rate (LIBOR) The Eurodollar rate at which London banks lend dollars to other London banks; considered to be the best representative rate on a dollar borrowed by a private, high-quality borrower.

Long The buyer of a derivative contract. Also refers to the position of owning a derivative.

Long position The buyer of a commodity or security or, for a forward contract, the counterparty who will be the eventual buyer of the underlying asset.

Long run A period of time in which the quantities of all resources can be varied.

Longitudinal data Observations on characteristic(s) of the same observational unit through time.

Long-lived assets Assets that are expected to provide economic benefits over a future period of time greater than one year.

Long-run aggregate supply curve The relationship between the real GDP supplied and the price level in the long run when real GDP equals potential GDP.

Long-run average cost curve The relationship between the lowest attainable average total cost and output when both capital and labor are varied.

Long-run industry supply curve A curve that shows how the quantity supplied by an industry varies as the market price varies after all the possible adjustments have been made, including changes in plant size and the number of firms in the industry.

Long-run macroeconomic equilibrium A situation that occurs when real GDP equals potential GDP-the economy is on its long-run aggregate supply curve.

Long-run Phillips curve Inflation rate equals the expected inflation rate.

Long-term assets Assets that have a useful life of more than one year, are used in the operation of a business, and are not intended for resale. Less commonly called *fixed assets*.

Long-term contract A contract that spans a number of accounting periods.

Long-term debt-to-assets ratio Ratio of long-term debt to total assets; the proportion of the company's assets that is financed with long-term debt.

Long-term equity anticipatory securities (LEAPS) Options originally created with expirations of several years.

Look-ahead bias A bias caused by using information that was unavailable on the test date.

Losses Asset outflows not directly related to the ordinary activities of the business.

Lower bound The lowest possible value of an option.

Lucas wedge The accumulated loss of output that results from a slowdown in the growth rate of real GDP per person.

M1 A measure of money that consists of currency and traveler's checks plus checking deposits owned by individuals and businesses.

M2 A measure of money that consists of M1 plus time deposits, savings deposits, and money market mutual funds and other deposits.

Macaulay duration The duration without dividing by 1 plus the bond's yield to maturity. The term, named for one of the economists who first derived it, is used to distinguish the calculation from modified duration. See also *modified duration.*

Macroeconomic factor A factor related to the economy, such as the inflation rate, industrial production, or economic sector membership.

Macroeconomic factor model A multifactor model in which the factors are surprises in macroeconomic variables that significantly explain equity returns.

Macroeconomic long run A time frame that is sufficiently long for real GDP to return to potential GDP so that full employment prevails.

Macroeconomic short run A period during which some money prices are sticky and real GDP might be below, above, or at potential GDP and unemployment might be above, below, or at the natural rate of unemployment.

Macroeconomics The study of the performance of the national economy and the global economy.

Maintenance margin The required proportion that the investor's equity value must be to the total market value of the stock. If the proportion drops below this percent, the investor will receive a margin call.

Maintenance margin requirement The margin requirement on any day other than the first day of a transaction.

Management fee The compensation an investment company pays to the investment management company for its services. The average annual fee is about 0.5 percent of fund assets.

Manufacturing resource planning (MRP) The incorporation of production planning into inventory management. A MRP analysis provides both a materials acquisition schedule and a production schedule.

Margin The amount of money that a trader deposits in a margin account. The term is derived from the stock market practice in which an investor borrows a portion of the money required to purchase a certain amount of stock. In futures markets, there is no borrowing so the margin is more of a down payment or performance bond.

Margin account The collateral posted with the futures exchange clearinghouse by an outside counterparty to insure its eventual performance; the *initial* margin is the deposit required at contract origination while the *maintenance* margin is the minimum collateral necessary at all times.

Margin call A request by an investor's broker for additional capital for a security bought on margin if the investor's equity value declines below the required maintenance margin.

Marginal benefit curve A curve that shows the relationship between the marginal benefit of a good and the quantity of that good consumed.

Marginal benefit The benefit that a person receives from consuming one more unit of a good or service. It is measured as the maximum amount that a person is willing to pay for one more unit of the good or service.

Marginal cost The opportunity cost of producing one more unit of a good or service. It is the best alternative forgone. It is calculated as the increase in total cost divided by the increase in output.

Marginal cost pricing rule A rule that sets the price of a good or service equal to the marginal cost of producing it.

Marginal probability *See* Unconditional probability.

Marginal product The increase in total product that results from a one-unit increase in the variable input, with all other inputs remaining the same. It is calculated as the increase in total product divided by the increase in the variable input employed, when the quantities of all other inputs are constant.

Marginal product of labor The additional real GDP produced by an additional hour of labor when all other influences on production remain the same.

Marginal propensity to consume The fraction of a change in disposable income that is consumed. It is calculated as the change in consumption expenditure divided by the change in disposable income.

Marginal revenue The change in total revenue that results from a one-unit increase in the quantity sold. It is calculated as the change in total revenue divided by the change in quantity sold.

Marginal revenue product The change in total revenue that results from employing one more unit of a resource (labor) while the quantity of all other resources remains the same. It is calculated as the increase in total revenue divided by the increase in the quantity of the resource (labor).

Marginal social benefit The marginal benefit enjoyed by society-by the consumer of a good or service (marginal private benefit) plus the marginal benefit enjoyed by others (marginal external benefit).

Marginal social cost The marginal cost incurred by the entire society-by the producer and by everyone else on whom the cost falls-and is the sum of marginal private cost and the marginal external cost.

Marginal tax rate The part of each additional dollar in income that is paid as tax.

Margins (or profit margin ratios and return-on-sales ratios) Ratios that are useful for evaluating a company's ability to manage its expenses to generate profits from its sales.

Marked to market The settlement process used to adjust the margin account of a futures contract for daily changes in the price of the underlying asset.

Market demand The relationship between the total quantity demanded of a good and its price. It is illustrated by the market demand curve.

Market failure A state in which the market does not allocate resources efficiently.

Market order An order to buy or sell a security immediately at the best price available.

Market portfolio The portfolio that includes all risky assets with relative weights equal to their proportional market values.

Market power The ability to influence the market, and in particular the market price, by influencing the total quantity offered for sale.

Market price of risk The slope of the capital market line, indicating the market risk premium for each unit of market risk.

Market risk premium The expected excess return on the market over the risk-free rate.

Market risk The risk associated with interest rates, exchange rates, and equity prices.

Market Value The current listed price at which investors buy or sell securities at a given time.

Market Value (Real Estate) The most probable price that a property should bring in a competitive and open market under all conditions requisite to a fair sale, the buyer and seller each acting pru-

dently and knowledgeably, and assuming the price is not affected by undue stimulus. Implicit in this definition is the consummation of a sale as of a specified date and the passing of title from seller to buyer under conditions whereby: (a) Buyer and seller are typically motivated. (b) Both parties are well informed or well advised and each acting in what they consider their own best interests. (c) A reasonable time is allowed for exposure in the open market. (d) Payment is made in terms of currency or in terms of financial arrangements comparable thereto. (e) The price represents the normal consideration for the property sold unaffected by special or creative financing or sales concessions granted by anyone associated with the sale.

Market value added (MVA) External management performance measure to compare the market value of the company's debt and equity with the total capital invested in the firm.

Market-oriented investors With reference to equity investors, investors whose investment disciplines cannot be clearly categorized as value or growth.

Marking to market A procedure used primarily in futures markets in which the parties to a contract settle the amount owed daily. Also known as the *daily settlement.*

Markowitz decision rule A decision rule for choosing between two investments based on their means and variances.

Mark-to-market The revaluation of a financial asset or liability to its current market value or fair value.

Matching principle The accounting principle that expenses should be recognized when the associated revenue is recognized.

Matching strategy An active investment strategy that includes intentional matching of the timing of cash outflows with investment maturities.

Materiality The condition of being of sufficient importance so that omission or misstatement of the item in a financial report could make a difference to users' decisions.

Matrix pricing In the fixed income markets, to price a security on the basis of valuation-relevant characteristics (e.g. debt-rating approach).

Maturity premium An extra return that compensates investors for the increased sensitivity of the market value of debt to a change in market interest rates as maturity is extended.

McCallum rule A rule that adjusts the growth rate of the monetary base to target the inflation rate but also to take into account changes in the trend productivity growth rate and fluctuations in aggregate demand.

Mean   The sum of all values in a distribution or dataset, divided by the number of values summed; a synonym of arithmetic mean.

Mean absolute deviation   With reference to a sample, the mean of the absolute values of deviations from the sample mean.

Mean excess return   The average rate of return in excess of the risk-free rate.

Mean reversion   The tendency of a time series to fall when its level is above its mean and rise when its level is below its mean; a mean-reverting time series tends to return to its long-term mean.

Mean–variance analysis   An approach to portfolio analysis using expected means, variances, and covariances of asset returns.

Means of payment   A method of settling a debt.

Mean-variance analysis   An approach to portfolio analysis using expected means, variances, and covariances of asset returns.

Measure of central tendency   A quantitative measure that specifies where data are centered.

Measure of location   A quantitative measure that describes the location or distribution of data; includes not only measures of central tendency but also other measures such as percentiles.

Measurement scales   A scheme of measuring differences. The four types of measurement scales are nominal, ordinal, interval, and ratio.

Median   The value of the middle item of a set of items that has been sorted into ascending or descending order; the 50th percentile.

Mesokurtic   Describes a distribution with kurtosis identical to that of the normal distribution.

Microeconomics   The study of the choices that individuals and businesses make, the way those choices interact, and the influence governments exert on them.

Minimum efficient scale   The smallest quantity of output at which the long-run average cost curve reaches its lowest level.

Minimum wage   A regulation that makes the hiring of labor below a specified wage rate illegal.

Minimum-variance frontier   The graph of the set of portfolios that have minimum variance for their level of expected return.

Minimum-variance portfolio   The portfolio with the minimum variance for each given level of expected return.

Minority interest   The portion of consolidated subsidiaries' net assets not owned by the parent.

Mismatching strategy   An active investment strategy whereby the timing of cash outflows is not matched with investment maturities.

Mixed factor models   Factor models that combine features of more than one type of factor model.

Modal interval   With reference to grouped data, the most frequently occurring interval.

Mode   The most frequently occurring value in a set of observations.

Model risk   The use of an inaccurate pricing model for a particular investment, or the improper use of the right model.

Model specification   With reference to regression, the set of variables included in the regression and the regression equation's functional form.

Modified duration   A measure of a bond's price sensitivity to interest rate movements. Equal to the Macaulay duration of a bond divided by one plus its yield to maturity.

Monetarist   An economist who believes that the economy is self regulating and that it will normally operate at full employment, provided that monetary policy is not erratic and that the pace of money growth is kept steady.

Monetary base   The sum of the Federal Reserve notes, coins, and banks' deposits at the Fed.

Monetary policy   The Fed conducts the nation's monetary policy by changing interest rates and adjusting the quantity of money.

Money   Any commodity or token that is generally acceptable as a means of payment.

Money market fund   A fund that invests in short-term securities sold in the money market. (Large companies, banks, and other institutions also invest their surplus cash in the money market for short periods of time.) In the entire investment spectrum, these are generally the safest, most stable securities available. They include Treasury bills, certificates of deposit of large banks, and commercial paper (short-term IOUs of large corporations).

Money market mutual fund   A fund operated by a financial institution that sells shares in the fund and holds liquid assets such as U.S. Treasury bills and short-term commercial bills.

Money market yield (or CD equivalent yield)   A yield on a basis comparable to the quoted yield on an interest-bearing money market instrument that pays interest on a 360-day basis; the annualized holding period yield, assuming a 360-day year.

Money market   The market for short-term debt instruments (one-year maturity or less).

Money multiplier   The amount by which a change in the monetary base is multiplied to determine the resulting change in the quantity of money.

Money price   The number of dollars that must be given up in exchange for a good or service.

Money wage rate   The number of dollars that an hour of labor earns.

Moneyness   The relationship between the price of the underlying and an option's exercise price.

Money-weighted rate of return   The internal rate of return on a portfolio, taking account of all cash flows.

Monopolistic competition   A market structure in which a large number of firms compete by making similar but slightly different products.

Monopoly   A market structure in which there is one firm, which produces a good or service that has no close substitute and in which the firm is protected from competition by a barrier preventing the entry of new firms.

Monte Carlo simulation   A risk analysis technique in which probable future events are simulated on a computer, generating estimated rates of return and risk indexes.

Monte Carlo simulation method   An approach to estimating VAR that produces random outcomes to examine what might happen if a particular risk is faced. This method is widely used in the sciences as well as in business to study a variety of problems.

Mortgage bonds   Bonds that pledge specific assets such as buildings and equipment. The proceeds from the sale of these assets are used to pay off bondholders in case of bankruptcy.

Moving average   The continually recalculating average of security prices for a period, often 200 days, to serve as an indication of the general trend of prices and also as a benchmark price.

Multicollinearity   A regression assumption violation that occurs when two or more independent variables (or combinations of independent variables) are highly but not perfectly correlated with each other.

Multifactor model   An empirical version of the APT where the investor chooses the exact number and identity of the common risk factors used to describe an asset's risk-return relationship. Risk factors are often designated as *macroeconomic* variables (e.g., inflation, changes in gross domestic product) or *microeconomic* variables (e.g., security-specific characteristics like firm size or book-to-market ratios).

Multiple linear regression   Linear regression involving two or more independent variables.

Multiple linear regression model   A linear regression model with two or more independent variables.

Multiple R   The correlation between the actual and forecasted values of the dependent variable in a regression.

Multiplication rule for probabilities   The rule that the joint probability of events A and B equals the probability of A given B times the probability of B.

Multiplier   The amount by which a change in autonomous expenditure is magnified or multiplied to determine the change in equilibrium expenditure and real GDP.

Multi-step format   With respect to the format of the income statement, a format that presents a subtotal for gross profit (revenue minus cost of goods sold).

Multivariate distribution   A probability distribution that specifies the probabilities for a group of related random variables.

Multivariate normal distribution   A probability distribution for a group of random variables that is completely defined by the means and variances of the variables plus all the correlations between pairs of the variables.

Must   A required provision for claiming compliance with the GIPS standards.

Mutual fund   An investment company that pools money from shareholders and invests in a variety of securities, including stocks, bonds, and money market securities. A mutual fund ordinarily stands ready to buy back (redeem) its shares at their current net asset value, which depends on the market value of the fund's portfolio of securities at the time. Mutual funds generally continuously offer new shares to investors.

Mutually exclusive events   Events such that only one can occur at a time.

Mutually exclusive projects   Mutually exclusive projects compete directly with each other. For example, if Projects A and B are mutually exclusive, you can choose A or B, but you cannot choose both.

n Factorial   For a positive integer n, the product of the first n positive integers; 0 factorial equals 1 by definition. n factorial is written as n!.

Nasdaq InterMarket   A trading system that includes Nasdaq market makers and ECNs that quote and trade stocks listed on the NYSE and the AMEX. It involves dealers from the Nasdaq market and the Intermarket Trading System (ITS). In many ways, this has become what had been labeled the third market.

Nash equilibrium   The outcome of a game that occurs when player A takes the best possible action given the action of player B and player B takes the best possible action given the action of player A.

National saving   The sum of private saving (saving by households and businesses) and government saving.

Natural monopoly   A monopoly that occurs when one firm can supply the entire market at a lower price than two or more firms can.

Natural rate of unemployment   The unemployment rate when the economy is at full employment. There is no cyclical unemployment; all unemployment is frictional and structural.

Natural resources   Long-term assets purchased for the economic value that can be taken from the land and used up.

Near-term, high-priority goal   A short-term financial investment goal of personal importance, such as accumulating funds for making a house down payment or buying a car.

Needs-tested spending   Government spending on programs that pay benefits to suitably qualified people and businesses.

Negative relationship   A relationship between variables that move in opposite directions.

Negative serial correlation   Serial correlation in which a positive error for one observation increases the chance of a negative error for another observation, and vice versa.

Negotiated sales   An underwriting arrangement wherein the sale of a security issue by an issuing entity (governmental body or a corporation) is done using an investment banking firm that maintains an ongoing relationship with the issuer. The characteristics of the security issue are determined by the issuer in consultation with the investment banker.

Neoclassical growth theory   A theory of economic growth that proposes that real GDP grows because technological change induces a level of saving and investment that makes capital per hour of labor grow.

Net asset value   The market value of the assets owned by a fund.

Net book value   The remaining (undepreciated) balance of an asset's purchase cost.

Net borrower   A country that is borrowing more from the rest of the world than it is lending to it.

Net exports   The value of exports minus the value of imports.

Net income (loss)   The difference between revenue and expenses; what remains after subtracting all expenses (including depreciation, interest, and taxes) from revenue.

Net investment   Net increase in the capital stock–gross investment minus depreciation.

Net lender   A country that is lending more to the rest of the world than it is borrowing from it.

Net operating cycle (or cash conversion cycle)   An estimate of the average time that elapses between paying suppliers for materials and collecting cash from the subsequent sale of goods produced.

Net present value (NPV)   The present value of an investment's cash inflows (benefits) minus the present value of its cash outflows (costs).

Net profit margin (profit margin or return on sales)   An indicator of profitability, calculated as net income divided by revenue; indicates how much of each dollar of revenues is left after all costs and expenses.

Net revenue   Revenue after adjustments (e.g., for estimated returns or for amounts unlikely to be collected).

Net taxes   Taxes paid to governments minus transfer payments received from governments.

Net-of-Fees Return   The gross-of-fees return reduced by the investment management fee.

Netting   When parties agree to exchange only the net amount owed from one party to the other.

New issue   Common stocks or bonds offered by companies for public sale.

New Keynesian   A Keynesian who holds the view that not only is the money wage rate sticky but that prices of goods and services are also sticky.

Node   Each value on a binomial tree from which successive moves or outcomes branch.

No-load fund   A mutual fund that sells its shares at net asset value without adding sales charges.

Nominal GDP   The value of the final goods and services produced in a given year valued at the prices that prevailed in that same year. It is a more precise name for GDP.

Nominal rate   Rate of interest based on the security's face value.

Nominal risk-free interest rate   The sum of the real risk-free interest rate and the inflation premium.

Nominal scale   A measurement scale that categorizes data but does not rank them.

Nominal yield   A bond's yield as measured by its coupon rate.

Noncash investing and financing transactions   Significant investing and financing transactions involving only long-term assets, long-term liabilities, or stockholders' equity that do not affect current cash inflows or outflows.

Nonconventional cash flow   In a nonconventional cash flow pattern, the initial outflow is not followed by inflows only, but the cash flows can flip from positive (inflows) to negative (outflows) again (or even change signs several times).

Noncurrent Not due to be consumed, converted into cash, or settled within one year after the balance sheet date.

Noncurrent assets Assets that are expected to benefit the company over an extended period of time (usually more than one year).

Nondeliverable forwards (NDFs) Cash-settled forward contracts, used predominately with respect to foreign exchange forwards.

Nonlinear relation An association or relationship between variables that cannot be graphed as a straight line.

Nonparametric test A test that is not concerned with a parameter, or that makes minimal assumptions about the population from which a sample comes.

Nonrenewable natural resources Natural resources that can be used only once and that cannot be replaced once they have been used.

Nonstationarity With reference to a random variable, the property of having characteristics such as mean and variance that are not constant through time.

Nontariff barrier Any action other than a tariff that restricts international trade.

Normal backwardation The condition in futures markets in which futures prices are lower than expected spot prices.

Normal contango The condition in futures markets in which futures prices are higher than expected spot prices.

Normal distribution A continuous, symmetric probability distribution that is completely described by its mean and its variance.

Normal good A good for which demand increases as income increases.

Normal profit The expected return for supplying entrepreneurial ability.

North American Free Trade Agreement An agreement, which became effective on January 1, 1994, to eliminate all barriers to international trade between the United States, Canada, and Mexico after a 15-year phasing in period.

Notes Intermediate-term debt securities with maturities longer than 1 year but less than 10 years.

Notes payable Amounts owed by a business to creditors as a result of borrowings that are evidenced by (short-term) loan agreements.

Notional principal The principal value of a swap transaction, which is not exchanged but is used as a scale factor to translate interest rate differentials into cash settlement payments.

n-**Period moving average** The average of the current and immediately prior $n - 1$ values of a time series.

NPV rule An investment decision rule that states that an investment should be undertaken if its NPV is positive but not undertaken if its NPV is negative.

Null hypothesis The hypothesis to be tested.

Number of days of inventory Ratio of the amount of inventory on hand to the average day's cost of goods sold; an indication of the number of days a company ties up funds in inventory.

Number of days of payables An activity ratio equal to the number of days in a period divided by the payables turnover ratio for the period; an estimate of the average number of days it takes a company to pay its suppliers.

Number of days of receivables Ratio of accounts receivable to average day's revenue; an indication of the length of time between a sale (i.e. an account receivable is created) and the collection of the account receivable in cash.

Objective probabilities Probabilities that generally do not vary from person to person; includes a priori and objective probabilities.

Objectives The investor's goals expressed in terms of risk and return and included in the policy statement.

Obsolescence The process of becoming out of date, which is a factor in the limited useful life of tangible assets.

Offensive competitive strategy A strategy whereby a firm attempts to use its strengths to affect the competitive forces in the industry and, in so doing, improves the firm's relative position in the industry.

Official reserves The amount of reserves owned by the central bank of a government in the form of gold, Special Drawing Rights, and foreign cash or marketable securities.

Official settlements account A record of the change in a country's official reserves.

Off-market FRA A contract in which the initial value is intentionally set at a value other than zero and therefore requires a cash payment at the start from one party to the other.

Offsetting A transaction in exchange-listed derivative markets in which a party re-enters the market to close out a position.

Okun gap The gap between real GDP and potential GDP, and so is another name for the output gap.

Oligopoly A market structure in which a small number of firms compete.

One-sided hypothesis test (or one-tailed hypothesis test) A test in which the null hypothesis is rejected only if the evidence indicates that the population parameter is greater than (smaller than) θ_0. The alternative hypothesis also has one side.

Open market operation The purchase or sale of government securities—U.S. Treasury bills and bonds—by the Federal Reserve System in the open market.

Open-End Fund (Private Equity) A type of investment fund where the number of investors and the total committed capital is not fixed (i.e., open for subscriptions and/or redemptions).

Operating activities Activities that are part of the day-to-day business functioning of an entity, such as selling inventory and providing services.

Operating cycle An estimate of the average time needed for a company to convert raw materials into cash from a sale.

Operating efficiency ratios Financial ratios intended to indicate how efficiently management is utilizing the firm's assets in terms of dollar sales generated per dollar of assets. Primary examples would be: total asset turnover, fixed asset turnover, or equity turnover.

Operating leverage The use of fixed costs in operations.

Operating profit (operating income) A company's profits on its usual business activities before deducting taxes.

Operating profit margin A profitability ratio calculated as operating income divided by revenue; indicates how much of each dollar of revenues is left after both cost of goods sold and operating expenses are considered.

Operating profitability ratios Financial ratios intended to indicate how profitable the firm is in terms of the percent of profit generated from sales. Alternative measures would include: operating profit (EBIT)/net sales; pretax profit (EBT)/net sales; and net profit/sales.

Operating return on assets A profitability ratio calculated as operating income divided by average total assets; a measure of the operating income resulting from the company's investment in total assets.

Operating risk Risk that is attributable to a company's operating cost structure.

Operations risk or operational risk The risk of loss from failures in a company's systems and procedures (for example, due to computer failures or human failures) or events completely outside of the control of organizations (which would include "acts of God" and terrorist actions).

Opportunity cost The value that investors forgo by choosing a particular course of action; the value of something in its best alternative use.

Opportunity set The set of assets available for investment.

Optimal portfolio The portfolio on the efficient frontier that has the highest utility for a given investor. It lies at the point of tangency between the efficient frontier and the curve with the investor's highest possible utility.

Optimizer A specialized computer program or a spreadsheet that solves for the portfolio weights that will result in the lowest risk for a specified level of expected return.

Option A financial instrument that gives one party the right, but not the obligation, to buy or sell an underlying asset from or to another party at a fixed price over a specific period of time. Also referred to as contingent claims.

Option contract An agreement that grants the owner the right, but not the obligation, to make a future transaction in an underlying commodity or security at a fixed price and within a predetermined time in the future.

Option premium The initial price that the option buyer must pay to the option seller to acquire the contract.

Option price, option premium, or premium The amount of money a buyer pays and seller receives to engage in an option transaction.

Option-adjusted spread A type of yield spread that considers changes in the term structure and alternative estimates of the volatility of interest rates.

Ordinal scale A measurement scale that sorts data into categories that are ordered (ranked) with respect to some characteristic.

Ordinary annuity An annuity with a first cash flow that is paid one period from the present.

Ordinary least squares (OLS) An estimation method based on the criterion of minimizing the sum of the squared residuals of a regression.

Ordinary shares (common stock or common shares) Equity shares that are subordinate to all other types of equity (e.g., preferred equity).

Orthogonal Uncorrelated; at a right angle.

OTC Electronic Bulletin Board (OTCBB) A regulated quotation service that displays real-time quotes, last-sale prices, and volume information for a specified set of over-the-counter (OTC) securities that are not traded on the formal Nasdaq market.

Other comprehensive income   Items of comprehensive income that are not reported on the income statement; comprehensive income minus net income.

Other receivables   Amounts owed to the company from parties other than customers.

Outcome   A possible value of a random variable.

Outliers   Small numbers of observations at either extreme (small or large) of a sample.

Out-of-sample forecast errors   The differences between actual and predicted value of time series outside the sample period used to fit the model.

Out-of-sample test   A test of a strategy or model using a sample outside the time period on which the strategy or model was developed.

Out-of-the-money   Options that, if exercised, would require the payment of more money than the value received and therefore would not be currently exercised.

Out-of-the-money option   (1) An option that has no value if exercised immediately. For example, a call when the strike price is above the current price of the underlying asset, or a put when the strike price is below the current price of the underlying asset. (2) An option that has no intrinsic value. (3) Options that, if exercised, would require the payment of more money than the value received and therefore would not be currently exercised.

Overnight index swap (OIS)   A swap in which the floating rate is the cumulative value of a single unit of currency invested at an overnight rate during the settlement period.

Overweighted   A condition in which a portfolio, for whatever reason, includes more of a class of securities than the relative market value alone would justify.

Owners' equity   The excess of assets over liabilities; the residual interest of shareholders in the assets of an entity after deducting the entity's liabilities.

Paid-In Capital (Private Equity)   The amount of committed capital a limited partner has actually transferred to a venture fund. Also known as the cumulative drawdown amount.

Paired comparisons test   A statistical test for differences based on paired observations drawn from samples that are dependent on each other.

Paired observations   Observations that are dependent on each other.

Pairs arbitrage trade   A trade in two closely related stocks involving the short sale of one and the purchase of the other.

Panel data   Observations through time on a single characteristic of multiple observational units.

Par value   *See* Principal.

The principal amount repaid at maturity of a bond. Also called face value.

Parameter   A descriptive measure computed from or used to describe a population of data, conventionally represented by Greek letters.

Parameter instability   The problem or issue of population regression parameters that have changed over time.

Parametric test   Any test (or procedure) concerned with parameters or whose validity depends on assumptions concerning the population generating the sample.

Partial regression coefficients or partial slope coefficients   The slope coefficients in a multiple regression.

Passive strategy   In reference to short-term cash management, it is an investment strategy characterized by simple decision rules for making daily investments.

Patent   A government-sanctioned exclusive right granted to the inventor of a good, service, or productive process to produce, use, and sell the invention for a given number of years.

Payables turnover   An activity ratio calculated as purchases divided by average trade payables.

Payback   The time required for the added income from the convertible security relative to the stock to offset the conversion premium.

Payer swaption   A swaption that allows the holder to enter into a swap as the fixed-rate payer and floating-rate receiver.

Payment date   The date on which a firm actually mails dividend checks.

Payment netting   A means of settling payments in which the amount owed by the first party to the second is netted with the amount owed by the second party to the first; only the net difference is paid.

Payoff   The value of an option at expiration.

Payoff matrix   A table that shows the payoffs for every possible action by each player for every possible action by each other player.

Pegged exchange rate regime   A system in which a country's exchange rate in relation to a major currency is set at a target value (the peg) but allowed to fluctuate within a small band around the target.

Percentage-of-completion   A method of revenue recognition in which, in each accounting period, the company estimates what percentage of the contract is complete and then reports that percentage of the total contract revenue in its income statement.

Percentiles   Quantiles that divide a distribution into 100 equal parts.

Perfect collinearity The existence of an exact linear relation between two or more independent variables or combinations of independent variables.

Perfect competition A market in which there are many firms each selling an identical product; there are many buyers; there are no restrictions on entry into the industry; firms in the industry have no advantage over potential new entrants; and firms and buyers are well informed about the price of each firm's product.

Perfect price discrimination Price discrimination that extracts the entire consumer surplus.

Perfectly elastic demand Demand with an infinite price elasticity; the quantity demanded changes by an infinitely large percentage in response to a tiny price change.

Perfectly inelastic demand Demand with a price elasticity of zero; the quantity demanded remains constant when the price changes.

Performance appraisal The evaluation of risk-adjusted performance; the evaluation of investment skill.

Performance guarantee A guarantee from the clearinghouse that if one party makes money on a transaction, the clearinghouse ensures it will be paid.

Performance measurement The calculation of returns in a logical and consistent manner.

Period costs Costs (e.g., executives' salaries) that cannot be directly matched with the timing of revenues and which are thus expensed immediately.

Periodic rate The quoted interest rate per period; the stated annual interest rate divided by the number of compounding periods per year.

Permutation An ordered listing.

Perpetuity A perpetual annuity, or a set of never-ending level sequential cash flows, with the first cash flow occurring one period from now.

Personal trust An amount of money set aside by a grantor and often managed by a third party, the trustee. Often constructed so one party receives income from the trust's investments and another party receives the residual value of the trust after the income beneficiaries' death.

Pet projects Projects in which influential managers want the corporation to invest. Often, unfortunately, pet projects are selected without undergoing normal capital budgeting analysis.

Phillips curve A curve that shows a relationship between inflation and unemployment.

Physical deterioration A decline in the useful life of a depreciable asset resulting from use and from exposure to the elements.

Plain-vanilla Refers to a security, especially a bond or a swap, issued with standard features. Sometimes called generic.

Plain vanilla swap An interest rate swap in which one party pays a fixed rate and the other pays a floating rate, with both sets of payments in the same currency.

Platykurtic Describes a distribution that is less peaked than the normal distribution.

Plowback ratio An indication of the proportion of earnings that are reinvested in the company rather than paid out as dividends; calculated as 1 − dividend payout ratio.

Point estimate A single numerical estimate of an unknown quantity, such as a population parameter.

Point of sale Systems that capture transaction data at the physical location in which the sale is made.

Policy statement A statement in which the investor specifies investment goals, constraints, and risk preferences.

Pooled estimate An estimate of a parameter that involves combining (pooling) observations from two or more samples.

Population All members of a specified group.

Population mean The arithmetic mean value of a population; the arithmetic mean of all the observations or values in the population.

Population standard deviation A measure of dispersion relating to a population in the same unit of measurement as the observations, calculated as the positive square root of the population variance.

Population variance A measure of dispersion relating to a population, calculated as the mean of the squared deviations around the population mean.

Portfolio An individually managed pool of assets. A portfolio may be a subportfolio, account, or pooled fund.

Portfolio performance attribution The analysis of portfolio performance in terms of the contributions from various sources of risk.

Portfolio possibilities curve A graphical representation of the expected return and risk of all portfolios that can be formed using two assets.

Position trader A trader who typically holds positions open overnight.

Positive relationship A relationship between two variables that move in the same direction.

Positive serial correlation Serial correlation in which a positive error for one observation increases the chance of a positive error for another observation, and a negative error for one observation increases the chance of a negative error for another observation.

Posterior probability An updated probability that reflects or comes after new information.

Potential credit risk   The risk associated with the possibility that a payment due at a later date will not be made.

Potential GDP   The quantity of real GDP at full employment.

Poverty   A situation in which a household's income is too low to be able to buy the quantities of food, shelter, and clothing that are deemed necessary.

Power of a test   The probability of correctly rejecting the null-that is, rejecting the null hypothesis when it is false.

Precautionary stocks   A level of inventory beyond anticipated needs that provides a cushion in the event that it takes longer to replenish inventory than expected or in the case of greater than expected demand.

Predatory pricing   Setting a low price to drive competitors out of business with the intention of setting a monopoly price when the competition has gone.

Preferences   A description of a person's likes and dislikes.

Preferred stock   An equity investment that stipulates the dividend payment either as a coupon or a stated dollar amount. The firm's directors may withhold payments.

Pre-investing   The strategy of using futures contracts to enter the market without an immediate outlay of cash.

Premium   A bond selling at a price above par value due to capital market conditions.

Prepaid expense   A normal operating expense that has been paid in advance of when it is due.

Present (price) value of a basis point (PVBP)   The change in the bond price for a 1 basis point change in yield. Also called *basis point value* (BPV).

Present value   The amount of money that, if invested today, will grow to be as large as a given future amount when the interest that it will earn is taken into account.

Present value (PV)   The present discounted value of future cash flows: for assets, the present discounted value of the future net cash inflows that the asset is expected to generate; for liabilities, the present discounted value of the future net cash outflows that are expected to be required to settle the liabilities.

Pretax profit margin   A profitability ratio calculated as earnings before taxes divided by revenue; useful for isolating the effects of taxes on a company's profitability.

Price ceiling   A regulation that makes it illegal to charge a price higher than a specified level.

Price continuity   A feature of a liquid market in which there are small price changes from one transaction to the next due to the depth of the market.

Price discovery   A feature of futures markets in which futures prices provide valuable information about the price of the underlying asset.

Price discrimination   The practice of selling different units of a good or service for different prices or of charging one customer different prices for different quantities bought.

Price effect   The effect of a change in the price on the quantity of a good consumed, other things remaining the same.

Price elasticity of demand   A units-free measure of the responsiveness of the quantity demanded of a good to a change in its price, when all other influences on buyers' plans remain the same.

Price floor   A regulation that makes it illegal to charge a price lower than a specified level.

Price level   The average level of prices as measured by a price index.

Price limits   Limits imposed by a futures exchange on the price change that can occur from one day to the next.

Price momentum   A portfolio strategy in which you acquire stocks that have enjoyed above-market stock price increases.

Price multiple   The ratio of a stock's market price to some measure of value per share.

Price relative   A ratio of an ending price over a beginning price; it is equal to 1 plus the holding period return on the asset.

Price risk   The component of interest rate risk due to the uncertainty of the market price of a bond caused by changes in market interest rates.

Price taker   A firm that cannot influence the price of the good or service it produces.

Price to book value   A valuation ratio calculated as price per share divided by book value per share.

Price to cash flow   A valuation ratio calculated as price per share divided by cash flow per share.

Price to sales   A valuation ratio calculated as price per share divided by sales per share.

Price/earnings (P/E) ratio   The number by which expected earnings per share is multiplied to estimate a stock's value; also called the *earnings multiplier.*

Priced risk   Risk for which investors demand compensation for bearing (e.g. equity risk, company-specific factors, macroeconomic factors).

Price-setting option   The operational flexibility to adjust prices when demand varies from forecast. For example, when demand exceeds capacity, the company could benefit from the excess demand by increasing prices.

Price-weighted index An index calculated as an arithmetic mean of the current prices of the sampled securities.

Primary market The market in which newly issued securities are sold by their issuers, who receive the proceeds.

Principal The amount of funds originally invested in a project or instrument; the face value to be paid at maturity.

Principal-agent problem The problem of devising compensation rules that induce an agent to act in the best interest of a principal.

Prior probabilities Probabilities reflecting beliefs prior to the arrival of new information.

Private Equity Private equity includes, but is not limited to, organizations devoted to venture capital, leveraged buyouts, consolidations, mezzanine and distressed debt investments, and a variety of hybrids, such as venture leasing and venture factoring.

Private information Information that is available to one person but is too costly for anyone else to obtain.

Private placement A new issue sold directly to a small group of investors, usually institutions

Private sector surplus or deficit An amount equal to saving minus investment.

Probability A number between 0 and 1 describing the chance that a stated event will occur.

Probability density function A function with non-negative values such that probability can be described by areas under the curve graphing the function.

Probability distribution A distribution that specifies the probabilities of a random variable's possible outcomes.

Probability function A function that specifies the probability that the random variable takes on a specific value.

Probit model A qualitative-dependent-variable multiple regression model based on the normal distribution.

Producer surplus The price of a good minus the opportunity cost of producing it, summed over the quantity sold.

Product differentiation Making a product slightly different from the product of a competing firm.

Production efficiency A situation in which the economy cannot produce more of one good without producing less of some other good.

Production-flexibility The operational flexibility to alter production when demand varies from forecast. For example, if demand is strong, a company

may profit from employees working overtime or from adding additional shifts.

Production function The relationship between real GDP and the quantity of labor when all other influences on production remain the same.

Production method A method of depreciation that assumes depreciation is solely the result of use and that allocates depreciation based on the units of use or output during each period of an asset's useful life.

Production possibilities frontier The boundary between the combinations of goods and services that can be produced and the combinations that cannot.

Production quota An upper limit to the quantity of a good that may be produced in a specified period.

Productivity growth slowdown A slowdown in the growth rate of output per person.

Profit The income earned by entrepreneurship.

Profitability ratios Ratios that measure a company's ability to generate profitable sales from its resources (assets).

Project sequencing To defer the decision to invest in a future project until the outcome of some or all of a current project is known. Projects are sequenced through time, so that investing in a project creates the option to invest in future projects.

Property rights Social arrangements that govern the ownership, use, and disposal of resources or factors of production, goods, and services that are enforceable in the courts.

Prospective P/E *See* Leading P/E.

Protective put An option strategy in which a long position in an asset is combined with a long position in a put.

Provision In accounting, a liability of uncertain timing or amount.

Pseudo-random numbers Numbers produced by random number generators.

Public good A good or service that is both nonrival and nonexcludable—it can be consumed simultaneously by everyone and from which no one can be excluded.

Pull on liquidity When disbursements are paid too quickly or trade credit availability is limited, requiring companies to expend funds before they receive funds from sales that could cover the liability.

Purchasing power parity The equal value of different monies.

Purchasing power parity (PPP) A theory stating that the exchange rate between two currencies will exactly reflect the purchasing power of the two currencies.

Relative frequency   With reference to an interval of grouped data, the number of observations in the interval divided by the total number of observations in the sample.

Relative price   The ratio of the price of one good or service to the price of another good or service. A relative price is an opportunity cost.

Renewable natural resources   Natural resources that can be used repeatedly without depleting what is available for future use.

Rent   The income that land earns.

Rent ceiling   A regulation that makes it illegal to charge a rent higher than a specified level.

Rent seeking   Any attempt to capture a consumer surplus, a producer surplus, or an economic profit.

Replacement value   The market value of a swap.

Report format   With respect to the format of a balance sheet, a format in which assets, liabilities, and equity are listed in a single column.

Required rate of return   The return that compensates investors for their time, the expected rate of inflation, and the uncertainty of the return.

Required reserve ratio   The ratio of reserves to deposits that banks are required, by regulation, to hold.

Reserve ratio   The fraction of a bank's total deposits that are held in reserves.

Reserves   Cash in a bank's vault plus the bank's deposits at Federal Reserve banks.

Residual autocorrelations   The sample autocorrelations of the residuals.

Residual claim   The owners' remaining claim on the company's assets after the liabilities are deducted.

Residual value   The estimated net scrap, salvage, or trade-in value of a tangible asset at the estimated date of its disposal. Also called *salvage value* or *disposal value.*

Resistance level   A price at which a technician would expect a substantial increase in the supply of a stock to reverse a rising trend.

Retail method   An inventory accounting method in which the sales value of an item is reduced by the gross margin to calculate the item's cost.

Return on assets (ROA)   A profitability ratio calculated as net income divided by average total assets; indicates the company's net profit generated per dollar invested in total assets.

Return on common equity   A profitability ratio calculated as (net income − preferred dividends) divided by average common equity; equal to the return on equity ratio when no preferred equity is outstanding.

Return on equity (ROE)   A profitability ratio calculated as net income divided by average shareholders' equity; indicates the return generated per dollar of shareholders' investment in the company.

Return-on-investment ratios   Ratios that are useful for comparing the net benefits generated from investments.

Return on total capital   A profitability ratio of net income to total capital (i.e., average interest-bearing debt + average total equity); indicates the return to the investments made by both creditors and shareholders.

Return prediction studies   Studies wherein investigations attempt to predict the time series of future rates of return using public information. An example would be predicting above-average returns for the stock market based on the aggregate dividend yield—e.g., high dividend yield indicates above average future market returns.

Revenue   The amount charged for the delivery of goods or services in the ordinary activities of a business over a stated period; the inflows of economic resources to a company over a stated period.

Revenue bond   A bond that is serviced by the income generated from specific revenue-producing projects of the municipality.

Revenue expenditure   An expenditure for ordinary repairs and maintenance of a long-term asset, which is recorded by a debit to an expense account.

Revolving credit agreements   The strongest form of short-term bank borrowing facilities; they are in effect for multiple years (e.g., 3–5 years) and may have optional medium-term loan features

Rho   The sensitivity of the option price to the risk-free rate.

Ricardo-Barro effect   The equivalence of financing government purchases by taxes or by borrowing.

Rising trend channel   The range defined by security prices as they move progressively higher.

Risk averse   The assumption about investors that they will choose the least risky alternative, all else being equal.

Risk budgeting   The establishment of objectives for individuals, groups, or divisions of an organization that takes into account the allocation of an acceptable level of risk.

Risk governance   The setting of overall policies and standards in risk management

Risk management   The process of identifying the level of risk an entity wants, measuring the level of risk the entity currently has, taking actions that bring the actual level of risk to the desired level of risk, and monitoring the new actual level of risk so that it continues to be aligned with the desired level of risk.

Risk premium The expected return on an investment minus the risk-free rate.

Risk premium (RP) (1) The difference between the expected return on an asset and the risk-free interest rate. (2) The increase over the nominal risk-free rate that investors demand as compensation for an investment's uncertainty. (3) The expected return on an investment minus the risk-free rate.

Risk-free asset An asset with returns that exhibit zero variance.

Risk-neutral probabilities Weights that are used to compute a binomial option price. They are the probabilities that would apply if a risk-neutral investor valued an option.

Risk-neutral valuation The process by which options and other derivatives are priced by treating investors as though they were risk neutral.

Risky asset An asset with uncertain future returns.

Rival A good or services or a resource is rival if its use by one person decreases the quantity available for someone else.

Robust The quality of being relatively unaffected by a violation of assumptions.

Robust standard errors Standard errors of the estimated parameters of a regression that correct for the presence of heteroskedasticity in the regression's error term.

Root mean squared error (RMSE) The square root of the average squared forecast error; used to compare the out-of-sample forecasting performance of forecasting models.

Roy's safety first criterion A criterion asserting that the optimal portfolio is the one that minimizes the probability that portfolio return falls below a threshold level.

Rule of 72 The principle that the approximate number of years necessary for an investment to double is 72 divided by the stated interest rate.

Runs test A test of the weak-form efficient market hypothesis that checks for trends that persist longer in terms of positive or negative price changes than one would expect for a random series.

Safety stock A level of inventory beyond anticipated needs that provides a cushion in the event that it takes longer to replenish inventory than expected or in the case of greater than expected demand.

Safety-first rules Rules for portfolio selection that focus on the risk that portfolio value will fall below some minimum acceptable level over some time horizon.

Sales Generally, a synonym for revenue; "sales" is generally understood to refer to the sale of goods, whereas "revenue" is understood to include the sale of goods or services.

Sales returns and allowances An offset to revenue reflecting any cash refunds, credits on account, and discounts from sales prices given to customers who purchased defective or unsatisfactory items.

Salvage value The amount the company estimates that it can sell the asset for at the end of its useful life.

Sample A subset of a population.

Sample excess kurtosis A sample measure of the degree of a distribution's peakedness in excess of the normal distribution's peakedness.

Sample kurtosis A sample measure of the degree of a distribution's peakedness.

Sample mean The sum of the sample observations, divided by the sample size.

Sample selection bias Bias introduced by systematically excluding some members of the population according to a particular attribute-for example, the bias introduced when data availability leads to certain observations being excluded from the analysis.

Sample skewness A sample measure of degree of asymmetry of a distribution.

Sample standard deviation The positive square root of the sample variance.

Sample statistic or statistic A quantity computed from or used to describe a sample.

Sample variance A sample measure of the degree of dispersion of a distribution, calculated by dividing the sum of the squared deviations from the sample mean by the sample size (n) minus 1.

Sampling The process of obtaining a sample.

Sampling distribution The distribution of all distinct possible values that a statistic can assume when computed from samples of the same size randomly drawn from the same population.

Sampling error The difference between the observed value of a statistic and the quantity it is intended to estimate.

Sampling plan The set of rules used to select a sample.

Sandwich spread An option strategy that is equivalent to a short butterfly spread.

Sarbanes-Oxley Act An act passed by the U.S. Congress in 2002 that created the Public Company Accounting Oversight Board (PCAOB) to oversee auditors.

Saving The amount of income that households have left after they have paid their taxes and bought their consumption goods and services.

plans remain the same. It is described by a supply schedule and illustrated by a supply curve.

Supply curve   A curve that shows the relationship between the quantity supplied and the price of a good when all other influences on producers' planned sales remain the same.

Supply of labor   The relationship between the quantity of labor supplied and the real wage rate when all other influences on work plans remain the same.

Supply-side effects   The effects of fiscal policy on employment, potential GDP, and aggregate supply.

Support level   A price at which a technician would expect a substantial increase in price and volume for a stock to reverse a declining trend that was due to profit taking.

Surprise   The actual value of a variable minus its predicted (or expected) value.

Survey approach   An estimate of the equity risk premium that is based upon estimates provided by a panel of finance experts.

Survivorship bias   The bias resulting from a test design that fails to account for companies that have gone bankrupt, merged, or are otherwise no longer reported in a database.

Sustainable growth rate   The rate of dividend (and earnings) growth that can be sustained over time for a given level of return on equity, keeping the capital structure constant and without issuing additional common stock.

Swap   An agreement between two parties to exchange a series of future cash flows.

Swap spread   The difference between the fixed rate on an interest rate swap and the rate on a Treasury note with equivalent maturity; it reflects the general level of credit risk in the market.

Swaption   An option to enter into a swap.

SWOT analysis   An examination of a firm's *S*trengths, *W*eaknesses, *O*pportunities, and *T*hreats. This analysis helps an analyst evaluate a firm's strategies to exploit its competitive advantages or defend against its weaknesses.

Symmetry principle   A requirement that people in similar situations be treated similarly.

Synthetic call   The combination of puts, the underlying, and risk-free bonds that replicates a call option.

Synthetic forward contract   The combination of the underlying, puts, calls, and risk-free bonds that replicates a forward contract.

Synthetic index fund   An index fund position created by combining risk-free bonds and futures on the desired index.

Synthetic put   The combination of calls, the underlying, and risk-free bonds that replicates a put option.

Systematic factors   Factors that affect the average returns of a large number of different assets.

Systematic risk   The variability of returns that is due to macroeconomic factors that affect all risky assets. Because it affects all risky assets, it cannot be eliminated by diversification.

Systematic sampling   A procedure of selecting every *k*th member until reaching a sample of the desired size. The sample that results from this procedure should be approximately random.

Tangible assets   Long-term assets that have physical substance.

Tangible book value per share   Common shareholders' equity minus intangible assets from the balance sheet, divided by the number of shares outstanding.

Tap   Procedure by which a borrower can keep issuing additional amounts of an old bond at its current market value. This procedure is used for bond issues, notably by the British and French governments, as well as for some short-term debt instruments.

Target balance   A minimum level of cash to be held available—estimated in advance and adjusted for known funds transfers, seasonality, or other factors.

Target capital structure   The proportion of component sources of capital (e.g. equity, debt) that a company strives to maintain

Target semideviation   The positive square root of target semivariance.

Target semivariance   The average squared deviation below a target value.

Tariff   A tax that is imposed by the importing country when an imported good crosses its international boundary.

Tax incidence   The division of the burden of a tax between the buyer and the seller.

Tax multiplier   The magnification effect of a change in taxes on aggregate demand.

Tax risk   The uncertainty associated with tax laws.

Tax wedge   The gap between the before-tax and after-tax wage rates.

Taylor rule   A rule that adjusts the federal funds rate to target the inflation rate and to take into account deviations of the inflation rate from its target and deviations of real GDP from potential GDP.

_t_-Distribution   A symmetrical distribution defined by a single parameter, degrees of freedom, that is largely used to make inferences concerning the mean of a normal distribution whose variance is unknown.

Technical analysis   Estimation of future security price movements based on past price and volume movements.

Technological change The development of new goods and better ways of producing goods and services.

Technological efficiency A situation that occurs when the firm produces a given output by using the least amount of inputs.

Technology Any method of producing a good or service.

Temporary New Account A tool that firms can use to remove the effect of significant cash flows on a portfolio. When a significant cash flow occurs in a portfolio, the firm may treat this cash flow as a "temporary new account," allowing the firm to implement the mandate of the portfolio without the impact of the cash flow on the performance of the portfolio.

Tenor The original time to maturity on a swap.

Term structure of interest rates The relationship between term to maturity and yield to maturity for a sample of comparable bonds at a given time. Popularly known as the *yield curve.*

Term to maturity Specifies the date or the number of years before a bond matures or expires.

Termination date The date of the final payment on a swap; also, the swap's expiration date.

Terms of trade The quantity of goods and services that a country exports to pay for its imports of goods and services.

Test statistic A quantity, calculated based on a sample, whose value is the basis for deciding whether or not to reject the null hypothesis.

Theta The rate at which an option's time value decays.

Third market Over-the-counter trading of securities listed on an exchange.

Thrift institutions Thrift institutions include savings and loan associations, savings banks, and credit unions.

Tick The minimum price movement for the asset underlying a forward or futures contract; for Treasury bonds, one tick equals $1/32$ of 1 percent of par value.

Time series A set of observations on a variable's outcomes in different time periods.

Time to expiration The time remaining in the life of a derivative, typically expressed in years.

Time value decay The loss in the value of an option resulting from movement of the option price toward its payoff value as the expiration day approaches.

Time value of money The principles governing equivalence relationships between cash flows with different dates.

Time value or speculative value The difference between the market price of the option and its intrinsic value, determined by the uncertainty of the underlying over the remaining life of the option.

Time-period bias The possibility that when we use a time-series sample, our statistical conclusion may be sensitive to the starting and ending dates of the sample.

Time-series analysis An examination of a firm's performance data over a period of time.

Time-series data Observations of a variable over time.

Time-series graph A graph that measures time (for example, months or years) on the *x*-axis and the variable or variables in which we are interested on the *y*-axis.

Time-weighted rate of return The compound rate of growth of one unit of currency invested in a portfolio during a stated measurement period; a measure of investment performance that is not sensitive to the timing and amount of withdrawals or additions to the portfolio.

Top-down analysis With reference to investment selection processes, an approach that starts with macro selection (i.e., identifying attractive geographic segments and/or industry segments) and then addresses selection of the most attractive investments within those segments.

Total asset turnover An activity ratio calculated as revenue divided by average total assets; indicates the extent to which the investment in total assets results in revenues.

Total cost The cost of all the productive resources that a firm uses.

Total Firm Assets Total firm assets are all assets for which a firm has investment management responsibility. Total firm assets include assets managed outside the firm (e.g., by subadvisors) for which the firm has asset allocation authority.

Total fixed cost The cost of the firm's fixed inputs.

Total invested capital The sum of market value of common equity, book value of preferred equity, and face value of debt.

Total probability rule for expected value A rule explaining the expected value of a random variable in terms of expected values of the random variable conditional on mutually exclusive and exhaustive scenarios.

Total probability rule A rule explaining the unconditional probability of an event in terms of probabilities of the event conditional on mutually exclusive and exhaustive scenarios.

Total product The maximum output that a given quantity of factors of production can produce.

Total return A return objective in which the investor wants to increase the portfolio value to meet a future need by both capital gains and current income reinvestment.

Total return swap A swap in which one party agrees to pay the total return on a security. Often used as a credit derivative, in which the underlying is a bond.

Total revenue The value of a firm's sales. It is calculated as the price of the good multiplied by the quantity sold.

Total revenue test A method of estimating the price elasticity of demand by observing the change in total revenue that results from a change in the price, when all other influences on the quantity sold remain the same.

Total variable cost The cost of all the firm's variable inputs.

Tracking error The standard deviation of the difference in returns between an active investment portfolio and its benchmark portfolio; also called tracking error volatility, tracking risk, and active risk.

Tracking portfolio A portfolio having factor sensitivities that are matched to those of a benchmark or other portfolio.

Tracking risk The standard deviation of the differences between a portfolio's returns and its benchmark's returns; a synonym of active risk.

Trade balance The balance of a country's exports and imports; part of the current account.

Trade credit A spontaneous form of credit in which a purchaser of the goods or service is, effectively, financing its purchase by delaying the date on which payment is made.

Trade Date Accounting The transaction is reflected in the portfolio on the date of the purchase or sale, and not on the settlement date. Recognizing the asset or liability within at least 3 days of the date the transaction is entered into (Trade Date, T 1 1, T 1 2 or T 1 3) all satisfy the trade date accounting requirement for purposes of the GIPS standards. (See settlement date accounting.)

Trade receivables (commercial receivables or accounts receivable) Amounts customers owe the company for products that have been sold as well as amounts that may be due from suppliers (such as for returns of merchandise).

Trademark A registered symbol that can be used only by its owner to identify a product or service.

Tradeoff An exchange–giving up one thing to get something else.

Trading effect The difference in performance of a bond portfolio from that of a chosen index due to short-run changes in the composition of the portfolio.

Trading Expenses The costs of buying or selling a security. These costs typically take the form of bro-

kerage commissions or spreads from either internal or external brokers. Custody fees charged per transaction should be considered custody fees and not direct transaction costs. Estimated trading expenses are not permitted.

Trading rule A formula for deciding on current transactions based on historical data.

Trading securities (held-for-trading securities) Securities held by a company with the intent to trade them.

Trading turnover The percentage of outstanding shares traded during a period of time.

Trailing P/E (or current P/E) A stock's current market price divided by the most recent four quarters of earnings per share.

Tranche Refers to a portion of an issue that is designed for a specific category of investors. French for "slice."

Transaction cost The cost of executing a trade. Low costs characterize an operationally efficient market.

Transaction Expenses (Private Equity) Include all legal, financial, advisory, and investment banking fees related to buying, selling, restructuring, and recapitalizing portfolio companies.

Transaction exposure The risk associated with a foreign exchange rate on a specific business transaction such as a purchase or sale.

Transactions costs The costs that arise from finding someone with whom to do business, of reaching an agreement about the price and other aspects of the exchange, and of ensuring that the terms of the agreement are fulfilled. The opportunity costs of conducting a transaction.

Transactions motive In the context of inventory management, it refers to the need for inventory as part of the routine production–sales cycle.

Translation exposure The risk associated with the conversion of foreign financial statements into domestic currency.

Treasury bill A negotiable U.S. government security with a maturity of less than one year that pays no periodic interest but yields the difference between its par value and its discounted purchase price.

Treasury bond A U.S. government security with a maturity of more than 10 years that pays interest periodically.

Treasury note A U.S. government security with maturities of 1 to 10 years that pays interest periodically.

Treasury stock method A method for accounting for the effect of options (and warrants) on earnings per share (EPS) that specifies what EPS would have been if the options and warrants had been exercised and the company had used the proceeds to repurchase common stock.

Tree diagram A diagram with branches emanating from nodes representing either mutually exclusive chance events or mutually exclusive decisions.

Trend A long-term pattern of movement in a particular direction.

Trimmed mean A mean computed after excluding a stated small percentage of the lowest and highest observations.

Trust receipt arrangement The use of inventory as collateral for a loan. The inventory is segregated and held in trust, and the proceeds of any sale must be remitted to the lender immediately.

t-Test A hypothesis test using a statistic (t-statistic) that follows a t-distribution.

Two-sided hypothesis test (or two-tailed hypothesis test) A test in which the null hypothesis is rejected in favor of the alternative hypothesis if the evidence indicates that the population parameter is either smaller or larger than a hypothesized value.

Type I error The error of rejecting a true null hypothesis.

Type II error The error of not rejecting a false null hypothesis.

U.S. interest rate differential A gap equal to the U.S. interest rate minus the foreign interest rate.

U.S. Official reserves The government's holdings of foreign currency.

Unbiasedness Lack of bias. A desirable property of estimators, an unbiased estimator is one whose expected value (the mean of its sampling distribution) equals the parameter it is intended to estimate.

Unbilled revenue (accrued revenue) Revenue that has been earned but not yet billed to customers as of the end of an accounting period.

Uncertainty A situation in which more than one event might occur but it is not known which one.

Unclassified balance sheet A balance sheet that does not show subtotals for current assets and current liabilities.

Unconditional heteroskedasticity Heteroskedasticity of the error term that is not correlated with the values of the independent variable(s) in the regression.

Unconditional probability (or marginal probability) The probability of an event *not* conditioned on another event.

Uncovered interest rate parity The assertion that expected currency depreciation should offset the interest differential between two countries over the term of the interest rate.

Underlying An asset that trades in a market in which buyers and sellers meet, decide on a price, and the seller then delivers the asset to the buyer and receives payment. The underlying is the asset or other derivative on which a particular derivative is based. The market for the underlying is also referred to as the spot market.

Underweighted A condition in which a portfolio, for whatever reason, includes less of a class of securities than the relative market value alone would justify.

Unearned fees Unearned fees are recognized when a company receives cash payment for fees prior to earning them.

Unearned revenue (deferred revenue) A liability account for money that has been collected for goods or services that have not yet been delivered.

Unemployment rate The percentage of the people in the labor force who are unemployed.

Unidentifiable intangible An intangible that cannot be acquired singly and that typically possesses an indefinite benefit period; an example is accounting goodwill.

Unit elastic demand Demand with a price elasticity of 1; the percentage change in the quantity demanded equals the percentage change in price.

Unit normal distribution *See* Standard normal distribution.

Unit root A time series that is not covariance stationary is said to have a unit root.

Univariate distribution A distribution that specifies the probabilities for a single random variable.

Unlimited funds An unlimited funds environment assumes that the company can raise the funds it wants for all profitable projects simply by paying the required rate of return.

Unrealized capital gains Capital gains that reflect the price appreciation of currently held unsold assets.

Unsystematic risk Risk that is unique to an asset, derived from its particular characteristics. It can be eliminated in a diversified portfolio.

Unweighted index An indicator series affected equally by the performance of each security in the sample regardless of price or market value. Also referred to as an *equal-weighted series*.

Unwind The negotiated termination of a forward or futures position before contract maturity.

Up transition probability The probability that an asset's value moves up.

Utilitarianism A principle that states that we should strive to achieve "the greatest happiness for the greatest number of people."

Utility   The benefit or satisfaction that a person gets from the consumption of a good or service.

Utility of wealth   The amount of utility that a person attaches to a given amount of wealth.

Valuation   The process of determining the value of an asset or service.

Valuation analysis   An active bond portfolio management strategy designed to capitalize on expected price increases in temporarily undervalued issues.

Valuation process   Part of the investment decision process in which you estimate the value of a security.

Valuation ratios   Ratios that measure the quantity of an asset or flow (e.g., earnings) in relation to the price associated with a specified claim (e.g., a share or ownership of the enterprise).

Value   The amount for which one can sell something, or the amount one must pay to acquire something.

Value at risk (VAR)   A money measure of the minimum value of losses expected during a specified time period at a given level of probability.

Value chain   The set of transformations to move from raw material to product or service delivery.

Value investors   With reference to equity investors, investors who are focused on paying a relatively low share price in relation to earnings or assets per share.

Value stocks   Stocks that appear to be undervalued for reasons besides earnings growth potential. These stocks are usually identified based on high dividend yields, low *P/E* ratios, or low price-to-book ratios.

Value-weighted index   An index calculated as the total market value of the securities in the sample. Market value is equal to the number of shares or bonds outstanding times the market price of the security.

Variable costs   Costs that rise proportionally with revenue.

Variance   The expected value (the probability-weighted average) of squared deviations from a random variable's expected value.

Variation margin   Additional margin that must be deposited in an amount sufficient to bring the balance up to the initial margin requirement.

Vega   The relationship between option price and volatility.

Velocity of circulation   The average number of times a dollar of money is used annually to buy the goods and services that make up GDP.

Venture Capital (Private Equity)   Risk capital in the form of equity and/or loan capital that is pro-vided by an investment institution to back a business venture that is expected to grow in value.

Vertical analysis   Common-size analysis using only one reporting period or one base financial statement; for example, an income statement in which all items are stated as percentages of sales.

Vertical common-size analysis   An analysis in which financial statement accounts are compared to a benchmark item in that same year. For the income statement, all items are restated as a percentage of revenues; for the balance sheet, all items are restated as a percentage of total assets.

Vintage Year (Private Equity)   The year that the venture capital or private equity fund or partnership first draws down or calls capital from its investors.

Volatility   As used in option pricing, the standard deviation of the continuously compounded returns on the underlying asset.

Voluntary export restraint   An agreement between two governments in which the government of the exporting country agrees to restrain the volume of its own exports.

Wages   The income that labor earns.

Warehouse receipt arrangement   The use of inventory as collateral for a loan. . It is similar to a trust receipt arrangement except that there is a third part (i.e., a warehouse company) that supervises the inventory.

Warrant   An instrument that allows the holder to purchase a specified number of shares of the firm's common stock from the firm at a specified price for a given period of time.

Weak-form efficient market hypothesis   The belief that security prices fully reflect all security market information.

Wealth   The market value of all the things that people own.

Weighted average cost method   An inventory accounting method that averages the total cost of available inventory items over the total units available for sale.

Weighted-average cost of capital   A weighted average of the after-tax required rates of return on a company's common stock, preferred stock, and long-term debt, where the weights are the fraction of each source of financing in the company's target capital structure.

Weighted average cost of capital (or marginal cost of capital)   The required rate of return that investors demand for the average-risk investment of a company and the cost that a company incurs for additional capital. Found as the average of the company's component costs of capital, weighted by their proportions in the company's capital structure.

Weighted mean   An average in which each observation is weighted by an index of its relative importance.

White-corrected standard errors   A synonym for robust standard errors.

Winsorized mean   A mean computed after assigning a stated percent of the lowest values equal to one specified low value, and a stated percent of the highest values equal to one specified high value.

Working capital   The excess of current assets over current liabilities.

Working capital management   The management of a company's short-term assets (such as inventory) and short-term liabilities (such as money owed to suppliers).

Working capital turnover   An activity ratio calculated as revenue divided by average working capital; an indication of the efficiency with which working capital is employed to produce revenues.

Working-age population   The total number of people aged 16 years and over who are not in jail, hospital, or some other form of institutional care.

World Trade Organization   An international organization that places greater obligations on its member countries to observe the GATT rules.

Yankee bonds   Bonds sold in the United States and denominated in U.S. dollars but issued by a foreign firm or government.

Yield   The promised rate of return on an investment under certain assumptions.

Yield beta   A measure of the sensitivity of a bond's yield to a general measure of bond yields in the market that is used to refine the hedge ratio.

Yield spread   The difference between the yield on a bond and the yield on a default-free security, usually a government note, of the same maturity. The yield spread is primarily determined by the market's perception of the credit risk on the bond.

Yield to maturity   The total yield on a bond obtained by equating the bond's current market value to the discounted cash flows promised by the bond.

Yield to worst   Given a bond with multiple potential maturity dates and prices due to embedded call options, the practice is to calculate a yield to maturity for each of the call dates and prices and select the lowest yield (the most conservative possible yield) as yield to worst.

Zero-cost collar   A transaction in which a position in the underlying is protected by buying a put and selling a call with the premium from the sale of the call offsetting the premium from the purchase of the put. It can also be used to protect a floating-rate borrower against interest rate increases with the premium on a long cap offsetting the premium on a short floor.

4⅝ 4¹¹/₁₆
4⅝ 4¹¹/₁₆ — ⅜
5½ 5½ — ⅛
5½ 21³/₁₆ — ¹/₁₆
20⅝ 21³/₁₆ — ⅛
17⅜ 18⅛ + ⅞
18½ 18⅛ + ½
6½ 6½ — ½
7¼ 6½ 6½ — ⅛
15/₁₆ 31/₃₂ —
⅞/₁₆ ⁹/₁₆
⁹/₁₆ ⁹/₁₆
¹/₃₂ 7¹³/₁₆ 7¹⁵/₁₆
7¹⁵/₁₆ 7¹³/₁₆ 7¹⁵/₁₆
2⅝ 2¹¹/₃₂ 2½ +
2¾ 2¼ 2¼
12¹/₁₆ 11⅜ 11¾ +
6⅛ 33¾ 33 33¼ —
87 25⅝ 24⁹/₁₆ 25⅝ +
602 11⅝ 11⅝ +
833 12 11⅝ +
16 10½ 10½ 10½ —
78 15⅝ 15¹³/₁₆ 15⅞ —
4608 9¹/₁₆ 8¼ 8⅞ +
430 11¼ 10¼
4⅞ 4

Page numbers followed by n refer to footnotes.